SPORT, CULTURE AND THE MEDIA

in CULTURAL and MEDIA STUDIES

Series editor: Stuart Allan

Published titles

Media Risk and Science
Stuart Allan

News Culture
Stuart Allan

Television, Globalization and Cultural Identities
Chris Barker

Cultures of Popular Music
Andy Bennett

Masculinities and Culture
John Beynon

Cinema and Cultural Modernity
Gill Branston

Violence and the Media
Cynthia Carter and C. Kay Weaver

Ethnic Minorities and the Media
Edited by Simon Cottle

Moral Panics and the Media
Chas Critcher

Modernity and Postmodern Culture
Jim McGuigan

Sport, Culture and the Media, 2nd edn
David Rowe

Critical Readings: Sport, Culture and the Media
David Rowe

Compassion, Morality and the Media
Keith Tester

SPORT, CULTURE AND THE MEDIA

The Unruly Trinity – 2nd edition

David Rowe

OPEN UNIVERSITY PRESS

Open University Press
McGraw-Hill Education
McGraw-Hill House
Shoppenhangers Road
Maidenhead
Berkshire
England
SL6 2QL

email: enquiries@openup.co.uk
world wide web: www.openup.co.uk

First edition 1999
Second editon 2004

Copyright © David Rowe 2004

A catalogue record of this book is available from the British Library

ISBN 0 335 21075 9 (pb)   0 335 21076 7 (hb)

Library of Congress Cataloging-in-Publication Data
CIP data has been applied for

Typeset by RefineCatch Limited, Bungay, Suffolk
Printed in the UK by Bell & Bain Ltd, Glasgow

To the Rowes and Henders:
great prizes in the lottery of families

CONTENTS

SERIES EDITOR'S FOREWORD

This second edition of David Rowe's *Sport, Culture and the Media: The Unruly Trinity* explores the extraordinarily dynamic linkages between media and sport, and their significance for contemporary society. Where other books in this area typically focus on a particular sport and its depiction in a single medium, Rowe's book covers both production and interpretation across the full spectrum of what he calls the 'media sports cultural complex'. In Part I, *Making Media Sport*, he traces the history of the media-sport nexus, surveys the production of sports journalism, and closely examines the political economy of the sports media. In Part II, *Unmaking the Media Sports Text*, he teases out the cultural meanings and social ideologies of a wide range of media sport forms and genres, including sports television, radio, films, books, newspapers, photography and the Internet. This new edition discusses the latest developments in the ownership and control of media sport and in media sport technology, consumption and use; incorporates new scholarly contributions to the international field of sports media studies; and reviews the most recent global sports events like the Sydney 2000 Olympics and the 2002 World Cup. It sets out to provide readers with the tools to analyse and understand the sports media for themselves as 'cultural citizens', and 'to take back a little of the cultural power that we have ceded to it'.

The *Issues in Cultural and Media Studies* series aims to facilitate a diverse range of critical investigations into pressing questions considered to be central to current thinking and research. In light of the remarkable speed at which the conceptual agendas of cultural and media studies are changing, the series is committed to contributing to what is an ongoing process of re-evaluation and critique. Each of the books is intended to provide a lively, innovative and comprehensive introduction to a specific topical issue from a fresh perspective. The reader is offered a thorough grounding in the most salient debates indicative of the book's subject, as well as important insights into how new modes of enquiry may be established for future explorations. Taken as a whole, then, the series is designed to cover the core components of cultural and media studies courses in an imaginatively distinctive and engaging manner.

Stuart Allan

ACKNOWLEDGEMENTS (FIRST EDITION)

Why would anyone not a dedicated masochist write an academic book? A relish for self-inflicted punishment must be the best qualification for the task. What really sustains the author (apart from ego and stimulants) is that, one day, the work (in both senses) will no longer be theirs. The book, conceived and executed in solitude, is finally a social product – it is written for people and, without those precious people, the book could never be written.

With the usual nervousness about advertent and inadvertent omissions, I thank on this occasion those who come to mind as indispensable: my family in the UK, especially the ones who haven't been acknowledged before – Joanna, Oliver, Alex and Tony – and my family in Australia who always get a mention – the inimitable Daniel and Madeleine. The longstanding and more recent friends and colleagues I honourably mention this time around are Therese and Grace Davis, Sue Dean, Mick Dwyer, Geoff and Dimity Lawrence, Helen Macallan, Kevin Markwell, Jim McKay, Toby Miller, Chuck Morris, Jules Pavlou Kirri, Deborah Stevenson, Alan Tomlinson, Garry Whannel and Dave Whitson.

I thank my other immediate academic colleagues for being exemplary workmates, and publicly acknowledge my debt to the life-saving, ever-engaging administrative double act, Shelagh Lummis and Kerry Beaumont (deft architect of the index). Richard Lever also provided some very handy research assistance at strategically significant moments. The Research Management Committee of the University of Newcastle provided generous funding for the study of sports journalists. Finally, Stuart Allan was as congenial a series editor as Justin Vaughan and Gaynor Clements were encouraging publisher and editorial assistant (respectively). I hope that this book bears some reasonable resemblance to the object they had in mind.

David Rowe

PREFACE AND ACKNOWLEDGEMENTS (SECOND EDITION)

The opportunity to publish a second edition is both irresistible and problematic. The great advantage is that the work can be updated and enhanced, and some of its more embarrassing moments 'airbrushed' for posterity. But there is also a question of fidelity to the spirit of the original work and to the historical conditions of its creation. To take an example from the world of popular music, my first academic love, this is analogous to using digital re-mastering to make a recording sound cleaner, glitch-free and more contemporary. The result may be technically superior but something intangible can be lost in the mix, usually some of the distinctiveness and boldness that was a strong aspect of the music's first appeal. This book is not a collection of tunes, but it is a considered reflection, after some five years, of changes to the 'media sports cultural complex' and in ways of analysing it within Cultural and Media Studies. It represents, therefore, the author's response to these shifts in the field and to its object of analysis in ways that are consistent with the principal concerns of the first edition of *Sport, Culture and the Media: The Unruly Trinity*.

I have tried to avoid obsessive tinkering with the original text, but I have not always succeeded in resisting the temptation of performing some fine-grained adjustment. In mitigation I plead that most of us, knowing what we (didn't) know five years later, would do things differently given the chance. More importantly, I have attempted to register and interrogate as necessary the major changes in media sport and its analysis that have occurred since I completed the first manuscript in 1998. These are of such consequence as to make me wish that I worked in a narrower, less contemporary field that doesn't mutate every time I glance away from it. Genetic engineering and nanotechnology come to mind as tranquil research areas by comparison. The changes that I wish to chart principally involve:

- New developments in the political economy of media sport, especially the end to the media-fuelled financial boom in sport, which, like the dot.com bonanza, has produced many casualties and re-drawn its lineaments.
- Shifts in media sport technology, consumption and use discussed briefly in the Afterword to the first edition that require elaboration in tracing the future nature and shape of the 'media sports cultural complex'.
- New theoretical and empirical work in the field that is making a significant contribution to the understanding of the relationships between sport, culture and the media, and an expansion of the discussions of reception, audiences, cultural citizenship and spectatorship in the first edition.
- Reflections on recent mega-media sports events (such as the Sydney 2000 Olympics and the 2002 World Cup) and new media texts (such as the films *Any Given Sunday* and *Bend It Like Beckham*) that are now available for textual analysis.

These additions, it is hoped, will make the second edition useful and relevant for the many researchers, scholars and students in interdisciplinary fields like Cultural, Media, Communication, Sport and Leisure Studies and for those in disciplines such as Sociology, Economics and History attracted to the subject of media sport and its wider socio-cultural significance. I have also edited a new work, *Critical Readings: Sport, Culture and the Media* (2004), that has the same structure as this book and is designed to provide readers with a solid, stimulating foundation on which to launch their own critical analytical adventures in an area of study that continues to fascinate, thrill and appal in almost equal measure.

Books are never the sole creation of their author and I cannot imagine how impoverished this one would have been without the direct and indirect contribution of many people. The individuals that I would like to single out for their international intellectual comradeship in recent years are Liesbet van Zoonen, Richard Giulianotti and Alina Bernstein. Collegiality and conviviality have been crucial bywords in the Cultural Industries and Practices Research Centre (CIPS) and in the former Department of Leisure and Tourism Studies at the University of Newcastle, Australia. My close collaborators, especially Deborah Stevenson, Geoffrey Lawrence, Jim McKay and Toby Miller, have been sustaining resources in the fullest sense. I would also like to acknowledge the grant support of the Australian Research Council and the University of Newcastle that has made possible the empirical research on which substantial elements of this book are based. The Man with Many Qualities, Peter Wejbora, provided excellent research assistance.

At Open University Press, Stuart Allan was, as ever, a delightfully constructive series editor, while Justin Vaughan was a very supportive publisher before his departure to new pastures. Cathy Thompson, and then Chris Cudmore recruited at the death, adeptly cyber-soothed the author during the darker moments when it all seemed too much. I am also grateful to the people who reviewed the first edition, commented on it in print, or contacted me directly to discuss aspects of it. This feedback has been invaluable to the writing of the second edition and has given me a precious sense of unfolding critical analytical debate that is an essential motivation to take to the field of inquiry once more.

Finally, nobody can be an academic and author in the contemporary world without exacting an unfair toll on those around them. I thank my family in south-western England for their forbearance over all those times that I haven't 'been there'. To my children, Maddy and Dan, I hope that I've taught some valuable lessons in how to lead rewarding adult lives by not repeating the keyboard-tethered sins of the father.

David Rowe

INTRODUCTION: IMMERSED IN MEDIA SPORT

A day in the life of the media sports consumer

All over the world, spanning many time zones, people of otherwise very different cultures, languages, religions and political ideologies are having a similar daily experience. Various aspects of the 'typical' day I am about to describe are representative of life in the more affluent reaches of late capitalist societies, but they are by no means unknown in even the poorest and least economically developed (by western standards) nations.

This daily round goes something like this: You wake up to the sound of the alarm clock radio and, as the news of the day is reported and anticipated, considerable prominence is given to seemingly bizarre cultural practices. They involve individuals and groups getting together and agreeing to engage in physical activities bound by rules (or even laws) in which people may be allowed to strike various parts of others' bodies with various parts of their own. Or they may be forbidden from having any kind of bodily contact at all. Often, they will be required to propel objects of various shapes and sizes using various implements or body parts towards designated targets of diverse kinds, while others do their best to stop them. Some people are paid huge sums of money for partaking in these activities, while others do it for fun or by compulsion at school. The ones who get paid do so because many more people want to watch them in operation in the same time and space or by means of electronic transmission. Those spectators also want to watch, read and listen to other people who get paid for talking and writing about what those exerting themselves are doing or what others have said or written about it. All that is shown, said and written provides many opportunities in many contexts (like playgrounds, pubs, bus queues, traffic jams and Internet chat rooms) for people to discuss what has happened and has been communicated about it in a spiralling and self-amplifying discourse.

To an inter-planetary visitor, this movement by a few people and interest in it by many more would seem like some kind of viral contagion, a collective insanity (or at least irrationality) perhaps brought back in the dust attached to moon rocks. For earthlings, however, it is an omnipresent part of their lives whether they like it or not. It is so pervasive that, like water or electricity, it is really acknowledged only when its supply is interrupted by natural disasters or industrial disputation. We on earth call it **sport**. As we have seen, however, this phenomenon is only partially about its actual practice. In fact, the activities on fields, courts, courses and other prescribed venues are at the bottom of an inverted pyramid of sports watching, selling, marketing, sponsorship, presentation and discourse. Sport is a contemporary medium for performing many tasks and carrying multiple messages and, as such, is increasingly indistinguishable from the *sports media*. This constellation of institutions and practices that supplies the means by which messages involving sport are communicated is not restricted to the print and electronic forms as they are conventionally conceived. 'Data' about sport are all around, with seemingly every animate and inanimate object capable of functioning as a *medium of sports culture*.

This point becomes clear as we resume the routine daily tasks commenced above and observe the extent to which sport has insinuated itself into the warp and weft of everyday life. At the breakfast table there is plenty to read. Not only does the morning paper carry many pages of sports results and analysis (usually conveniently placed on the back page or in a 'pull out' supplement), but the cereal boxes may be covered with the bright endorsements of prominent sportspeople. Befuddled breakfast conversation can stay on safe ground if it covers only the results of the previous night's games or the latest engagement between a 'sexy' female pop singer and a 'hunky' footballer. As the breakfast dishes are stacked for washing, regular sports news updates are given by the radio or by breakfast television. The visit to the bathroom may well involve contact with the range of soaps, deodorants and colognes promoted by runners, tennis players, boxers and the like. Patches of tattooed skin proclaiming undying love for Manchester United or the Chicago Bulls could be in need of cleansing. Next comes the big decision about what to wear, often meaning a difficult choice over which company's sports logo will emblazon T-shirts, shoes, hats, socks and jackets. The Nike 'swoosh', perhaps, or the Reebok flag insignia or, then again, maybe the three stripes of adidas?

Once out over the threshold, public space is suffused with signs of sport – much to the chagrin of dedicated sports haters and to the mild irritation of the merely indifferent. Billboards, hoardings, the sides of buses and numerous other available surfaces carry advertisements featuring celebrity sports-people endorsing fast food chains, new car models, leisurewear brands, health insurance and sundry other goods and services. Many fellow travellers and pedestrians have also turned themselves into walking brand promotions, displaying corporate sports logos and colours. Some are seemingly cut off from the surrounding world as they listen to sports reports and live commentaries on personal 'walkmans', or chat and send 'text' messages via mobile phones to distant others about their latest sporting idols and villains. Flashing electronic signs and newspaper stands on street corners carry news about footballers transferring between teams for multi-million sums of money, coaches and managers sacked, and forthcoming sports fixtures on television. Shop windows and street stalls display all manner of sports paraphernalia for sale, from collectors' cards to supporters' scarves and, if a local team is about to take part in a significant sports contest, messages of support decorate the streetscape, 'go the Blues, Reds, Cowboys, Bruisers, etc.' urgings in respectable shop windows are visible alongside the illicit fan signatures, endorsements, insults and threats characteristic of sports graffiti.

Leaving public territory for the institutional world does not mean entering a sports-free zone. In workplaces and educational establishments, conversational space in available breaks is likely to be filled with talk of sport and about sports talk as athlete-endorsed hamburgers and isotonic drinks are consumed, and personal boundaries and identities are marked with photographs and banners on desks and walls declaring sporting affiliations. The sports cyberworld will be illicitly contacted when employers and teachers think that computers and their Internet access are being put to more 'serious' work and educational use. The predictive and analytical skills of workmates are likely to be applied to 'sweeps' at the time of famous horse races, sports result 'tipping' competitions, online sports betting and, in pursuit of the perennial dream of a rich retirement, by accurately predicting the results of a number of sports contests and so winning the 'pools'. On the journey home, **media** headlines may be sighted about the latest sports scandal (Rowe 1997a) – a famous sportsman and film star on trial for the murder of his wife, a swimmer caught with performance-enhancing drugs in her bloodstream, a basketball player announcing that he's HIV-positive, allegations of corruption of referees and match-fixing connected to international sports betting rings. Back again at the domestic hearth, there will be myriad opportunities to receive information about sport in the electronic and print media, or via home computers (which might be loaded with inter-active sports games), and there is likely to be 'live' sports coverage or edited highlights on the multi-channels of free-to-air or pay television. As the alarm clock radio is being checked for the morning and the sleep timer switched on to guide the listener into slumber, quite possibly the last sounds of the day to be registered by the conscious and unconscious self, as at the moment of waking, will be of sport.

This is a picture of a sports impregnated world that does not rely on actual engagement in physical activity. People do so, of course, and in large numbers – but to nothing like the extent that they watch, talk and read about it (McKay 1990; Brown and Rowe 1998). It is increasingly hard to remember a time when sport and the media were not deeply entwined in a relationship of such systematic intensity that it has been characterized as a 'complex', with any apparent primacy given to sport or media varying between Jhally's (1989) conception of the 'sports/media complex' and Maguire's (1993) notion of the 'media/sport production complex'. The adjusted formulation used in this book is that of the **media sports cultural complex**, which signifies both the primacy of symbols in contemporary sport and the two-way relationship between the sports media and the great cultural formation of which it is part. As I have noted above, the sights, sounds and 'feel' of sport are everywhere – shrilly piping out of televisions and radios, absorbing acres of newsprint, and decorating bodies whose major physical exertion has commonly entailed walking between different leisurewear stores in suburban shopping malls. Media sports **texts**, of course, do not appear *ex nihilo* – that is, they are not beamed in from outer space, already formed and with unknown origins. An industrial infrastructure of daunting proportions manufactures them for us, peopled by specialists who are unequivocally in the sports discourse business. As a consequence, whether certified 'sports nuts' or the vaguely interested, largely indifferent to or actively dismissive of sport, we are all required to confront and negotiate the power and presence of the sports media.

Sport, Culture and the Media: structure and outline

In seeking to comprehend the phenomena and accomplish the task set out above, *Sport, Culture and the Media: The Unruly Trinity* is divided into two parts, which reflect the different emphasis on sports production and reception. Part I, 'Making media sport', focuses on the organizational structures and professional ideologies that shape the production of media sports texts. It opens with an introduction to the field, 'Understanding sport and media: a socio-historical approach' (Chapter 1), which provides a brief historical and sociological overview of the developing relationship between sport and media as a prerequisite for the production of media sports texts, showing how the institutions became mutually dependent in an increasingly extensive exchange of exposure and rights fees for content and audience capture. The heightened prominence of sport in print reportage (including specialist sports, business and general journalism), magazines, still photography, radio, film, video, television and new media is outlined. Themes of media power, the reproduction of ideologies of dominance and the position of the sports media in contemporary culture are highlighted as crucial to the ensuing analysis. The links between the conditions under which media sports texts are made, and the meanings and ideologies that they generate, are proposed as the key twin foci of a cogent and instructive understanding of the relationships between sport, culture and the media.

This is not to suggest that the production and reception of texts are distinct processes that have no bearing on each other. The reverse is the case, because what is produced in the media always operates with notions of how a text might be received, just as how it is received (positively, negatively or not at all) depends first on whether the text has been produced for consumption in the first place, and then on the conditions which are only partially under the control of the text producer (such as whether it is being 'displayed' to a man or woman, sports fan or sports hater, and so on). By provisionally separating media sports text production and reception along these lines, it is possible to grasp the complex ways in which media sports texts are made and unmade in a continuous process involving the representation of a cultural form by media organizations, its transformation through these acts of representation, and then its further transformation (including challenges to the media's representation of sport) by other interested parties (such as sports administrators, performers and fans). In so doing, it is possible to challenge two common, flawed and opposing arguments (both partially defensible) – either that the media are so powerful that they are progressively exterminating sport 'as we know it' (with sports fans reduced to the playthings of media moguls) or that sport is so powerful that the media are forced to fawn over it like hungry dogs (with sports fans ever more indulged and pampered by sports television, radio and the press).

The macro analysis of Chapter 1 underpins a focus on actual sites of media sport production. Chapter 2, 'Working in media sport: the discipline of sports journalism', examines one key area of media institutional practice in addressing the professional status of sports journalism as a sector of journalism in general. Based on a study of sports journalists in the print and electronic media, it demonstrates how the makers of media sports texts have difficulty in securing high professional standing, not least because they are expected to observe the strictures of journalistic objectivity while also developing close ties both to their subjects (athletes and other sports workers) and to their audiences (predominantly sports fans). The resulting tension is shown to have a significant impact on the formation of stories and to produce sharp divisions between different sub-disciplines within sports journalism. The cultural significance of what otherwise might be seen as merely an internal power struggle within a media profession is, it is argued, symptomatic of a more general societal ambivalence concerning the importance and seriousness of popular culture and a squeamishness about its commercial dimensions. Hence, 'Money, myth and the big match: the **political economy** of the sports media' (Chapter 3) concludes the first part of the book by assessing the relative power of major sports and sports organizations, and of media corporations and proprietors, in a world showing signs of advancing **globalization**.

The development of new economic synergies and media technologies is examined in this chapter along with sharply contrasting local and 'amateurist' sports media. Economic forces are shown to be central to the manufacture of the form and content of media sports texts without exercising absolute powers of determination over them. The constantly shifting institutional structures and practices in the media sport economy inevitably involve questions of cultural politics and there follows an examination of familiar debates about politics in and of sport from a largely unfamiliar perspective – the rights associated with the concept of cultural citizenship. The sports media are shown to be caught between a 'neutralist' entertainment stance, their traditional 'Fourth Estate' role, and the Olympian ideology of sport as supra-political. The media sports scandal is briefly discussed as a massively conspicuous media event that cannot be contained by the 'sport-and-politics don't mix' edict, which, to a substantial degree, problematizes the notion of a separate sphere of sports journalism. This discussion prompts a reconsideration of the political responsibilities of the sports media where economic imperatives threaten to compromise journalistic ethics. This semiotic and ideological instability and 'contestability' are then addressed in Part II, 'Unmaking the media sports text'.

In this second part of the book, the activities of reading, decoding and deconstructing sports images and information are shown to be connected to, but not entirely governed by, the industrial forces that have 'supplied' them. A series of readings of 'typical' media sports texts of various kinds is conducted in which each text is shown to be deeply inscribed with ideologies of power, so demanding an overall critique of the concept of an entirely open text amenable to an infinite range of meanings. At the same time, media sports texts are shown to be available for multiple readings according to time, context and readership, and can be seen to be subject to general representational shifts as responses to organizational and wider social changes. In Chapter 4, 'Taking us through it: the "art" of sports commentating and writing', there is an analysis of several types of spoken and printed media sports texts (such as 'live' commentary, routine sports reports and sports gossip), noting how each constructs particular versions of the sporting and surrounding worlds. The language of sport – sometimes called 'sportuguese' (Hargreaves 1986) – is also appraised alongside the role of sports metaphors in non-sporting discourses as bearers of populist meaning, thereby tracing the two-way flow of media sports texts and social ideologies.

Words, although a vital component of media sports culture, are by no means its only vectors. In 'Framed and mounted: sport through the photographic eye' (Chapter 5), the still, visual media sports text is appraised, concentrating on the aesthetic **codes** that govern the composition of sports photographs. Particular attention is given to the representation of gendered and racialized athletes' bodies in orthodox sports news photographs and publicity stills. Visual metaphors, especially in advertising, are shown to work alongside print captions in the accomplishment of various sporting associations and connotations. In concluding Part II, 'Screening the action: the moving sports image' (Chapter 6) interrogates media sports texts in sound and vision – the television broadcast, filmic treatment of sport and sport-related themes. The ways in which sport as myth makes itself readily accessible for the discharge of a variety of narrative and ethical functions are appraised, alongside the efficacy of such symbolic deployments of sport in the light of their substantial dependence on specific and pre-existing audience histories.

This discussion returns us to the territory traversed in this Introduction – the relationships between sport, culture and the media that are always everywhere in process, influencing and being influenced by each other in a perpetual dance of assertion and counter-assertion. There are both traditional and novel aspects of this process, but also little doubt that, at the much-hyped dawn of a new millennium, it is subject to profound and rapid change. An Afterword looks to the future of media sport, which, in technological capability if not yet in widespread cultural practice, has arrived. 'Sport into the ether(net): new technologies, new consumers' closes the book with a consideration of the trajectory of media sport in terms of the texts being generated ('reality' media sport), the relationship between the institutions of sport and media, and the exchanges between sport producers and consumers. The capacity of new media technologies to subvert current prevailing textual relations and practices in sport is assessed in the light of what is already known of the history of media sports development. Once again, the linkage between the conditions under which media sports texts are made and the meanings and ideologies that they generate is shown to be in need of constant review.

Conclusion: looking towards sport and media

A trained capacity to decode media sports texts and to detect the forms of ideological deployment of sport in the media is, irrespective of cultural taste, a crucial skill. It is no exaggeration to assert that such a key critical competency is an important aspect of a fully realized cultural citizenship (Murdock 1992; Stevenson 1995; Rowe 2003) in the era of the omnipresent sports image. It is important, then, to understand the dynamics of the relationship between sport and the media. We need to be able to analyse their mutual roles as social institutions (including assessment of the traditional sports fan's lament that 'TV has taken over sport'), and to develop a knowledge of the institutional processes, practices and motivations that bring media sports texts of various kinds to their willing and unwilling audiences. It is also incumbent on us to be able to criticize their (separate and mutual) interaction with other social institutions, groups and individuals, not least by interrogating the ideologies of repression and exclusion embedded within such seemingly innocent and exhaustingly available elements of popular culture.

In examining the production and content of mainstream media sport texts, we also encounter the points of dissonance and resistance, the places where different meanings and practices of and for sport are made and played out. The requirement is not to treat the sport–media nexus as a closed system of commercial exploitation, massified communication and unreflexive image consumption, but to acquire the critical means to establish an authoritative grasp of the structural, institutional and organizational framework governing their production, dissemination and reception. This is not as grim a task as it sounds, because to gain critical knowledge and acumen in this or any other corner of the popular world involves the pleasure of trading heedless absorption or numb indifference for knowing reflection and informed appreciation (in its broadest sense). In engaging with sport and media, the personal and the political, the serious and the fun-loving, the po-faced and the ironic, can be combined in the most surprising and productive of ways.

Part I
MAKING MEDIA SPORT

UNDERSTANDING SPORT AND MEDIA:
A SOCIO-HISTORICAL APPROACH

The world of sports in the age of mass media has been transformed from nineteenth century amateur recreational participation to late twentieth [and early twenty-first] century spectator-centered technology and business.

(Michael Real 1998: 14)

Introduction: when two worlds collide

Before launching into an extended analysis of how media sports texts are made and interpreted, it is necessary to have an historical and sociological under-standing of the relationship between the institutions of sport and media. There is, after all, no necessary reason why they should be connected in any but the most perfunctory of manners. The practice of sport, in the first instance, is physical play: it is an embodied experience, demanding movement, the cor-poreal manipulation of time and space, and often the hard clash of bodies against other bodies or against immobile hard surfaces. In fact, it is this bodily aspect of sport that prevents game contests like chess and Scrabble from being fully recognized as sports. Most conventional definitions of sport stress that, whatever else happens when we are in the presence of sport, whole bodies or their selected parts are in motion (or, in the case of sports like shooting and archery, exhaustively trained to minimize it). A conservative but, in terms of the analytical sports literature, representative approach like that of J. Bowyer Bell separates sport and other playful activity in a straightforward way:

Certainly, all sports are games but equally certainly not all games are sports. War games or diplomatic games are matters of analogy, not sports events. Sports are play in a closed universe, seemingly isolated from society's other activities. More to the point, some play is a game, not a sport. Essentially a sport is a *repeatable, regulated, physical contest producing a clear winner.*

(Bell 1987: 2, original emphasis)

Such prescriptions of what ought to be called a sport are often contested, but at both official and unofficial levels dispute is not so much over whether a game contest has to be physical to count as sport, as about the physical status of the activity that claims to be a sport. Thus, Bell (1987: 3) rules out chess as a sport because 'structurally, the physical element is irrelevant' and dice because 'winning depends, if honesty rules, on lady luck not an adept toss', but admits darts to the sporting pantheon despite its lack of 'intellectual challenge or a vastly demanding physical strain'. The strong sense of physically based hierarchy in according the title of sport is made clear in the reluctant admission that 'For the purist, there is the problem of video [or computer] games. Alack, it appears that, however crude the game, the winner, physically adept, is playing a sport' (Bell 1987: 3). The sports spectator, therefore, is witnessing a physical activity predicated on the precise calculation of winners and losers, or, in the 'unfortunate' (certainly for sports marketers) absence of a clear result, stated and measurable criteria for declaring a draw or tie.

The 'practice' of media – in terms of both production and reception – is much less physically dependent. Film and television directors, camera operators, music producers, writers and so on may require plenty of physical stamina and, in some cases, an extraordinary 'eye' or 'ear', but, the question-ably accountable area of awards aside, tend to be assessed on aesthetic rather than physical, quantitatively measurable criteria (such as the influence of writers rather than their ability in a head-to-head contest to put assessable words on the page). As text reception activities, viewing and reading are, of course, sensory and sensual activities, and can elicit physiological responses (by provoking fear, sexual arousal, and so on), but they are hardly in the same league (forgive the pun) as completing a marathon or knocking an opponent to the canvas. While the value and status of different media texts is hotly disputed – Milton versus Mills and Boon, or Verdi versus The Verve, etc. – the outcome is rarely as self-evident as Brazil 3 Germany 0 or an individual world record in swimming.

Similarly, sport and media, as organizational complexes, have different reasons for being, personnel, skill requirements, relations with government and non-government agencies, and so on. In short, 'getting physical' in sport and 'making symbols' in media might be expected to remain different cultural pursuits with few compelling reasons to engage each other on a regular basis. Yet, over the past century, the boundaries between these two institutions have blurred sometimes to the point of near invisibility, and they have become so mutually indispensable that, as asserted in the Introduction, one is literally unthinkable without the other (literally, because it is almost impossible now to 'imagine' sport without the mind's eye conjuring up replay, slow motion and multi-perspectival images, accompanied by the inner voice of phantom sports commentators). How did this intermeshing of sport and media occur? In search of an answer, we must look to the great changes that have refashioned the structure and rhythm of the lives of most of the world's inhabitants – the rise of **capitalism** and industrialism in general and the advent of mass consumption and the **commodification** of leisure time in particular. To develop this argument, I shall first sketch in very briefly the twin histories of the institutions whose convergence provides the rationale for this book.

The rise of sport

Most scholarly histories of sport (such as Guttmann 1978) trace the origins of structured physical play in different societies and epochs, but argue that what we have come to recognize as sport, like the nation-state or adolescence, is of much more recent and specific origin. There are many 'folk' games still played today in human groups organized around tribes, small to medium-sized settlements, and even extending to the 'urban villages' of the metropolis. The ancient Olympic Games are routinely judged to be the birthplace of sport, but it would be historically fallacious to conceive of the development of sport into its modern manifestation as arising out of a steady evolutionary process, the origins of which can be traced directly to the ancient Greeks. This is not only because the original, 'ancient' Games were discontinued for at least sixteen centuries (according to Hill 1992: 6, terminating in either AD 261 or 393) until revived in 1896 by the French aristocrat Baron Pierre de Coubertin, although there had been attempted revivals in both Greece and England in the intervening period. It is also because sport as a recognizable social and cultural institution is not universal but emerged in a particular location (Britain) at a particular time (early industrialization). There is a danger, of course, in proposing such a foundational argument, of trying to clean up the messy origins of contemporary sport and of failing to acknowledge its qualitative and directional changes. Without wishing to 'essentialize' the diverse and chaotic world of sport, it is nonetheless important to appreciate that the constituent elements of what is now globally identifiable as sport became manifest in response to a unique combination of historical factors, which, once established, took on a logic and life of its own – an argument not unlike, perhaps, Max Weber's (1930: 182) thesis that an historically contingent meeting of Calvinism and Protestantism created the 'spirit of capitalism', which, once it had taken firm hold, then 'escaped from the cage'. What were these formative forces and conditions out of which sport was created in Britain, and especially that part of it that 'is forever England'? An Anglo imprint so strong that the German writer Agnes Bain Stiven stated that 'England was the cradle and the loving "mother" of sport', while an aristocratic compatriot remarked that in Germany the English word ' "Sport" is as untranslatable as "gentleman" ' (Prince Puechlser-Muskau, quoted in Elias 1986a: 127).

First, there is the longstanding practice of physical or 'rough' play and of periodic competition. Elias and Dunning (1986a) describe the 'folk football' events when the inhabitants (especially the young men) of small settlements engaged in playful activities like the attempted conveyance of inflated pigs' bladders from one village to the other, and a corresponding obstruction of this passage – both tasks to be achieved by any means possible! Not only did such events take many hours (even days), but they also sometimes resulted in serious injury and even death. The more organized game contests such as boxing, wrestling, football, horseracing and cock fighting took place principally on market, feast, harvest and holy days well into the nineteenth century (Clarke and Critcher 1985: 53). They often incurred the wrath or moral concern of dominant political and religious forces who abhorred the wasteful and dissolute behaviour – drunkenness, wagering, violence and sexual promiscuity – that often accompanied these 'proto-sports' tournaments. Ruling elite anxiety concerning the leisure pursuits of the general populace is a feature of all social history. Elias and Dunning (1986b: 176), for example, describe an order by 'King Edward III in 1365 to the Sherriffs of the City of London' that 'able bodied men' who were at 'leisure' on feast days should engage only in militarily useful 'sports' using bows, arrows and other approved weapons. Those who engaged in 'vain games of no value' like stone throwing, handball and football did so 'under pain of imprisonment'. Not all authorities have taken quite such a draconian stance, but they have recognized the highly political nature of permitting, prescribing and proscribing popular pastimes. Weber (1930: 167), for example, notes that it was even necessary for Kings James I and Charles I to make the *Book of Sports* (sport used here in the most general sense of pleasurable diversions) into law to permit 'certain popular amusements on Sunday outside of Church hours', legislation that was inspired by a struggle for power with the Puritans, for whom:

> Sport was accepted if it served a rational purpose, that of recreation necessary for physical efficiency. But as means for the spontaneous expression of undisciplined impulses, it was under suspicion; and in so far as it became purely a means of enjoyment, or awakened pride, raw

instincts or the irrational gambling instinct, it was of course to be strictly condemned.

(Weber 1930: 167)

There is little doubting what would have been the Puritans' disapproval of almost everything that characterizes the culture of sport today – the ecstasy of the moment of victory, the chauvinistic pride when a fan's team wins, and the rawest of human feeling from high states of euphoria to violent impulses (Kerr 1994). They would have condemned righteously the ever-expanding possibilities to gamble not only on the outcome of a sports contest (or, in the case of the 'pools', many simultaneous sports contests), but also on the seemingly infinite range of mini-outcomes (such as predictions of scores, scorers, timing of significant game developments, and so on) now made available on a 24-hour basis by a global Internet betting industry. Sport can be seen to be an important symptom and a partial cause of a move away from a social order founded on the repression of physical play and its pleasurable *accoutrements* to one that not only accepts such pursuits, but also promotes and 'makes capital' from them. The constituents of the contemporary 'carnivalesque' (Bakhtin 1968) may have changed, but – as Hughson (1998) notes in his analysis of soccer hooliganism – sport is still a significant site of struggle between the controllers of social space and the controlled.

From the late eighteenth century onwards, the sea change in social organization caused by the spread of factory labour, the growing concentration of the new industrial proletariat in the cities, the circulation of popular democratic and revolutionary ideas, and the mobilization of radical political movements – in short, the capitalist, industrial, urban and political revolutions that unfolded across the nineteenth century (Nisbet 1967) – made control and surveillance of popular amusements more difficult. This increased degree of social licence provoked an intensified 'moral panic' (Cohen 1980) about popular leisure among the established landed class and the emerging capitalist class alike. Pressure built up, therefore, for greater control over working-class activities outside paid labour hours as part of a more general subjection to industrial capitalism's time and work-discipline (Thompson 1967). Workers were expected to turn up for work on time and in a fit state for arduous and often dangerous shifts in mines, mills and factories – any residual tolerance of seasonal, intermittent and ill-disciplined agricultural labour was being swept away by the industrial capitalist demand for efficiency and reliability. Such calls for commitment to work and restrained leisure led, for example, to the banning in 1860 of the ancient football game in Ashbourne, Derbyshire, leading to a Court Circular carrying an 'Obituary: Death of the Right Honourable Game Football' (Anon. 1992: 5). At the same time, there was a movement to promote healthy physical activity and to discharge 'unhealthy' urges among the citizenry.

It was this line of moral thought that led, somewhat bizarrely, to the staging from 1850 of the 'Olympian Games' in the small English town of Much Wenlock, Shropshire. The Games' founder, Dr William Penny Brookes (who developed a close association with Baron de Coubertin), was strongly in favour of school physical education (especially in state-supported, non-fee-paying institutions) and believed that farm labourers (whose work under more intensive farming methods was becoming as rigidly prescribed as that of their industrial counterparts) should be given compulsory physical training. In extolling the virtues of outdoor exercise, he observed that 'true manliness shows itself not merely in skill and field sports, but in the exercise of those moral virtues which it is one of the objects of religion to inculcate' (quoted in Hill 1992: 10). Hence, through compulsory physical education and sport in state schools, and the imposition of more rigid rules governing sports like boxing, cricket and football outside it, elite and religious groups believed that they could maintain discipline within the working class.

The fear that the 'idle' leisure of the 'common man' would lead to physical degeneracy, a weakened kingdom unable to defend itself (or to attack and colonize others), and a debauched nation sapped of moral fibre, spread in the nineteenth century to the young men of the 'officer' class. For example, Thomas Arnold, the headmaster of Rugby (an English 'public', which is to say private, fee-paying) School, famously advocated sport as a means of promoting discipline, cooperation, leadership and 'purity'. As Clarke and Critcher note:

> The encouragement of organized sport was simultaneously a means of controlling the characteristically anarchic behaviour of public schoolboys and of redirecting the public school ethos towards a model of what would subsequently be defined as 'muscular Christianity'. Thus both the traditional clientele of the aristocracy and the new market of the sons of the bourgeoisie could be retained for the public schools, refurbishing an image tarnished by low morality and dubious academic accomplishment.
>
> (Clarke and Critcher 1985: 62)

Baron Pierre de Coubertin was much taken with this 'healthy body, healthy mind' aspect of sport and by the noble idea that, while excelling at sport would make the citizenry more able to wage war effectively (France, after all, had suffered an ignominious recent defeat in the Franco-Prussian War), meeting other physically and morally fit young people from all over the world in international sporting competition every four years would enhance international understanding and make actual military combat less likely. This residual notion of a *pax Olympia* was highly visible during the Winter Olympics in Nagano, Japan, in February 1998, when the then President of the International Olympic

Committee (IOC), Juan Antonio Samaranch (strongly backed by Michael Knight, the New South Wales minister responsible for the 2000 Summer Olympics in Sydney, Australia), called on all countries to observe an 'Olympic truce', just as US-led forces massed for a threatened military strike against Iraq. No such call was made by the IOC as troops and planes were again poised to invade Iraq in a quest for 'weapons of mass destruction' and 'regime change' in 2003, which was not an Olympic year. The motives of the Olympic truce were, however, more pragmatic than moral. During the ancient Olympics, runners were sent out, torch in hand, requesting safe passage through areas troubled by military strife to enable the athletes to reach Elis to compete in the Ancient Games (Hill 1992: 7–8). The strong moral impulse (much degraded, as I shall later discuss) behind the modern Olympics, which were first staged in Athens in 1896 near the Gods' home on Mount Olympus, was, then, less a legacy of the ancient Greeks than the product of a model of competition influenced by the English, adapted by the French, exported to the world and, in 2004, re-imported to Greece.

Profitable play

If there was a powerful morally and physically improving element fostering the development of organized sport in nineteenth-century Britain, there was a less edifying, baser force at work also – capital and profit. Importantly, the commercialization of sport and the commodification of athletes (transformed from casual 'players' into sportsworkers selling their athletic labour power as 'products' bought and sold on the sport market) opened up a deep schism within the institutional **ideology** of sport itself. For lovers of sport like de Coubertin and Arnold, being an *amateur* (derived directly from the French word for lover) was to adhere to higher values of selfless devotion to the sport, fellow team members and competitors. Indeed, the ethos of sport they were promoting explicitly opposed the 'unworthy' practice of 'playing for pay' or of constructing entire sports (like prize fighting) around gambling and money-making. Attitudes to the business and work possibilities of sport were clearly marked by social class at both ends of the hierarchy. For those who had inherited wealth (especially through land ownership), there was no material need to earn money from sport, but for the emergent entrepreneurial capitalist class who accumulated wealth by making and selling goods and services, and for the members of the working class who had no means of support other than their own labour power, professionalized sport held many attractions. Thus, while 'upper-crust' sports like rugby split into two codes in England in 1895 (and in Australia in 1907) over the issue of player payment and compensation for loss of work through travel or injury, and the International Olympic Committee to this day eschews the paying of prize money to athletes (since 1981 questions of eligibility to compete and remuneration have been left to the individual international federations; Hill 1992: 240), the penetration of the logic of capital accumulation into sport has been such that, as Cashmore (2000) has noted, the term 'amateur' has increasingly become a term of abuse in sporting culture.

'Pure' amateurism in sport, if it ever existed, quickly died and, in the case of rugby union (the amateur side of the split), a long period of 'shamateurism' ended in 1995 with such suddenness that it now threatens to swamp in commercial terms its long-time professional antagonist – rugby league – while multi-millionaire tennis players like Andre Agassi, Serena Williams, Venus Williams and Pete Sampras are now permitted to take part in Olympic competition. A suggestion to introduce golf as an Olympic sport has been opposed due to concerns that the best players would not compete because they would earn much more money on the international golf circuit. Estimating the current global value of the 'sportsbiz' is no mean task, given the range of economic activities which it can claim to embrace, but in 1988 Neil Wilson (1988: 8) noted that 'Official figures in Britain estimate that more than [US]$4 billion is spent on sport each year, more than on motor vehicles. In Britain, sport-related activity employs 376,000 people, more than the chemical industry, or agriculture or the combined electricity and gas industries'. A decade later, a report by the Confederation of Australian Sports valued sport's economic activity in that country (with a population less than one-third of Britain's) at AUS$8 billion, with the sports sector directly employing '95,000 people in 1995–96 – more than the rail, grain, electricity and clothing industries' (Boreham and Pegler 1998: 3). In the same year as this report was released in Australia, the eight-year TV rights to the National Football League in the United States alone were sold for US$17.6 billion (Attwood 1998: 39; see Chapter 3). In 2000, La Fédération Internationale de Football Association (FIFA), soccer's world governing body, estimated that annual world expenditure on this sport alone was US$250 billion (Miller *et al.* 2001: 13). It can easily be seen, then, that the sports industry (without factoring in its contribution to ancillary industries like clothing, food, beverages and transport) has grown enormously over recent decades – and in global proportions.

How can such large sums of money be generated in and through sport? In examining the flow of capital, the initial source lies in the willingness of some people to pay for the privilege of sport spectating. This ability and desire to be entertained by those who specialize in and excel at particular activities – a phenomenon periodically present in pre-industrial societies in the shape of travelling groups of troubadours and actors – grew as part of a more general development of the division of labour in capitalist and industrial societies, as the new complexity and profusion of mass-produced goods and available services demanded a much wider range of occupations, skills and tasks (Durkheim 1960; Marx 1967). Furthermore, the now rigid and carefully calculated segments of work time in factory (and later office) labour created its own alternative – leisure time – that demanded an equivalent level of planning and organization to be utilized to the full (Brown and Rowe 1998). This 'rationalization' (Weber 1968) of the rhythms of work and leisure in the eighteenth and nineteenth centuries was accompanied, as we have seen, by the growing standardization of the rules of various sports and strong pressure from the authorities to stamp out the most dangerous and destructive pursuits – in the name both of propriety and also of labour force efficiency (a gin-sodden or injured worker is also an unproductive one). This process, which he links to a more general 'civilizing process', is described by Elias as the 'sportization of pastimes', whereby:

> The framework of rules, including those providing for 'fairness', became more precise, more explicit and more differentiated. Supervision of the observance of the rules became more efficient; hence penalties for offences against the rules became less escapable. In the form of 'sports', in other words, game-contests involving muscular exertion attained a level of orderliness and of self-discipline on the part of participants not attained before. In the form of 'sports', moreover, game-contests came to embody a rule-set that ensures a balance between the possible attainment of a high-combat tension and a reasonable protection against physical injury.
>
> (Elias 1986b: 151)

This 'figurational' perspective judges the development of organized sport to be evidence of a general shift away from the unrestrained bodily expressions that left the participants in some physical jeopardy (ranging from pub brawls to 'knock down', bare knuckle fighting) to a more disciplined activity in which a clear division existed between spectators and performers. In the case of fist fighting, for example, it evolved under the 1867 'Queensbury Rules' and subsequent restrictions into a boxing contest in a ring of prescribed size over a specified number of rounds of limited duration between only two fighters of similar size, both wearing padded gloves, permitted only to strike particular parts of the body ('no hitting below the belt!'), and so on. Bouts are now quickly ended by the referee when one boxer becomes defenceless and risks (even more) serious injury, while medical staff closely monitor the boxers' health. The efficacy of these measures is disputed – Eric Dunning (1999: 59), for example, cites research that gloves enable boxers to punch harder and more often – but regular public contests and, importantly for this book, television scrutiny, have had a clear 'disciplinary' effect on sport.

As the discretionary income of the industrial proletariat increased, especially by organizing through trade unions to wrest a little more of the capital surplus from the bourgeoisie, the possibility arose of reclaiming and expanding that capital surplus by packaging and selling spectator access to those sports that could attain the requisite, pleasurable 'high-combat tension'. Nineteenth-century entrepreneurs (in the case of the first cricket tours these were often, not too surprisingly, publicans – to the extent that Cashman (1994: 71) describes them as 'the first cricket administrators, [who] viewed cricket as an extension of public-house entertainment') created the conditions for a sports business in much the same way as other leisure pursuits became paying concerns. They relied on supplying services that were attractive to consumers – and made to seem even more so by lively advertising and promotion – but which could be accessed only at a cost. This viewing fee was set at a level that reflected the 'scarcity' of what was to be watched and the superiority of the perspective on proceedings. In this way, sport became another component of the burgeoning entertainment industry, which, as Goldlust notes, has over the past two centuries supplanted so much uncommodified, self-reliant leisure:

> The successful growth of spectator sport was premised on a set of well established entrepreneurial principles that applied throughout the 'enter-tainment' industry. As determined by the organisers, a price, or a range of prices was fixed, the payment of which entitled any member of the public to be admitted to a venue in which the performance or event would take place. The venue, be it a circus, vaudeville house, concert hall, theatre, cinema or stadium, was physically constructed in a manner that limited the potential audience to a finite number of paying customers who, from variably privileged vantage points – depending on the price they were prepared to pay – could experience that performance or event. Through the construction of some form of physical barrier or boundary, those unwilling to pay the cost of admission or unable to gain entry to the venue, because all the legally sanctioned audience space was already committed, were excluded.
>
> (Goldlust 1987: 73–4)

The ease with which sports contests could be enclosed and 'screened' for paying customers varied with the nature of the sport: it was much harder, for example, in large, open-air football, cricket and baseball grounds than for roofed boxing or wrestling buildings and tents. It was also more profitable to set up permanent venues in the large, population-dense urban centres than to rely on travelling sports exhibitions, where transport and sustenance costs were high and venue security and comfort standards were low. The 'classical' mass production capitalist principle of producing as much of the same commodity as cheaply as possible took hold in spectator sport from the late nineteenth century onwards. By the second decade of the twentieth century, 'Spectator sport was [now] attracting massive crowds' (Clarke and Critcher 1985: 74), especially of working-class men. On this basis, a whole economy of sport developed as:

- sporting clubs and associations were formed by subscribing members;
- competitions were established with attractive prize money;
- imposing venues with large crowd capacities were built;
- a labour market (often feudalistic until player revolts) grew up to handle the transfer and valuation of professional and semi-professional 'sportsworkers';
- state funds were donated to the development of sport;
- sportswear and fan merchandise were manufactured and sold;
- and (of particular significance for this book) newspapers, magazines, newsreels, films, radio (and, later, television) programmes became devoted to sport.

The initial development of the commercial side of sport paralleled that of other forms of entertainment, with more and more information about sports events and the people involved in them (especially the new sports celebrities) provided by a panoply of publications from newspaper sports columns to specialist sports newspapers and magazines. But prime dependency on paying spectators physically transporting themselves to particular events limited its potential for expansion. A vast, untapped audience existed that could, by means of developing audiovisual technology, be relieved of the necessity to travel to sports events – instead, the games would come to the audience (Rowe 1996). Yet how could this large, dispersed 'crowd', which was neither never likely to meet each other nor approach a sports stadium, be turned into a market capable of turning a profit? The answer, of course, is that listeners and viewers – especially the latter, on account of television's power to simulate 'real time', sensory experience – would not pay directly to see sport (except by bearing the cost of electronic equipment, electricity and, in some countries, a licence). Instead, another party (advertised businesses) would arrange and pay for them to watch sport and selected messages through a third party (television). While this 'free-to-air' television transmission of sport is now supplemented and even threatened by a re-instatement of direct payment for service through subscription and pay-per-view TV (Roche 2000; Rowe 2003), it is still overwhelmingly dominant on the most important sports media occasions (like the Olympics and the Super Bowl) when the sheer size of the audience generates enormous advertising, sponsorship and TV rights revenue. The popularity of sport, then, became an economic resource in its own right that can be readily harnessed by external economic interests. For this reason, the economy of sport in the twentieth century has developed in such a way that it is no longer reliant on a direct, monetary exchange between spectator and 'exhibitor'. These important economic aspects of sport, however, should not obscure the political and cultural dimensions that illuminate the appeal of sport in making it marketable in the first place.

Political football

National governments, on behalf of the nation-state, have invested heavily in sport and sports television (including through sports institutes and national, public broadcasters) because of the highly effective way in which sport can contribute to nation building. In countries divided by class, gender, ethnic, religious, regional and other means of identification, there are few opportunities for the citizens of a nation to develop a strong sense of 'collective consciousness', of being one people. One significant exception is war, for which sport is often claimed to be a substitute, so that 'in the course of the twentieth century, the competitive bodily exertions of people in the highly regulated form that we call "sport" have come to serve as symbolic representations of a non-violent, non-military form of competition between states' (Elias 1986c: 23). The idea of sport as a 'symbolic representation' of war has sometimes been taken further, to the extent that it is seen as a functional substitute for it, discharging military aggression between countries in a relatively harmless way. This 'war minus the shooting' proposition is most famously associated with George Orwell, but he saw sport as anything but a benign diversion, instead judging international competitions to be malign manifestations of militaristic nationalism:

> I am always amazed when I hear people saying that sport creates good-will between the nations, and that if only the common peoples of the world could meet one another at football or cricket, they would have no inclination to meet on the battlefield. Even if one didn't know from concrete examples (the 1936 Olympic Games [the so-called Nazi Olympics], for instance) that international sporting contests lead to orgies of hatred, one could deduce it from general principles.
>
> (Orwell 1992: 37–8)

The English, according to Orwell, were leading 'young countries' like India and Burma (at least in 1945 when his article was published) astray by exporting their 'obsession' and arousing 'even fiercer passions'. In the ensuing half century and into a new millennium, there have been many more examples of what Orwell would have regarded as 'nations who work themselves into furies over these absurd contests, and seriously believe – at any rate for short periods – that running, jumping and kicking a ball are tests of national virtue' (Orwell 1992: 38). Sometimes the consequences of such heightened emotion can be fatal, as in the 1994 'revenge' murder of Colombian footballer Andres Escobar, who was summarily executed outside a bar by an enraged fan after Escobar had scored the own goal that precipitated his team's exit from the World Cup finals. Probably the most famous direct linkage of sport and military combat is the so-called 'soccer war' in 1969 between El Salvador and Honduras, where border tensions were touched off by riots following a soccer World Cup qualifying match between the countries. Not only has the entwining of national and sports culture tightened in many countries and spread to others, but also the possibilities of exposing all of the globe's citizens to such 'symbolic representations' of national progress and international competition have grown with the institutions of sport and media.

Just as it was in Britain that the social institution and cultural form of sport first emerged, it was the British state, through its public broadcaster the British Broadcasting Corporation (BBC), that pioneered the use of great sporting occasions as festivals of nationhood, so that 'broadcasting would produce a new form of national event: in extending major occasions of state and of sport throughout the land it would make a royal wedding a nation's wedding', and demonstrating 'the centrality of the BBC's sport coverage of notions of Britishness and national identity' (Whannel 1992: 20, 21). Other countries quickly appreciated this symbolically unifying power of national and, especially, of international sport, so that great sporting moments like the Super Bowl in the USA, the Melbourne Cup in Australia, the FA Cup Final in the UK, Hockey Night in Canada (Kidd 1982; Gruneau and Whitson 1993) and global media mega sports events like the Olympics (Larson and Park 1993) and the soccer World Cup (Sugden and Tomlinson 1998), have become orgies of both nationalism and commodification ('commodified nationalism', perhaps).

Apart from the state political usages of sport – most notoriously, as Orwell noted above, Adolf Hitler's attempt to use the 1936 Berlin Olympic Games as a vehicle for the assertion of Aryan supremacy – the overall cultural significance of sport cannot be underestimated. For example, most of the historical accounts of sport drawn on above reproduce the inequality of its gender order, with women athletes and spectators rendered more or less invisible or marginal (Hargreaves 1993a, 1994). Yet there is a powerful 'herstory' in sport: a series of tales of women who have fought for the right to play sport, be paid properly for it, supported by sponsors at the level of their male counterparts, wear what they choose while competing, secure appropriate media coverage, and so on (Blue 1987; Guttmann 1991). If culture is the 'stuff' of everyday life – the frame through which we experience, interpret, mould and represent everything that surrounds us – then sport occupies, as noted in the Introduction, an uncommonly prominent position within it. The economy of sport is, then, more than the exchange of money for tickets, of wages for performance on the field of play. There is also a **cultural economy** of sport, where information, images, ideas and rhetorics are exchanged, where symbolic value is added, where metaphorical (and sometimes literal, in the case of publicly listed sports clubs) stocks rise and fall. This cultural (and material) economy of sport has developed through 'cottage industry' and early industrial and capital accumulative phases to a full-blown, sophisticated complex. Once elements of sport had become rationalized and industrialized, they necessarily entered into relations with other economic entities that acted as conduits, carrying sports culture far beyond its places of origin. As noted above, the institution (which, more accurately, is a constellation of diverse but related structures and practices) that has become crucial to the destiny of modern sport is the media.

The media have created the capacity for sport to reach its staggering global audience and to 'service' that audience, reproducing and transforming sports culture through an endless and pervasive process of showing, 'sounding', discussing, depicting – in short, of representing sport in myriad ways. Before we can proceed to an analysis of the sports media, we must first understand, through cultivating a socio-historical sensibility, not only why contemporary sport needs the media so desperately, but also why the media have an equal and urgent need for sport.

The rise of the mass media

As in the case of the physical play and game contests that mutated into sport, **communication** using a variety of aural and visual media is an ancient practice, from cave paintings and 'sagas' told around camp fires through religious icons and hand-written books, to satellite broadcasts and computer graphics. A key element of the rise of capitalism and industrialism was the transformation of small-scale and technologically rudimentary media into an institutional complex of enormous social, cultural, political and economic importance. These 'mass media comprise the institutions and techniques by which specialized social groups disseminate symbolic content to large heterogeneous and geographically-dispersed audiences' (Bennett *et al.* 1977: 9, adapted from Janowitz 1968). The standard accounts of the development of mass communication (such as Bittner 1983; McQuail 1987) chronicle the 'take off' points, such as the invention in 1450 of the Gutenberg press that gave birth to print and, later, the arrival of radio transmitters followed by the cathode ray tube that brought us television. To see these technological developments out of social context is, however, also to view the development of media as an inevitable, evolutionary process. But the history of media, like that of sport, is a much more complicated tale of struggle. In this case it is between powerful groups (first the church, then the state) to control the circulation of 'dangerous' texts, such as officially unapproved versions of the Bible, and other, often less powerful groups and individuals (political movements, trade unions, unaffiliated people asserting their rights of liberty) who wanted access to these texts and to the means to circulate their own texts. Not only did the rise of representative democracy, citizenship and the nation-state demand a free and efficient media as a political imperative, but so also did the new capitalist class require the capacity to display its goods nationally and, later, internationally in obedience to an economic one. McQuail traces our contemporary notions of the 'ideal' newspaper to:

> The 'high bourgeois' phase of press history, from about 1850 to the turn of the century, [which] was the product of several events and circumstances: the triumph of liberalism and the ending, except in more benighted quarters of Europe, of direct censorship or fiscal constraint; the establishment of a relatively progressive capitalist class and several emergent professions, thus forging a business-professional establishment; many social and technological changes favouring the operation of a national or regional press of high information quality.
>
> (McQuail 1987: 12)

The establishment of the values and practices of 'good' journalism (fearless independence from government and other powerful groups, a commitment to rooting out corruption, an authoritative voice on which the public can rely, and so on) was followed by a more overtly commercial concern with advertising. The 'quality' newspapers could exercise political influence by reaching a relatively small but powerful readership, as Hartley (1996) notes in his comment on the 1835 painting by B.R. Haydon, *Waiting for the Times*, in which one gentleman impatiently covets the broadsheet in the hands of another, anxious not to remain 'absent from the imagined community of VIP readership' (p. 14). As Curran (1981a) notes, attempts by the British ruling class to deny this level of power and influence through the media to others by imposing stamp duties and by harshly enforcing laws of libel and sedition, paradoxically also helped the nineteenth-century radical press (like *The Poor Man's Guardian* and the *Northern Star*) to flourish by slowing 'the development of a mass market for newspapers, and consequently the development of expensive print technology to service it, while the duty on advertisements limited the growth of advertising expenditure on the popular press' (p. 25). Campaigns against 'the taxes on knowledge' were as much driven by desires for capital accumulation as by appeals for freedom of thought and expression – the removal of many political impediments to newspaper production allowed the economic power of 'new money' entrepreneurs (especially press barons like Lord Northcliffe and, a little later, Lords Beaverbrook and Rothermere) to assert itself. Thus, cheaper, widely distributed papers, made attractive to advertisers by toning down political rhetoric and to readers by sensational copy, edged out the radical, 'disreputable' press (Curran 1981b) and created and then serviced a different market to that of 'highbrow' newspapers.

The new technological capabilities of the media meant that the content of the popular 'penny dreadful' scandal sheets that were sold on the streets could be readily disseminated in a manner that reflected the economic power generated simply by the exposure of large numbers of people to imprecations to buy products and services. The emerging 'yellow press' (associated in the USA with Joseph Pulitzer and William Randolph Hearst) was not much admired by the guardians of nineteenth-century media morality but, just as occurs in the contemporary world, the immediate riposte was that demonstrable public demand for 'bad' journalism had to be satisfied, and that no group of privileged individuals had the right to dictate what the 'masses' wanted to read and see. Disputes over media morality and ethics, and especially their political and economic power, are no less apparent long after the daily newspaper first made its mark. Indeed, as Schultz argues, they may have been exacerbated in the current 'information age':

> As the engines of global economic growth switch from industrial to information production, the rhetoric which, for two centuries, has legitimised the media as more than just another business needs to be re-examined. More than any other industry the media have been characterised by 'deeply ethical' debates about role and responsibility – profit was never the sole criteria [*sic*] on which the media were judged. But as the profits generated by the media continue to grow the tensions between serving the public and making money are also likely to escalate.
>
> (Schultz 1994: 61)

This idea that the media are 'not just another business' sits particularly uncomfortably with developments in the late twentieth and early twenty-first centuries that have seen the media's principal currency – information and images – become also the prime unit of exchange, and the role of the media far exceeds that of the idealized vocation of nineteenth-century quality journalism. Indeed, the development of new media technologies such as the Internet have not to date had the predicted impact of democratizing communication and reducing media concentration, leading instead to converged media interests and re-concentration as, for example, Internet service providers merge with media conglomerates (as occurred in the formation of AOL Time Warner; see Hesmondhalgh 2002) or in the case of the now standard practice of leading newspapers producing online editions (Wejbora 2003). The intensification of debates about media power and responsibility is, however, a product of expansion of the whole media sector, rather than, as media moralists often suggest, linked to a specific development like the invention of television, the circulation of glossy magazines or the marketing of paperback books.

News and entertainment

The mass media, as we have seen, had from the outset two major, sometimes conflicting functions. The first involved the 'serious' notion of news gathering and processing as part of the Fourth Estate, which acted (at least ostensibly) as a watchdog on the powerful and as an important influence in the key process of nation building by communicating the nation to itself (Gellner 1983; Schlesinger 1991). It was no longer necessary to listen to a town crier to hear the news of the day or to rely on rumour and gossip to be informed about what was happening outside the individual's or small group's immediate experience. The great journals of record and opinion leaders such as *The Times* of London and the *New York Times* and, later, public broadcasters like the BBC and those in the former British colonies or dominions on which they were modelled, like the Australian and Canadian Broadcasting Corporations (ABC and CBC, respectively), were and are key media organizations in the formation of an informed 'public sphere' (Habermas 1989). The extent to which the mass media successfully fulfil this important function of challenging the powerful and promoting informed citizenship has always been hotly disputed, not least because to own or control a major media organization (especially an 'empire' consisting of many different organizations operating in a single medium or, even more powerfully, across different media) is a significant form of power in its own right (Golding and Murdock 2000). However unflattering the 'verdict' might be on the capitalist press or on state broadcasters in regard to their sincerity and effectiveness in serving the people at large and protecting the weak from the abuse of power by ruling elites, there is no doubt that major media organizations are highly sensitive to allegations that they ruthlessly exploit their command of the channels of mass communication to their commercial and political advantage. As Windschuttle (1984) argues, the conventional defence of commercial media organizations (and, we might add, even of some increasingly entrepreneurial public media) against criticisms of dereliction of public duty is to construct the idea of the 'public interest' within a type of 'free market model', which, in the case of newspapers, positions them as:

> simply in the business of satisfying the demand for news. So the principal criterion of selection is public interest. The concept of 'public interest' is usually interpreted in two ways: what the public is interested in; and what is in the public's interest. This produces a dual approach to the business of editing. It means the news media have to both 'give the public what it wants', which is often taken to be 'human interest' or largely trivial material, and to fulfil its 'duty' to record the important events of the day.
>
> (Windschuttle 1984: 262)

Because the public interest can be invoked easily but never understood absolutely, and because terms like 'trivial' or 'human interest' can be endlessly debated, newspaper proprietors and editors (and their equivalents in television and radio) can claim that they are only biased against what is boring and off-putting for their publics. If they do not cover news stories about their commercial or political opponents, or represent them unfavourably if they do, it can be claimed by media organizations that it is in response to an audience-pleasing imperative. Here the rather abstract concept of the public interest can be easily translated into measurements (ratings, circulation, sales) of what the public can be shown to be interested in.

This second function of the mass media, then, has rather less lofty ambitions and a somewhat reduced emphasis on ethical accountability; it is to entertain the populace using the new media technologies (which allow texts to be rapidly reproduced and disseminated) to communicate cheaply with large numbers of people. In this way, it is no longer necessary to go to a concert to hear music or to watch a play in performance to experience drama. Furthermore, the popularity of this media content can be used to advertise the myriad goods whose mass production demands an equivalent level of mass consumption (Dyer 1982). As Brierley puts it with disarming directness:

> Advertising arose out of the industrial revolution. Overproduction of mass market goods through new manufacturing techniques and low consumption meant that consumer goods companies needed to stimulate demand. New channels of distribution such as transportation and mass retailing opened up the possibility of reaching new markets.
>
> (Brierley 1998: 39)

To be effective, advertising had to connect with the powerful social myths already in circulation (Leiss *et al.* 1990) and also be situated in a highly visible media site where it was available to facilitate the trade in goods and services. Popular media texts could, then, be used as a lure to bring unknowing and perhaps reluctant consumers into the orbit of commodity culture. In 'capturing audiences for advertisers' – as Smythe (1977) has influentially argued – for the purpose of mass consumer persuasion, the mass media could now be subsidized by those same advertisers to provide cheap (as in the case of newspapers whose cover price is only a fraction of their production cost) or free (as in much 'free-to-air' television) media content that would provide the opportunity for an unprecedentedly massive 'window display' for goods and services.

As the mass media developed into large-scale, formal, bureaucratic organizations in the business of producing news, culture and entertainment in a manner imitative of the continuous process production methods of factories, they also displayed an insatiable hunger for content – the vast spaces of print and air time had to be filled in fulfilling their dual informational and entertainment functions. It is impossible to imagine newspapers or radio news bulletins being cancelled on the grounds that nothing sufficiently newsworthy happened in the world today, or no new records or films being released this week because of a temporary talent shortage, or blank pages in magazines and empty TV screens on account of a failure to come up with anything sufficiently diverting. This is not only because news is always being made and culture produced that is of interest to somebody somewhere, but also because 'dead air', blank screens, empty pages and goods-free shops cannot be tolerated by the media and cultural industries and their business clients. The economics of the commercial media are premised on the continued availability of 'new' material (however familiar in form and predictable in content) that will constantly stimulate popular attention, and that will balance the comfortable expectations of audiences with elements of novelty and surprise (Cunningham and Miller (with Rowe) 1994). In this way, the mass media can be conceived as an institutional space that must be filled on a daily basis to function, rather than in more conventional terms as a supplier of cultural goods on the basis of established and measurable demand.

The publicly funded media, furthermore, are charged as we have seen with the additional responsibility of fostering national culture, a sense of belonging to the nation which brings its various citizens together across the barriers of locality, class, age, race, ethnicity, gender, and so on. The public media are no less required to provide continuous content than the commercial media, although their revenue does not derive directly from selling goods and exposing audiences. For public media to fail to produce copious quantities of information and entertainment would imply the unthinkable – that the nation is not being dutifully served or, worse, that during breaks in transmission it does not exist! All media – public or private, large or small – have to deal with the question of a public. While it is misleading to reduce media relations simply to one group of people (the audience) accepting or rejecting the product of another (journalists, film-makers, pop musicians, television directors, and so on), there is no doubt that, ultimately, audiences are crucial to the success of media enterprises.

The media, especially in corporate and public form, are expected to be accountable to their audiences – they are literally at their service. Despite widespread belief in the ease of audience manipulation by unscrupulous advertisers, television executives and press barons, it is striking that media professionals see their publics often as fickle, mysterious and essentially unknowable. In a crowded marketplace where most cultural products that are sold will lose money, or where success is dependent on stopping the listener from 'touching that dial' or the viewer from switching the remote control, it is necessary to minimize the risk of failure in an uncertain 'task environment' (Hirsch 1971). Managing that task environment is a delicate activity: it is necessary to 'second guess' what audiences want; to act on previous successes by giving them more of the same while judging when they have become bored or satiated with a particular format; to offer the requisite level of novelty without alienating the audience with something too far 'out of left field'. Making media texts is, then, both a creative and a conservative activity, requiring a judicious appreciation of the swings between cycles of standardization, when a successful formula (like TV 'infotainment' shows, teenage 'splatter' movies, 'reality' television, costume dramas or 'boy band' pop music) is found and reproduced, and cycles of diversification (like the sudden eruption of visually and sonically confrontational punk music, ironically 'postmodern' violent films with discontinuous narratives, or 'weird' TV serials about the dark underbelly of conventional community life), when novel approaches and material are desired. David Hesmondhalgh (2002: 233) has argued, correctly, that this model of standardization/diversification in the cultural industries (based on Peterson and Berger 1975) is flawed, but it does reflect something of the 'herd' behaviour of cultural producers who are always stealing ideas and formulae from each other while, contradictorily, going it alone in the perpetual search to be first with the 'next big thing'.

The producer–institution–text–audience relationship is revealed to be a highly complex one that is resistant to the simple accounting logic of attendances, ratings, readerships, 'hits', sales, and so on. In socio-cultural terms, audiences are highly artificial constructs, temporarily mobilized by the text in often widely varying circumstances, with different levels of commitment, knowledge and attention, and prone to dissolve just as analysts believe themselves to be in possession of the keys to unlock their secrets (Ang 1991; Ruddock 2001; Balnaves *et al.* 2002). Nonetheless, in all areas of cultural production there is a constant, institutionally rational attempt to match the produced text to viable aggregations of people who will respond positively to it and, better, demand more. What subject could possibly satisfy and stimulate the competing and disparate demands of diverse populations? The answer – for so many editors and programmers the dream solution to the perennial problem of contacting and holding media audiences – is sport.

Having it both ways: sport meets media

Sport provides the mass media with many precious qualities. In terms of audiences it is able regularly to deliver large (sometimes enormous), often extremely loyal cohorts of readers, listeners and viewers. The linkage between sport and media did not await the arrival of the age of television. As Michael Harris (1998: 19), for example, demonstrates, 'cricket was drawn into the content of the London newspapers' well before 1750 as part of the 'widening circle of commercialization within what might begin to be described as the leisure industries' and of the 'emergent urban activity which became closely associated with the elite groups in English society'. Newspapers, therefore, were key promotional tools as entrepreneurs began to 'construct a business around public recreation' (Harris 1998: 24). The core audience of sports fans (and the derivation from 'fanatic' is frequently appropriate) is a reliable 'commodity' that can be profitably sold to advertisers, and on occasions a much larger and less committed audience can be drawn in to take part in the great national and international spectacles which generate their own momentum of interest through their sheer size and 'cross-media' visibility. Just as television has, like fashion, its new seasons, sport has its equivalent of serials and blockbusters. The established sports can bubble away in their rolling time slots (in some cases becoming global, year-round offerings courtesy of satellite television), while the media machine periodically gears up for national and international mega media sports events, which, in self-fulfilling fashion, become compulsive viewing and reading matter (because they are nearly impossible to escape). Consider, for example, the scarcity of personal space impervious to images and information concerning the Summer Olympics or the soccer World Cup during the com-petition period in any society with a reasonably well-developed media infrastructure. Sport not only produces audiences faithful to the media which are displaying it, but also is productive of other forms of loyalty, such as to products (as the sponsors of sports competitions and the companies that invest heavily in sports-related advertising, like Benson and Hedges, Coca-Cola and McDonald's, can attest) and also to city, state, county, region or nation (an emotion much prized by governments and much exploited by commerce). In countries like Australia, where sensitivity to media and cultural imperialism exists as a result of its earlier colonial status and current openness to media products from the dominant English language centres of production, sport also supports the idea of local loyalty by counting towards legislated quotas of local audiovisual media content (Cunningham and Miller (with Rowe) 1994).

For all this valuable emphasis on predictability and loyalty – to the extent that many sports in the media take on the appearance of sought-after brand names with a high recognition factor (Lash and Urry 1994) – sport also possesses the highly desirable quality of novelty and unpredictability. Media **discourse** before, during and after sports events is variously about prediction, judging what has been predicted against what is actually unfolding, and then reflecting on and seeking to find explanations for what has transpired (Eco 1986). In other words, while, for example, 'live' sport on television may have the stylized and easily anticipated quality of the soap opera **genre** (see Chapter 6), it is always capable of a surprise outcome that refuses to follow slavishly a script that has been apparently prepared for it (Harriss 1990). This 'uncertainty principle' of sport – and hence media sport – explains why result fixing, like a boxer 'taking a dive' or a soccer goalkeeper deliberately letting in a goal, is so scandalous. In sport's famous clichés, 'it's never over until the fat lady sings' (in this case a scenario borrowed from opera) or 'the game is never over until the final whistle' (a tautology masquerading as wisdom). This 'emergent' quality of sport in the media helps meet the perpetual audience need for something new and different alongside what is familiar and known. It also provides the media with the cornerstones of news gathering and delivery – constant updates, reported results, highlights, behind-the-scenes information, and so on. Sport, then, stands at the confluence of the two principal functions of the mass media – news and entertainment – and is carefully structured into the 'softer' spaces of news bulletins and newspaper sections. It simultaneously supplies the material to be reported on and a substantial component of the infrastructure of reporting. As content, sport can absorb copious quantities of media space and time. A test cricket match, for example, is a single sports event that can occupy a television schedule from morning to early evening, followed by some packaged late night highlights and frequent news updates and reports, for five six-hour days. Variations on the same sports story can appear on the front, features and 'op ed' pages of newspapers, as well as in the regular sports sections, supplements or 'tear-outs'.

It is little wonder that the relationship between sport and the media (especially television) is commonly described as the happiest of marriages, with both institutions becoming mutually dependent in an increasingly extensive and expensive exchange of exposure and rights fees for sport in return for compelling content and audience capture for the media (Rowe 1996). Like all enduring relationships, however, there are many points of tension, power plays, negotiations, compromises, disagreements and secrets. Both parties can also claim that they are dominated by the other. So, while media companies may complain that the price of broadcast rights demanded by sport are extortionate (Milmo 2002), sports, sports fans and sports journalists (the latter two categories can usually be collapsed) often bemoan that everything in sport has been subordinated to the interests of the media. As one print sports journalist has stated:

> This year, Wimbledon has reversed the normal priorities. It is putting the tastiest match on last, rather than first. This is vexing for the paying punters, but good news for television, the biggest paying punter of them all. Another of professional sport's constant balancing acts is to please both punters and television. And it is the interests of punters and, perhaps more importantly, the leading players, that have come second . . .
>
> But all sporting events must balance the needs of pure sport and the needs of commerce. Without commerce there is no professional sport.
>
> (Barnes 2000: 34)

Many of these visible, partly obscured and hidden elements of the sport–media nexus will be analysed in the following chapters as we attempt to understand how media sports texts are manufactured, 'unwrapped' and consumed. This might be an all-very-interesting but not terribly enlightening exercise in the description of cultural production if making media sport was just a technical matter, a value-neutral process whereby sports information and action is disseminated and a little (or even a lot of) money is made on the side. But this is not the case: power over media sports production brings with it other forms of power – economic, social, cultural and ideological – which often seem elusive or the existence of which is denied altogether by those who believe that 'it's just business' or 'it's only a game'. The final task in this summary socio-historical analysis of sport and media is to propose that the (conscious or unconscious) exercise of power is not an unfortunate by-product of the media sport production process but is, in fact, central to it.

Conclusion: sport, media and cultural power

The heightened prominence of sport in print reportage (including specialist sports, business and general journalism), magazines, still photography, radio, film, video, television and the Internet is incontestable. What we are to make of this observation is much less easily established. Several propositions can be offered to explain the spectacular growth of the sports media. Blandly, it can be suggested that it is produced by the efficient operation of the market in cultural goods, services and information, a benign example of how popular taste is accommodated by the cultural industries. Alternatively and more sinisterly, wall-to-wall media sport can be seen as the extension of the 'bread and circuses' policies of dominant groups, perpetually distracting the population with trivia while getting on with the business of ruling a grossly unequal world to their own advantage by making sure that oppositional values are discredited and neglected. These well known polarized perspectives, described over a quarter of a century ago by Cohen and Young (1973) as the commercial *laissez-faire* and mass manipulative models of the media, have between them a range of different positions that gravitate, in emphasis rather than in their totality, towards one or other end of the analytical spectrum. Even less conclusive is the approach which stresses the inconsistent, contingent, negotiated or emergent relations between media, sport, culture and society. Instead of the master **narrative** of consumer freedom versus mass oppression, there is a more modest and qualified attention paid to the historical and institutional conditions which produce outcomes that can only be pronounced upon after close and unprejudiced inspections of particular instances of media sport on a case-by-case basis. From such a perspective it is not possible to speak of the state of the sports media in general, but only of the diverse complexity of sites and processes out of which are produced many different, historically conditioned but non-determinant circumstances (Sugden and Tomlinson 2002).

Here, then, commercial and media forces can be said to have wrested control of a sport from 'the people', but over here 'the people' have successfully resisted the blandishments of sports media commerce, or have accepted the need for economic rationalization, or have formed alliances with more 'sympathetic' commercial enterprises or governments to repel the clumsy incursions of 'buccaneering' businesspeople. The cost of such an open, flexible and indeterminate approach is, however, the loss of explanatory power arising from a concern with the uniqueness of each instance of media sport rather than with the common features out of which patterns and trends can be discerned. For this reason, the analysis of sport and media must move in different directions, carefully weighing the macro and micro, general and specific influences, which, in combination, work to fashion everyday life out of the social resources at hand. Thus, as Foucault (1980) observes, there are different forms and effects of power that are in play at different levels throughout the social world. Power is not necessarily a negative concept: it ranges in character from the exercise of the grossest and subtlest forms of oppression to the capacity to effect dramatic or cumulatively progressive change. Power also operates in environments – like the domain of the sports media – often dismissed as trivial and harmless. The 'trick' is to recognize the many forms, directions, sites and effects of power without optimistically inflating the success of resistive strategies or playing down the capacity of established power structures to assert themselves with an almost effortless and invisible force.

In this book I am interested in three main manifestations of power. The first is at the institutional level – the manner in which the institutions of media and sport have come together, the ways in which one may be said to have dominated (or even consumed) the other, the extent to which their interaction has had a mutually modifying effect. The second is at the symbolic level – how the institutionally provided and moulded media sports texts can be interpreted and used, sometimes accepted and revered, on other occasions rejected and ridiculed. The third is at the relational level – the wider social and cultural ramifications of the development of a giant, partially globalized media sports cultural complex; that is, the extent to which this great 'engine' of **signs** and **myths** itself symbolizes and helps create our current 'being in the world'. By gaining a better knowledge and understanding of how media sports texts are produced and what they might mean, it is possible to learn more about societies in which 'grounded' and 'mediated' experience intermesh in ever more insidious and seemingly seamless ways.

This chapter has covered a good deal of ground in attempting to establish a socio-historical framework for the study of sport, culture and the media. Many corners have been cut in the process, because to do a thorough job would have taken up the whole of this book – and probably several more volumes. I have tried to demonstrate something of how sport and the media developed as social institutions and then intersected and interpenetrated as the rapid growth in industrialized leisure and large-scale consumption, coupled with the require-ments of modern nation building, created the circumstances for a long-lasting and increasingly intense union. Such developments, I have argued, need to be interrogated rather than merely documented, because the enormous investment of capital, human labour, political rhetoric, social effort and cultural space that has produced contemporary media sport has also created the conditions for the playing out of many forms of power to:

- 'discipline' great proportions of the world's citizens to watch sports TV in escalating (though disputed) numbers, such as the estimated 3.7 billion people in 220 countries claimed to have watched the Sydney 2000 Olympics and the cumulative audience for the Korea/Japan 2002 World Cup of 28.8 billion people from 213 countries;
- determine the destiny of large companies and their employees, including giant media corporations like NBC, the now defunct Kirch media (who paid too much for the broadcast rights to the 2002 soccer World Cup and couldn't recoup the cost), sports apparel manufacturers like Nike, and soft drink makers like Pepsi;
- influence the policies of government in, for example, underwriting bids to host mega-media sports events, deciding on whether to participate in

sports boycotts, and setting regulatory parameters for broadcast rights and the advertising of unhealthy products like tobacco and bicycle shorts;
- constitute much of the verbal and visual imagery in circulation, from sports metaphors in business and politics to street billboards and television super-slow-motion replays;
- occupy the ground of so much social discourse, ranging from bar-room banter to the measured tones of the academic conference paper.

Clearly, all that the media sports cultural complex has at its disposal is a power that cannot be dismissed lightly with the old catchcry 'that's entertainment'.

Where is the point of entry for probing the media sport behemoth with the social scientific scalpel? It is as well to remember (in order not to 'fetishize' and reify them) that media sports texts, as the product of human activity, have to be manufactured by human subjects according to accepted and imposed procedures and values. The personnel traditionally charged with supplying and/or interpreting these texts are quite commonly regarded as the 'least cuddly' of their profession, 'notorious for going sour with drink and age' (McGuane 1992: xv). They are known by the professional title 'sports journalist'.

Further reading

Boyle, R. and Haynes, R. (2000) *Power Play: Sport, the Media & Popular Culture*. Harlow: Pearson Education.

Chandler, J.M. (1988) *Television and National Sport: The United States and Britain*. Urbana, IL: University of Illinois Press.

Elias, N. and Dunning, E. (1986) *Quest for Excitement: Sport and Leisure in the Civilising Process*. Oxford: Basil Blackwell.

Goldlust, J. (1987) *Playing for Keeps: Sport, the Media and Society*. Melbourne, VIC: Longman Cheshire.

Guttmann, A. (1978) *From Ritual to Record: The Nature of Modern Sports*. New York: Columbia University Press.

Wenner, L.A. (ed.) (1998) *MediaSport*. London: Routledge.

WORKING IN MEDIA SPORT: THE DISCIPLINE OF SPORTS JOURNALISM

> I have done every job in provincial journalism, everything but Saturday afternoon sport, because even vultures will throw up on something!
>
> (Terry Pratchett 1990: 13)

> I get paid for doing what normal people gladly pay to do. Through ridiculous luck, coincidence and deception, I seem to be the holder of a kind of fantasy job.
>
> (Simon Barnes 1989: 1)

Introduction: flesh, blood and sports journalists

There is something deeply paradoxical about the professional status of sports journalism, especially in the medium of print. In discharging their usual responsibilities of description and commentary, reporters' accounts of sports events are eagerly consulted by sports fans, while in their broader journalistic role of covering sport in its many manifestations, sports journalists are among the most visible of all contemporary writers. The ruminations of the elite class of 'celebrity' sports journalists are much sought after by the major newspapers, their lucrative contracts the envy of colleagues in other 'disciplines' of journalism. Yet sports journalists do not have a standing in their profession that corresponds to the size of their readerships or of their pay packets, with the old saying (now reaching the status of cliché) that sport is the 'toy department of the news media' still readily to hand as a dismissal of the worth of what sports journalists do. This reluctance to take sports journalism seriously produces the paradoxical outcome that sports newspaper writers are much read but little admired.

How can we explain, putting aside the wider question of the surprising lack of occupational prestige of journalists as a group – according to Curran (1998: 90) 'former standards of accuracy are declining, at least in the eyes of the public' – the rather low esteem in which sports journalists are held within their chosen profession? Or, even if journalists in general retain high or even growing repute, why does the American writer James Traub (1991: 35) note that after a short stint as a sports writer, 'The experience taught me that the trend of increasing prestige for the press, observable in such coverage sectors as business and politics, has not been universal'? In looking for an answer to these questions, it is necessary to understand the wider ambivalence concerning the value of popular culture and of attempts to take it seriously. Sports journalists, furthermore, are caught in a particularly difficult bind because of the different, sometimes contradictory professional demands made on them: they are expected, often at the same time, to be objective reporters, critical investigators, apologists for sports and teams, representatives of fans and, not unusually, to have performed in sport at elite levels. Their readers, listeners and viewers are more than a little uncertain about the value of their work. As Hornby (1992) pronounces in his obsessive fan's paean to soccer, *Fever Pitch* (the film of which is discussed in Chapter 6), 'Sports journalists and armchair Corinthians are the Amazon Indians who know more than we do – but in another way they know much, much less' (p. 136). Such questioning of authoritative knowledge recurs repeatedly in lounge and bar-room discussions of sports journalism: What do they know anyway? Can they really feel it? Are they too close to it? Maybe they're just overpaid sports groupies? Often lying behind such doubts is a lingering resentment, from non-sports colleagues and sports fans alike, that sports journalism is something of a 'lurk' – a case of 'nice work if you can get it'. Simon Barnes (1989: 1) in detailing *A Sports-writer's Year*, registers his acute awareness of this attitude of combined hostility and envy towards sports journalists in calling its introduction 'How to become a sportswriter by complete accident', and through self-deprecating humour. He also discloses a craft secret: 'I hope that it does not come as a complete shock to the world that the job involves a spot of work here and there' (p. 3).

These conflicts over the identity and conduct of sports journalists go beyond a little jockeying for position in the professional pecking order: they have far-reaching ramifications for the process of making media sports genres and texts. By inspecting the 'coalface' of media sports production, it is possible to 'de-naturalize' media sports texts and so to understand that they are particular creations and constructions arising from the complex, contradictory forces that make culture. At the same time, we begin to see something of the cultural politics of sports journalism, especially the ways in which sports texts mediate understandings of social issues within sport and between sport and the society in which it is embedded. The seemingly 'automatic', neutral procedures of media sports text production are thereby revealed as wedded to the negotiation and promotion of power relations in their various forms. This case study of sports journalism is, then, being used to exemplify the kind of critical analysis that could be applied to any area of media sport production. Specific questions might vary, but the crucial principle is that all media sports texts are manufactured, and that the process of production involves many decisions, calculations, dilemmas and disputes. The produced media sports text, in other words, has to be released from its mechanical appearance and *humanized*.

In this chapter, I shall explore the practice and status of sports journalism (with the major emphasis on print) in teasing out key aspects of the making of sports texts. In so doing, I shall draw on a research study (with some interview extracts presented here also found in Rowe and Stevenson 1995) I conducted in the mid-1990s, which involved over forty interviews (not all conducted by me) with working sports journalists (mostly print, but also television and radio) from three different English-speaking countries (Australia, the UK and New Zealand), and subsequently informed by discussions with journalists from various disciplines in the UK and the USA. A key element of the empirical study was the sports journalists' self-assessment of their own and their colleagues' work activities in different sports media (all identifying names of individuals, organizations and places, it should be noted, have been removed in presenting these interview data). It is important to understand (although not be limited to) what sports journalists think about what they do because, despite appearances to the contrary on occasions, they do not robotically churn out pre-programmed content. However urgent the deadlines, limited the vocabulary and familiar the organizational routine of sports journalism, it should never be forgotten that, as Schudson points out:

> Journalists write the words that turn up in the papers or on the screen as stories. Not government officials, not cultural forces, not 'reality' magically transforming itself into alphabetic signs, but flesh-and-blood journalists literally compose the stories we call news.
>
> (Schudson 1991: 141)

Despite the development in the early 1990s of computer programs like the 'Zybrainic Sportswriter', which can automatically compose sports data fed to it by non-journalists, so allowing '*The Monroe City News* in Missouri [to] become the world's first newspaper to use a computer instead of journalists to write its sports reports' (*Sydney Morning Herald* 1993: 79), there is a human body and brain behind the sports news.

My concentration on print sports journalists reflects the continuing pre-dominance of the written form as the vehicle for what we call journalism (rather than commentary or presentation) and the numerical strength of print journalists as compared with the rather smaller departments of the electronic media. Some have questioned whether most television sports journalism is recognizable as journalism in the accepted sense, because 'unfettered jour-nalism' is jeopardized by the commercial relationships between sports and television companies (Klatell and Marcus 1988: 220). Commercial and other close relations between sports organizations and newspapers are by no means unknown, but print does create much more space for the journalistic analysis of sport than television or radio. Henningham (1995), in a national survey of Australian sports journalists conducted in 1992, notes that 'Sport is the biggest single speciality in mainstream news media' (p. 14), accounting for almost 11 per cent of all Australian journalists, 80 per cent of whom worked for newspapers (as opposed to two-thirds of non-sports journalists). As the study did not 'count [the] many more journalists who work for specialist sports publications or non-news sports programs on television and radio' (Henningham 1995: 14), it can be seen that the number of 'accredited' and 'non-accredited' sports journalists is very substantial. Although there may be some peculiarities of the Australian context (to be discussed below), related studies in countries like the USA (such as Garrison and Salwen 1989; Salwen and Garrison 1998) indicate that sports journalism is, indeed, the largest sub-discipline in the profession and that print is at its heart. This is not to ignore the movement of sports journalists from print to radio to television to the Internet, and the increasing tendency for them to range across media so that, in a single day, a sports journalist might write stories, provide radio reports and commen-tary, and take part in a TV studio discussion or online forum. It is notable, however, that print credentials carry the most weight, reflecting the continuing power of newspapers to set the agenda for the electronic media. Although we see the 'imprint' of sports text production practices on the back (and, not infrequently, the front and middle) of every newspaper, we are somewhat less likely to observe and reflect on the factors that brought them to the page in the first place. A good starting point, then, is to consider what it might feel like to be a practising sports journalist.

Sports journalists: 'shabby reputations' and professional problems

To be a sports journalist is to engage in an occupational specialization that combines the general responsibilities of the profession with the particular demands imposed by the object to which those professional practices and ethics are directed. In principle, then, sports journalists are no different from those with any other assigned 'round' or 'beat'. Court reporters relate the events of important trials; law reporters address difficult legal issues; police reporters go to crime scenes and get unattributable briefings from the constabulary; business reporters watch the share market and pick up on the rumours (often planted) of corporate plays; and sports reporters get the best seats at the biggest games, inform others of what happened, and are meant to use this privileged vantage point to expose the hidden workings of the sports machine. This 'democracy' of journalistic disciplines does not, however, exist in pure form. A hierarchy of esteem (if not always one of salaries or profile) exists that places the 'serious' disciplines (like the politics round) at the top end and the 'lighter' ones (like the entertainment page) at the bottom. Sports journalists, whose subject suffers from the twin disadvantages of popular appeal and a focus on the body rather than the mind, tend to gravitate towards the lower echelons. As Salwen and Garrison discovered in their survey of over 200 members of the US Associated Press Sports Editors:

> Issues related to professionalism, which included ethics, were major con-
> cerns to both sports journalism and journalism in general, according to
> the respondents. Sports journalists who elaborated on these concerns as
> they relate to sports journalism believed that their shabby reputations
> cultivated over the years haunt them in this age of professional prestige and
> accountability. In this regard, we can see how the historical roots of sports
> journalism affect the field today.
>
> (Salwen and Garrison 1998: 98)

Two levels of response to the researchers' questions can be seen to be at work here. When asked to consider journalism in general, 30 per cent of Salwen and Garrison's respondents ranked 'professionalism' second only to the 'reader related' category (31 per cent) of the nine most important problem areas (Salwen and Garrison 1998: 93). These sports journalists appear to be reflecting on the overall decline of journalism's occupational prestige, a fate that it shares with other professions like medicine and law (Macdonald 1995). When addressing sports journalism in particular, respondents ranked 'profes- sionalism' first in the list of problem areas, although only 21 per cent of them did so (Salwen and Garrison 1998: 93). The probable explanation of this survey outcome is that the sports journalists saw their own discipline as so beleaguered that they spread the range of important problems rather more widely, with seven of the nine most important problem categories selected by 8 per cent or above of the total, compared with only four out of nine for journalism in general. Thus, if the profession of journalism is felt to be currently 'in trouble' by many journalists, then the discipline of sports journalism is believed never to have been out of it. Salwen and Garrison note that this 'historical baggage' weighs down sports journalism and allows sporting figures like the late A. Bartlett Giamatti, once president of Major League Baseball's National League, to state:

> My impression is that editors generally ignore the sports section. They ignore it in the sense, and it is an important one, that the same set of editorial standards for accuracy, competence, distinguishing fact from opinion, rewriting, and editing are simply not applied as consistently or rigorously to sports sections as they are applied to all other sections of the paper.
>
> (Giamatti, quoted in Salwen and Garrison 1998: 89)

In finding sports journalists guilty of sins of truth denial, dubious ethics and misplaced apostrophes, there is a suggestion – not uncommonly held within and without the sports discipline – that sports journalists are a breed apart. Indeed, this term was used by a provincial British sports journalist in describing the special demands of the job:

> I think the [sports] news is different, you are a different breed . . . it's a very specialist area, sports fans don't suffer fools, you need to know what you're talking about. You can't just put anybody on sport, you've got to be certain he's a fanatic . . . you have to live and breathe it to an extent, you have a vast knowledge, especially like myself, a special editor of a particular sport . . . because rugby in Barchester is the be-all-end-all, really . . . If you're giving statistical information you've got to be on the ball, you've got to get it right, because you can guarantee if you don't get it right somebody will pick it up. It only has to happen a couple of times and you get known as the person who gets it wrong, who can't get it right. So you have to live and breathe it, you have to be armed always with facts.
>
> (Alan)

In sharp contrast to Giamatti's notion of an indifferent tolerance of inaccuracy, this sports journalist is acutely aware of the demanding nature of the readership, to the extent that the journalist is expected to display, on pain of getting 'known as the person who gets it wrong', the same fanatical attention to sporting statistics and facts as the fans themselves. It is by meeting such demands that sports journalists sometimes seem to become detached from the wider profession and attached to the world of sports fandom (we could call this 'anorak' journalism).

As Henningham (1995: 13) points out, the almost uniquely isolated position of sport in media organizations helps foster such feelings of professional difference, with the 'ghetto structure of sports departments in newspapers and broadcast media organisations' turning them into something of an occupational one-way street. Young sports journalists, once they have entered the sports department, tend to remain there rather than moving on to other, more prestigious 'rounds'. With sports departments being their 'own little empires, with a sports editor, sub-editors and reporters, all of whom handle nothing but sport' (Henningham 1995: 13), sports journalists operate in a rather enclosed world, achieving upward mobility towards the position of sports editor by 'leapfrogging' between media organizations or gaining internal promotion. But they remain largely confined to the sports arena, according to Henningham (1995: 13), as 'sports editors never become editors of newspapers'. We could observe that they are trapped in the journalistic equivalent of the 'Land of Boobies' in the child's story *Pinocchio*, where boys never had to study but spent their time 'in play and amusement from morning till night' (Collodi 1911: 196). This is not such an unkind analogy in the light of Henningham's (1995: 14) finding that sports journalists are happier in their work than non-sports journalists, with only 17 per cent being 'dissatisfied' with their jobs, and have half (13 per cent) of the 'very high' job stress experienced by other journalists. This finding contradicts, it should be noted, the frequent complaint by many print sports journalists interviewed that they were subjected to punishing, stressful deadlines.

In my study of sports journalists, a young, university-educated journalist on a provincial newspaper, who subsequently transferred to different journalistic specialisms such as music and features, stated that he found 'sport a bit of a dead end', with less recognition than 'police or council or general reporting' (Christopher). On the sports desk, furthermore, there may be few opportunities to embrace the subject widely, as it is 'rare' for 'sports journalists to cover more than two or three sports, and, in many instances, journalists will report on the same sport throughout their careers, never seeking or being required to broaden their horizons in other sporting fields' (Boyle and Haynes 2000: 167). The price of specialization may be a conceptual vision that extends little beyond the tunnel through which the players pass onto the field of play. An experienced career British-born newspaper sports journalist working in New Zealand (interviewed, it should be noted in the interests of ethnographic colour, some 32,000 feet above Afghanistan and Turkey), reflected on the joys of travelling the world reporting on major sports events (especially golf tournaments) while also recognizing that 'we certainly are looked upon as rank old hacks by some other branches of journalism' (Rodney). This journalist noted that many promising young journalists were deterred from entering the sports specialism by this poor professional reputation. It is important to probe why it is widely believed – not uncommonly even by sports journalists themselves – that the sports pages are characterized by inaccuracy, incompetence, technical weakness and ethical failings. This is not a reputation confined to print, as one indigenous Australian journalist, who trained as a sports broadcaster before moving into other areas of radio, remarked of the cool reaction of his new non-sports colleagues to his career background: 'I mean there is that stigma attached to sport, that it's not really news as such' (William). What, then, are the prevailing standards by which all journalism is assessed and which determine what counts as 'news as such'?

While there is considerable disagreement about the core criteria of good journalism – we need only contrast the highly subjective 'new journalism' (Wolfe and Johnson 1975) with the canon of objective reportage – it is useful to outline a conservative prescription for what journalistic values and practices ought to be, and then to compare them with the failings – real or imagined – of sports journalists. In a diatribe against journalism educators who subscribe to a cultural studies approach, Windschuttle has outlined 'the three characteristics of journalism that most teaching in the field upholds':

> First, journalism is committed to reporting the truth about what occurs in the world . . . Second, the principal ethical obligations of journalists are to their readers, their listeners and their viewers . . . Third, journalists should be committed to good writing.
>
> (Windschuttle 1998: 11)

In another place I would take issue with Windschuttle's rather crude and mechanical journalistic manifesto, but it is probable that such prescriptions are frequently taken by journalists and non-journalists as the yardstick of 'good journalism'. It is immediately apparent that much contemporary (and no doubt previous) journalism of all kinds does not observe these strictures. 'Truth' can be manipulated by governments or proprietors or 'spin doctors' and sundry other media manipulators; the interests of readers may be sacrificed for those of advertisers or journalistic careerists; what appears on the page may be a ragbag of cliché and plagiarism (see, for example, the trenchant criticisms of con-temporary journalism by crusading public intellectuals like John Pilger (1998) and Noam Chomsky (1989; Herman and Chomsky 1988)). Yet, as we have seen, if journalism in general is open to such charges, sports journalism, lowly placed on the 'totem pole', is doubly so. In part, these criticisms are made by con-necting what sports journalists do with who they are. Garrison and Salwen (1994: 40–1) describe them as 'overwhelmingly white, male, college-educated and thirty-something'. For most journalistic disciplines, the bulk of this description would hold except for the 'overwhelming'. As Henningham (1995: 14), for example, notes of the sexual composition of the profession in Australia, there are almost nine male sports journalists for every one female, but among their non-sport counterparts, the ratios are still close to two-thirds male and one-third female. In teasing out what is common to journalism and specific to sports journalism, and reasonable critique from snobbish prejudice, we can make use of a technique developed by the FBI in tracking down serial killers and urban terrorists – profiling.

Profiler: the strange case of the sports journalist

Empirical studies of the sports journalism discipline (like those noted above) provide a handy snapshot from which to build up a more detailed picture of the social characteristics of sports journalists and attitudes to their professional practice. The areas covered in Henningham's (1995) study (which is succinctly interpreted in principally quantitative terms by its author and so demands considerable elaboration and cross-comparison) that I shall concentrate on are: social characteristics and related attitudes; work satisfaction; political orientation; and ideas on the media's role and ethics. The image of the sports journalist that emerges from the matches and mismatches of available data and attitude is of a journalistic specialism that benefits from the privileges of inherited social advantage while suffering from its association with the socially and culturally disadvantaged. This rather convoluted argument is necessitated by the contradictory and ambivalent attitudes that abound in constructing the image of the sports journalist.

Sports journalists (as briefly mentioned earlier) are not drawn from the ranks of the working class. This is a hardly surprising observation in an occupation requiring relatively advanced non-manual skills and, as Henningham (1995: 15) found, sports journalists are every bit as middle class in origin as other journalists. However, the research subjects in Henningham's Australian survey, unlike those in Garrison and Salwen's (1994) US-based study, had on average lower levels of educational attainment than non-sports journalists (but somewhat higher than those of the general population). Although this picture is variable, a perceived pattern of sports journalists moving into the specialism without a university education, coupled with the vexed issue (Rowe and Stevenson 1995) of the recruitment of untrained, unaccredited personnel on the basis of their achievements in the field of sport (the celebrity-athlete-turned-sports writer), contributes to the negative image of much sports journalism even from within the discipline. As one sports journalist working for an Australian broadsheet newspaper put it:

> Well I think in this country you've been able to get away with some pretty
> lazy writing being a sports journalist. I mean some of the career paths into

sports journalism have been ex-players who decide they want to do something with their sport when they finish playing. They might have been a great player who played a hundred times for Australia but whether they can string two words together is another matter, but they have been allowed to do that because of who they were. Or even, racing is a good example, a lot of people who got into racing journalism were strappers or kids who, you know, there was more of an opportunity if you were involved in a sport to become a sports writer. That is not to say that all people who have come out of an active sporting career can't write, it did mean in that sense that the standard of the writing was not as high, and they were not trained as closely or as professionally as other journalists.

(Martin)

The negative attitude of journalists (both sports and non-sports) who had trained 'in-house' in the orthodox way to those who had entered the profession on the basis of their sporting expertise is common. Suspicions of involvement in 'ghosting' – the common practice in the entertainment print media of celebrities putting their names to texts that they have not written – hang over the heads of all sports journalists (certainly in early career) who are practising or former elite sports performers. As one Australian print journalist, a former international sportsman who has now published widely in the international sports press, exclaimed:

I was highly offended in the first two articles I did [while still a player] that, you know, I got a great reaction and people said 'were they ghosted?' No, they fucking were not ghosted! And nothing I've done has ever been ghosted! I've done ghosting for friends and I don't mind doing it, but I think to have some resentment towards someone like me when I look at joining the *Messenger* now, you know, you've got to start out, basically. I don't know, I stand to be corrected but I think you've got to have a degree before you can be a first-year cadet – although I think if you have a degree they might start you at third year or something like that, but it is a very arduous process and circuitous route to get to a decent grading in journalism. Now the short cut that I took to that, to circumvent all that, was to have a field of expertise where I would have some authority to write things . . . [It's] by no means only sport, people make their names in computers, and don't come that route because people want to read what they have to say. Now I consider myself very fortunate to have circumvented that, I never would have had the wherewithal to have done it the other way. I stumbled into journalism, found that I loved it, but I never would have done it the other way. I never would have stuck it for a four-year cadetship, doing shipping rounds and nonsense like that. I was lucky and so far so good it's worked out well.

(Philip)

This experience of 'stumbling' into sports journalism from another occupational area – including elite sport – is a common and, in many cases, by no means an illegitimate one, but it does not do much, from a credentialist point of view, for the status of the specialism, especially when it is accompanied by the ethically dubious practice of ghosting. It is not helped in this case when the journalist resents accusations that his work is 'ghosted' but he is prepared to 'ghost' for others. In 'paying their dues' on the shipping and garden fete rounds, many journalists expect to bank up professional experience that is recognized as a qualification for the job, including sports reporting. The movement into their ranks of those unqualified or underqualified in journalistic terms not only questions the value of such experience, but also raises the broad issue of the authority of the writer and critic who has not been what he or she is describing at the highest level – an Olympic athlete, opera singer, chef, and so on. This tension between competing forms of authority – sporting and literary – in a discipline of journalism that is already subject to considerable scepticism concerning its quality and worth leads, as is noted below, to an anxious pressing of claims to professional and even artistic legitimacy.

This difficulty in restricting labour market entry – especially in cases where 'ingress' is on the basis of demonstrated physical rather than mental and literary prowess – may negatively affect sports journalism's prestige, but it does not automatically depress its social class composition. As McKay (1991) has noted, in terms of the general population, participants in sport 'have a relatively high level of income and education' (p. 11). Furthermore, Henningham (1995) found that, while indistinguishable from other journalists in socioeconomic class terms, sports journalists are more likely to be Anglo and male than their colleagues in the wider profession. A degree of caution is needed here – there are no doubt other equally WASP (White Anglo Saxon Protestant) dominated journalistic specialisms (business and political reporting spring to mind), but these may be protected from criticism by their concern with 'serious' matters of state and economics. In other words, the social homogeneity that is barely questioned in some areas of journalism becomes, in the negative stereotype of the sports journalist, a sign of the 'hack'. A 'clubbish' image of sport journalism begins to emerge when it is seen to be resistant to entry by women (according to Van Zoonen (1998: 129), masculinity and a subjective attachment to sport and sportspeople is definitive of sports journalism) and/or those of non-Anglo background. In my (qualitative) study it was sometimes remarked that, for example, in Britain there were few Asians and

Afro-Caribbeans coming through the ranks of young sports journalists. One British former editor and current sports columnist noted the irony of the largely mono racial/ethnic composition of sports journalism, 'Just as an increasing number of sportsmen have become black'. He went on to remark that:

> Barry Brain, the sports editor of *The Watchdog*, told me that he was very consciously bringing on black sports writers because he did feel they had a perspective that was missing in the sports pages, but not very many are doing that. Again, I just don't know how many guys there are who are any good at it.
>
> (Darren)

The under-representation of non-Anglo people in the sports media could be the journalistic equivalent of 'stacking', the practice in sport of (often unconsciously) assigning black athletes to 'race-appropriate' sports, team and coaching positions that rarely involve tactical decision making and leadership (Cashmore 2000). From this perspective, sports reporting and commentary largely involves white people in a non-manual occupation authoritatively judging the sporting deeds of largely silent and objectified non-white people using their bodies to make a living. The outcome (if not the intention) is racist and ethnocentric in that the culture of sports journalism can be seen to be replicating a very old and damaging structure of inequality that reserves key 'gatekeeping' positions for dominant social groups even as subaltern people appear to be making progress in the area in question. Eric Dunning (1999: 212–13) describes the agitation of some black sports journalists and the Black Newspaper Publishers Association in the USA in the 1940s to end racial segregation in baseball, the self-proclaimed 'national pastime'. It is ironic that, several decades later, the spectre of segregation, symbolic rather than formal, still haunts many sports desks.

The view that diversifying the 'body' of sports journalists not only is a matter of social equity but is also likely to produce fresh insights and approaches was again expressed by Darren when he reflected on the dearth of good female sports reporters in Britain, and the pattern of those who had specialized in sport becoming discouraged and moving to other specialisms:

> Every sports editor starts off paying lip service that he wants women to read the sports page, and one effective way of getting more women to read the sports pages is getting more women to write on sport pages – there is a natural identity there. And then they get bored with it or there aren't enough women around and it fades away again. I think it's a great shame because I think, I read a piece that Sue Knott wrote in *The Sunday Times* a few weeks ago, an interview with Ray Kennedy, the footballer with MS

[multiple sclerosis]. Now that was something very few men could have written – if any, I suspect – because it had a special sympathetic perspective, human perspective and did illuminate the situation for people very well indeed. He talked to her in a way he might not have talked to a man, there's a kind of macho culture in which they hold back some of these really personal things. I'd like to see a lot more of that.

(Darren)

The recruitment of female sports reporters was partly advocated here as a tactic to increase circulation and partly to supply a more traditionally nurturant, non-combative feminine quality to the sports page, yet it nevertheless reveals the predictability of approach of much current sports journalism and the limited experiential base of its practitioners. Three prominent women journalists interviewed by Amanda Smith (1997: 93) were rather more circumspect about being 'pigeonholed' in their approach to their work, for example that they would privilege women's sports or write what one describes as 'fluff pieces'. But they also reported some difficulties of gaining access to athletes and undue concentration on their sex and sexuality. Emma Lindsey's (2001) reflection on some of her experiences as that very rare bird (no sexism intended), a black woman sports journalist in Britain, illustrates the difficulty that a traditionally homogeneous workplace in racial, class and gender terms has with dealing with the 'Other' in its midst, and of its keenness to keep difference on the margins. Her difficulties with gaining access to restricted areas despite her press pass, exasperation with racial and sexual stereotyping of black athletes, and difficult professional journalistic relationship with those same black athletes (including a feud with champion sprinter Linford Christie) who often expect her unequivocal endorsement as a fellow person of colour, all attest to the hard labour in the sports department that awaits the small numbers of black and/or female journalists that venture into it. In describing 'how the media machine works to perpetuate, and indeed helps to create, certain stereotypes that exist elsewhere', Lindsey is also describing 'the role of business in the promotion of certain stereotypes, and its ever-tightening grip on sport's future' (Lindsey 2001: 188). Sports journalists, she argues, in subscribing to the 'Edenic view' (p. 198) of sport as the privileged space of innocence and nobility, are largely complicit in this process. It is easier to take this Panglossian position, she implies, when the closest that the sports journalist has come to the experience of social exclusion has been hearing snide remarks about junkets and free-loading uttered by other journalists who have to write about welfare policy or unemployment.

Henningham (1995: 15) records in his study that sports journalists were less likely than non-sports journalists to have 'experienced or had knowledge of newsroom prejudice' relating to race, ethnicity or sex. Of those few sports journalists in his study who were female, women journalists were far more likely than their male colleagues to agree that it is 'more difficult for women to get ahead in journalism' (36 per cent compared with 85 per cent, although their non-Anglo counterparts did not tend to attribute to ethnicity an equivalent level of obstruction to upward occupational mobility). Because they had not experienced prejudice and discrimination on the grounds of race, ethnicity or sex themselves, or had not been sensitized to the negative experience of others (not least because most of their immediate colleagues had similar backgrounds), most of the sports journalists in this study were not much troubled by social structural inequities.

This cosy picture of the sports desk as a WASP male enclave is reinforced to a degree by Henningham's findings that sports journalists tended to stay in the same job and, indeed, profession, for longer than their non-sports colleagues, and (as mentioned above) were generally more satisfied with, and less stressed by, their jobs than journalists in general. When questioned on the relative importance of different characteristics of those jobs, sports journalists were significantly (in statistical terms) attracted to their job's pay, security and fringe benefits, and significantly less concerned with the editorial policies of their organization (Henningham 1995: 16). This last characteristic connects with the pattern of political orientation of journalists. As we saw in Chapter 1, western news media workers have traditionally prided themselves (though sometimes only with the aid of self-delusion) on their fiercely guarded critical independence from governments and big business enterprises (even when the latter are their own employers). Yet, the sports journalists whose attitudes are recorded in studies like Henningham's are more politically conservative than non-sports journalists (almost twice as likely to vote on the Right), and more positive and optimistic about the current state of press freedom, concentration of ownership and control, and so on. The 'splendid isolation' of the sports department has no doubt partially insulated it from the improper interference by proprietors and managers that bothers journalists in other departments. Greater priority, as a result, is given to news functions like 'get information to the public quickly' and 'concentrate on news of interest to the widest possible public' rather than 'provide analysis and interpretation of complex problems' or taking the role of sceptical 'adversary' in dealing with public officials and businesses (Henningham 1995: 16). Here the traditional sports reporting and recording function comes to the fore at the expense of the analytical and investigative tasks of the news media.

Crusaders and cheerleaders

The engaged, 'crusading' media role is less appealing to those sports journalists (the majority, it seems) schooled in the work of describing sports events and passing on news about them, rather than interrogating and probing their subject with vigour. Henningham found that the Australian sports journalists in his sample are more ethically principled than other journalists on issues like 'using confidential business or government documents without authorization' or 'badgering unwilling informants to get a story'. Ethics is, of course, a highly contested area, and in the case of investigative journalism it might be claimed that a higher ethical duty is being observed when such tactics are used in the public interest. This ethical dilemma seems not to trouble many sports journalists, who may be less tempted to cut corners in the interests of the 'big scoop' not only because much of their work involves interpreting what is already publicly known and visible, but also because they are heavily dependent on cultivating good relationships with sportspeople, officials, sponsors, and so on. The penalties of being frozen out by the 'usual suspects' (the providers of off-the-record insider information) are serious for journalists on any round (Chibnall 1977) but are likely to be worse than most in sport, especially outside the capital cities or where the journalist has been overly reliant on sporting camaraderie and has not developed other analytical resources and 'quotable' sources. A provincial British print journalist whose main work task was to cover the local soccer team made clear the professional and ethical difficulties that may arise (what he called 'the big tightrope of doing the job') when there is a high level of dependency and concentration on a single sports operation:

> *Gareth*: If you are working for a national paper, for example, or even a paper covering a number of teams, you don't have the daily contact and you float in and out as it were. You may upset people at a particular club but that doesn't really matter because you're not going back for a few more weeks. But in this instance you have hit the nail on the head, my job does entail speaking to the manager, the Baddington manager Brian Snout, and my job is to speak to him basically every working day. But, yeah, that's right there can be occasion, OK you ring up in the morning and the manager, whoever it may be over the years, is not very happy about what you wrote last night and then you kick off with having to defend what you've written before you move onto, you know, what's happening today type of thing. It is important, of course, that you do manage to bridge that gap because at the end of the day you depend on ringing the manager to get the information, so if you criticize them a bit too heavily and, the

following morning he says, 'I'm not very happy with you', and puts the phone down, then the job is made that much more difficult.

D.R.: If there is a kind of embargo by the manager, and he refuses say to speak to you, would that make it virtually impossible to do your job?

Gareth: Um, no. In fact two or three years ago I did have a set to with Fred Wild, the previous manager. The team were doing badly and the paper generally, not totally what I'd written, but I'd been criticizing, and other writers on the paper as well on the sports desk were having their two pence worth . . . As a result of that he said we were trying to get him the sack and he had no intention of cooperating with us in future, so he refused to speak to us, to the paper in general. That meant that for a period we had to go along with, you know, we weren't banned from the club, there was no suggestion of that. It was just purely that I didn't have access to the manager to obtain the information on a daily basis, but I was still able to go along, report the matches in the normal way, and pick up information as best one can.

There are other contacts that a journalist has, naturally, he doesn't rely purely on the manager, although it is the manager that they normally deal with on a day-to-day basis, quote on a day-to-day basis. It doesn't mean that you don't get unidentified sources and, therefore, you can't quote people anymore, and you're having to say 'this is believed to be happening' and 'that may be happening'. In some ways it takes the pressure off a little bit right away, you no longer have the worry, as I mentioned earlier, of having to get back onto the manager the following morning and take flak for the criticism you might have given him overnight, because, you know, you've no longer got that worry of having to speak to him. Basically, you can sit back and let fly willy nilly. He's got to, the manager's got to suffer in a way, because you're going to feel even more free to criticize.

D.R.: And, of course, he did in the end get the sack.

Gareth: That was about twelve months later.

This exchange reveals the complexity (familiar, of course, to journalists on many other rounds where the 'object' to be reported on and the associated sources are fixed and limited) of the relationship between the sports journalist and their principal source. It is a relationship of mutual dependency – the sports entity needs media coverage and the media worker needs a story – which can break down or get out of balance. In this instance, 'normal service' was resumed without compromising journalistic integrity (indeed, the journalist felt liberated by not having to deal with the source on a 'daily basis', so being licensed to 'let fly willy nilly'), but it is not difficult to imagine less ethical outcomes (arising out of, as Murphy (1976) discovered in his study of provincial journalism, the network structure of local elites). Thus, the 'normal relation-ship between sporting organisations and media organizations' may be one of 'mutually beneficial interdependency' (Brookes 2002: 38), but it involves a delicate equilibrium that, to a substantial degree, can only be maintained where there is rough parity of power between those organizations. Where the media have little need for or interest in covering a sports organization, the usual result is (perhaps benign) neglect or occasional investigation and criticism. The commercial media might then be offered material inducements, such as a con-certed newspaper, radio or television advertising campaign, to encourage some positive editorial media coverage for the sports organization. If the sports organization holds the whip hand, however, sports journalists tend to become surrogate sports promoters.

Broader areas of ethics on which sports journalists were not questioned in Henningham's study include the perils of becoming too much of a 'cheerleader' for sports teams (see Chapter 4) and a 'mate' of athletes rather than an independent journalist, and on the inevitable temptations (not unknown to travel and wine journalists, among other specialisms) of the 'perks' that go with the job (travel, hospitality, the 'best seat in the house', free tickets, opportunities to consort with celebrities, and so on). It is at this point, where the ethics of journalism rub against the enviable 'on the side' opportunities of the sports round, that critics of sports journalism (in some cases, no doubt unreasonably) see it as the compromised ally of the sport and entertainment business rather than as a legitimate arm of the news media. Mark Lowes's (1997, 1999) study of the sports desk in a Canadian newspaper bears out many of the pressures on, and practices of, sports journalists discussed above. Journalists on the sports round receive copious materials in the form of press releases from the com-mercial sports organizations that they cover, and 'are assured of a full stomach' (Lowes 1997: 153) when covering their games. One of the reporters he 'shadowed', whose 'beat' was a National Hockey League team, was deeply dependent on them for information, making frequent calls during the day. Lowes (1997: 156) observed that, 'Colvin [a pseudonym] usually wraps up this news gathering component of his day around 5:30 p.m. or 6 p.m. with yet another phone call to the Hornets' [another pseudonym] media relations people, "just to see if there's anything else up"'. Through such routines and structured relations 'major commercial spectator sports' reproduce a little examined or questioned dominance over 'non-commercial sports' in the sports pages of newspapers. Margaret MacNeill (1998), also in a Canadian context, raises rather different issues of practices and ethics, surveying 1200 amateur athletes about their relationships with the sports media, and expressing concern about 'the confusion [that] elite athletes harbour about basic constitutional rights to free speech and about how they can effectively interact with the media'

(p. 101). The power of the media to ' "make or break" an athlete's reputation and level of fame', she argues, disadvantages sportspeople, leaving them so vulnerable to misquotation that they fear to challenge and are suspicious of sports journalists. MacNeill's advocacy of a new, international media sport-specific code of ethics suggests that current professional self-regulation of sports journalists is inadequate to protect athletes from unfair coverage. This is a rather different anxiety to the one previously discussed that sports journalists tend to be much more interested in back scratching than muck raking. These matters are, as we have seen, not limited to the Canadian context, but travel across continents and oceans to all the places where a sports journalist watches a game, and asks a breathless athlete, 'How does it feel to let the entire nation and your ancestors down?' or, alternatively, 'What's it like to be bigger than Jesus and Mohammed combined?', and files the story.

In this section, I have tried to flesh out the shadowy glimpse of the sports journalist schematically presented in Henningham's article. He concludes by judging contemporary sports journalism as something of a throwback – perhaps one that would be approved of, as discussed earlier, by Windschuttle (1998: 17) – to 'an older model of journalism, more objective and "fact based", more in tune with the commercial imperatives of the media, less questioning of the ideological and sociological role of journalism'. Henningham is also concerned by the lack of 'angst' and the absence of a 'self-critical approach' by sports journalists whose profile, as developed out of the survey, is of a rather complacent group of white male professionals from comfortable backgrounds with enviably 'cushy' jobs. This picture does not altogether match that emerging from my qualitative study of sports journalists or that reported in Salwen and Garrison's quantitative and qualitative studies. Methodologically, these variable findings may stem from the different types of data generated by 'pencil and paper' survey-style interviews and exploratory, semi-structured interviews.

It is likely that the more thoughtful and self-critical responses of the sports journalists in my study were artefacts of the selected research method, which involved interviews of at least twenty minutes' duration (often much longer) and a series of inquisitive and sometimes discomfiting questions. It is also possible that sports journalists are generally satisfied with their lot but feel less so when reminded by interviewers that they tend to be poorly regarded by their non-sports peers. Most of the interviewees in my study described both the pleasure and pain of their jobs as producers of media sports texts. For example, a female sports journalist on a broadsheet Australian newspaper (necessarily, as we have seen, unrepresentative of her occupational group) expressed a sense of international variation in the prestige of sports journalists, a desire for greater recognition and the joy of sports writing:

I think, perhaps, they're treated better in Britain than we are here, we're all dying to be treated the way they are in America, where they're generally seen as the top echelon of journalism in sport over there, and it would be lovely to be felt that way here. But people generally assume, that have nothing to do with it, that it's much easier than other forms of journalism, and because it's sport, it's a physical activity, that there's nothing intellectual about it. It's not true, I did all the other things when I was a cadet, but the thing that gave me most stimulation was sports writing. You have the most freedom, you make many more decisions on your own about how it should be approached, and particularly now that sport is so professional, you have to know about finance and economics and courts, because it's always ending up in the courts these days, and you've got to be able to encompass all those areas. If you can't do that then you're not going to survive in professional sports. The way it is, you really have to be able to turn your hand to anything, and you've also got to be a good writer, because sport is a very descriptive type of writing, expressive, you've got to be able to make people feel that they were there. So, that's why I like it, it just gives you so much [more] breadth than the other sections.

(Nancy)

Like virtually every interviewee in the study, this sports journalist was keen to assert the degree of difficulty and required skill of the specialism. Journalists, editors and other sports writers are often frustrated and resentful about their professional standing, and anxious to improve it. The shifting positions of sport in the general cultural hierarchy and in the narrower culture of journalism are the determinants of the standing of sports journalism. In Chapter 1, we noted how sport in its various forms, at different historical moments, is claimed by different social groups. Dominant groups (such as the nineteenth-century British aristocracy and the twentieth-century bourgeoisie) have often embraced sport and prescribed approved forms of it for subordinate groups in the interests of character building, discharging 'unhealthy' urges, physical fitness, and so on (Ingham and Loy 1993). We have also seen that great sporting events, especially when carried simultaneously to all parts of the country by the electronic media, have contributed vitally to the process of nation building (Whannel 1992). Yet the very popularity of many sports, the possibilities they offer of an inclusive cultural democracy, have made them also questionable to social elites, especially when they have moved beyond the noble 'disinterested practice' of amateurism (Bourdieu 1978) into the less edifying world of mass entertainment.

Sport's reliance on the moving body has also been at odds with those who have developed a culture of refinement through aesthetics and contemplation, as Urry (1990: 45) has noted in the social-class inflected split between forms of tourism typified by the 'collective' and the 'romantic' gaze. Organized sport, like other cultural forms, also moves in and out of fashion. For example, in the 1960s it was seen by many in the counter-culture as a popularly digestible form of militarism, but in the following decade supporting a sports team became a way for middle-class male intellectuals to demonstrate that they really were 'men of the people' (Rowe 1995). In contemporary Britain, soccer's remarkable recent wave of popularity has washed over groups in very different positions in the social hierarchy of 'Cool Britannia' (Miller *et al.* 2001). The consummate image-projecting politician of the post-Thatcher era, Prime Minister Tony Blair, has made much of a personal love for football that is of disputed intensity and longevity. This strategic deployment of 'football fever' is well captured on the cover of a recent sociology of sport book, which bears a well-known image of Blair practising his soccer and populist political skills with a former (and predictably unsuccessful) England manager (Sugden and Tomlinson 2002). Journalists from outside the sports round have neither been immune to this epidemic of sports fandom nor have they been blind to its possibilities for professional advancement, while proprietors, managers, programmers and editors have, in many cases somewhat belatedly, realized the commercial value of sport and have provided more capital and human resources for it.

What do these long-term trends and recent changes mean for the profile of the sports journalist? As I mentioned above (and not unlike the position of tabloid journalists in general), sports journalists are reasonably socially advantaged professionals whose 'patch' is a form of popular pleasure with a lowly reputation in some quarters. If the development of their professional discipline has been stunted by a somewhat comfortable, socially homogeneous male culture of giving 'the facts' and mixing with the players, it is, because of its expanding audiences, commercial clout and cultural profile, also currently in a state of flux. To improve our understanding of the making of the media sports text, it is helpful to examine more deeply, as Schudson (1991: 141) noted above, how in the specialism of sport the 'flesh-and-blood journalists [who] literally compose the stories we call news' negotiate the various and conflicting demands that are made on them.

Talking to the sports talkers

In the excerpts from interviews with sports journalists presented earlier in this chapter it was apparent that, in going about their everyday duties, they are subject both to the occupational problems that beset all types of journalists (such as their relationships with sources) and others that, while not altogether exclusive to sports journalists, are particularly common to and pressing for them (like their status with fans and professional peers). Because the stereotype of the hard-bitten sports journalist is such an established one, it is tempting to discount the differences between them. While it is unquestionable that sports journalists tend to be white, middle class and male – for example, Creedon (1994a: 100) notes that the US-based Association for Women in Sports Media found that 'only 3% of the nation's 10,000 print and broadcast sports journalists are women' – differences and tensions exist between practitioners with similar social 'profiles'. We can also anticipate that the breaches already made in the bastion of sports journalism by women and non-Anglo people will widen. That progress in diversifying the composition of the sports journalism labour force and its professional ideologies is slow and uneven is reflected, though, in the 'heteronormativity' of the workplace culture. There is little evidence to date that openly gay and lesbian sports journalists are making any more impression in their occupation than their athlete counterparts are making in professional sport (Dworkin and Wachs 2000). Various divisions of a professional nature may emanate from involvement in different genres in the same medium (such as between tabloid and broadsheet journalists) or in different sports media (such as print versus broadcast), and complicate even further an already complex process of media sports text production in which fans, fellow journalists, athletes, sports administrators and sponsors are also implicated.

If we consider, for example, the case of Caroline, a female sports editor on an Australian radio station using a contemporary pop music format, it is clear that she must negotiate rather different work-related issues than a male journalist on the sports desk of a major newspaper. First, there is the matter of gender affecting the conduct of her work, such as in the 'danger zone' of the male sports dressing room, the scene of various confrontations over rights of access by female sport journalists, most famously symbolized by the 'Lisa Olson "incident"' (Kane and Disch 1993) in which the *Boston Herald* reporter was subjected to 'locker room' sexual harassment in 1990 by some players from the New England Patriots football team. Caroline displayed acute aware-ness of the pioneering role of women sports journalists like Lisa Olson, whose public campaign against her treatment led to fines imposed by the National Football League and guarantees of gender equity in the conduct of sports journalism:

> I know I have come in on the shoulders of other women who have had to take football teams to court for not letting them in the dressing rooms. I know that, I know that a few years ago I probably wouldn't have been let within coo-ee [Australian slang for proximate] of a football dressing room,

but because other women have done that I have been fortunate, I have had a slightly easier ride . . . they make sure there is an area where the players and the media can be. The players if they want to be naked can be in another room, and then get dressed and come out and talk to all of us, male and female . . . and in the end instead of me having to trot over to them, they come trotting over to me because they know me.

(Caroline)

While acknowledging the preponderance of men in sport's journalism, Caroline saw the discipline as no more 'cliquey' than other rounds (like the parliamentary) that she had worked on. In replying to a question about whether she socialized (in bars and similar venues) with people in the sports industry, the reason given for not doing so was not exclusion on grounds of gender but the limited, straight news requirements of the radio station:

No, I have never done that, because I have never had the time, and also, too, because sport is not the huge priority of the station as a whole, and our news services as a whole, I don't have to go delving, delving and get all these little scoops, and bits and pieces. It's not the way our format really works with a music station, with news on the hour, and although I think it is a good news service and they do take it seriously here, it's not something where you need to have all this dirt digging and delving and finding out little whispers in corners over a beer. So, if I was strictly on a round and I had to do that, I would do it, but in this situation I don't have to.

(Caroline)

This female radio sports editor, who in response to the radio newsroom requirement, with its limited personnel and urgent deadlines, of being 'jacks and jills of all trades', became responsible for the area by default, because 'I discovered I was the only person in this newsroom who either (a) liked sport at all and (b) had any interest in it'. The station format required a clear division of labour between media, with the radio providing the kind of old-fashioned 'fact-based' reportage identified earlier by Henningham (1995), leaving the more investigative coverage to print and the more detailed match and game analysis to television:

Well, the parallel with print is very similar to what it does in news. With radio, with newspapers, it's almost the same as basic hard news, other news. I see radio as a means of getting information through fast, not deep information. At the newspaper end they can go digging and delving and they can talk about what happened minute by minute through the match [but] a lot of people out there like following their favourite team but they don't want to read the absolute nuts and bolts. They just want to know the score . . . With television again, I think television is like a different kettle of fish altogether because my view is the sort of people who are watching television aren't listening to us and vice versa, you can't really have two sound sources on at the same time, so we'll find our job is more very much just to give the brief stuff – who won, who was the highest scorer, and let the other media go with the big post-mortem stories.

(Caroline)

Another female radio journalist who was required to conduct in-depth interviews did not find gender unimportant in her work (as did Caroline) but, rather, was able to use traditional gender roles and identities in her favour:

I think it [being in a minority as a female sports journalist] is an absolute advantage because most of the people you have to speak to are men, and for whatever reason, I guess it comes back to playing mothers and fathers, men will tell women something that they won't tell other men. So if you're talking about getting an interview and getting somebody to say something different, it's a real advantage being a female because you can play the softer side, and make the person relax and they do start telling you more than they would tell somebody else if they had the curtains or the barriers up. And I think the same for women. Women obviously know how to talk to women, whereas I think some men don't. So I think it's an advantage, I really haven't struck any disadvantages yet.

(Teresa)

Such neutral or positive experiences of gender in sports journalism – which run counter to those that might be expected – are not, of course, universal. For example, one young female print journalist found it more difficult for a woman to get 'a rapport going' with the predominantly male sportspeople with whom she had to deal on a professional basis, stating that it was 'hard for a female reporter because there is a lot of sexist attitudes. I'm sure a lot of people would just say "what would you know about sport?" . . . It would be harder for them than a guy, I'm sure' (Diana). Yet a more experienced female sports journalist in a published interview, the late Wanda Jamrozik, turned this gender exclusion to her advantage, arguing that the 'insider trading' (journalists acquiring privileged information about sportspeople that they did not publish because 'it would betray the trust of friends') in sport 'was much greater than in other areas that I'd worked as a journalist'. By being forced to be on the outer in male-dominated sport (although less so when assigned to cover female sport, an editorial practice that many female sports journalists feel to be a form of ghettoization and marginalization), Jamrozik experienced less 'foreclosing on the things you might write about' after 'selling your soul' like, for example, the mostly male journalists on the 'traveling media circus that follows the professional tennis around' (quoted in Smith 1997: 91).

While it is not possible from my qualitative study to make claims of statistical representativeness and validity, it was striking that most of the female sports reporters interviewed were, on average, younger and with higher levels of educational attainment than their male counterparts. Baird's (1994) study of Australian women sports journalists (which used both quantitative and qualitative methods) found this to be precisely the case. Compared with Henningham's mostly male respondents, Baird's sample of women was twice as likely to be tertiary educated than sports journalists in general (although well behind US levels of education), with only 21 per cent over 30 years of age compared with 60 per cent of all Australian sports journalists as found in Henningham's (larger) study. In Britain and Australia, at least, there is an apparent gap in 'cultural capital' and formal credentials between new entrants to the discipline of sports journalism (including university-educated women) and longer serving reporters (mostly men) who had received only a secondary education – and in some cases had not even completed that. This division is often replicated in the journalists' location in tabloid and broadsheet newspapers.

Tabloids, broadsheets and fanzines

A copious amount of sports copy is often taken to be a sign of the tabloid, yet the intensive coverage of sport by the broadsheets replicates the familiar, wider classification of the press into 'worthy' and 'unworthy'. One veteran British tabloid sports journalist saw this split in explicitly hierarchical terms, and inverted it by strongly asserting the high levels of skill (such as those of economy and speed) required by the tabloid sports press and expressing great antipathy towards 'patronizing' colleagues on the broadsheets with their 'wonderful degrees' who fail to appreciate such professional accomplishments:

> What pisses me off about my so-called colleagues on the broadsheets is their patronizing manner when it comes to tabloid journalists. They give the impression they want to wash their mouths out when they refer to tabloid journalism. Well, I can assure nearly all of them that I can do their job, they can't do mine. They're not good enough. And I mean that sincerely, they're not good enough to work for *The Daily Front* newspaper, they'd be totally lost. To be able to write and inform their readers in five hundred words of exactly what's happened and why, they couldn't do it. They need two thousand words and bore the arse off people. You know, I mean I fall asleep on a Sunday reading some of them, you know they go

on and on with their long words and they think they're clever. I mean this patronizing crap that they come out with . . . The good broadsheet journalists, the McIlvanneys of this world, they will never patronize their colleagues on the tabloids, they're too big for that, they're big men in every sense of the word. They know we have a difficult job and most of us do it extremely well . . . Most of them wouldn't last a month on a tabloid newspaper because they're not good enough. I have no hesitation. They've all got wonderful degrees, no doubt, all went to university, but they couldn't do our job, wouldn't know where to start. It would destroy them . . . We've all got a job to do and most of us do it extremely well, otherwise we wouldn't still be doing it.

(Calvin)

The unflattering image of the tabloid sports reporter is, indeed, powerfully imprinted on the minds of many university-educated sports reporters and editors. As one sports editor on a British weekly magazine put it, 'I think sports journalists just tend to be real, particularly with the tabloids, the tabloid hack element. I find it's a stereotype that is actually largely, really true' (Alistair), while his counterpart on a broadsheet newspaper stated, 'there are very great differences between what, say, a tabloid soccer man does . . . and what one of the quality people [does], especially the people on the *Independent* or the *Guardian*, which are very much writer driven' (Philip). This assertion of the 'quality' writing function over and against that of 'hack' journalism is constantly made by those who wish to elevate media sports texts, especially of the print variety, almost to the status of art. Sports journalism is not the only specialism where aspiration and current standing are strangers. One British freelance sports journalist and academic placed the sports round at 'second bottom of the pile, second only to media journalists. Media journalists have got a real chip on their shoulder, they believe they are seen to be the lowest of the low – and very often they are' (Sidney). Once again, the status of journalists who cover popular culture is believed to be poor, the lowly cultural status of sport and television rubbing off onto the journalist responsible for reporting on them. The possibility of transcendence is offered by turning formulaic writing into artistic expression:

there are people who have turned it into such an art, feature writing and the atmosphere, who recognize sport as being much more than just a knockabout between two competing sides of individuals but as part of the culture of the country and the society and the sociological aspects of sport . . . They elevate their own sport to something bigger and greater really, and they write, and because they can write well and capture the atmosphere and the social reflections in sport, then I think they actually become recognized as rather better than your average results recorder. I think that's particularly true again of the broadsheet press. It's less true of the tabloid press. I have to say on the tabloid side . . . on reflection it might be, given the number of pages devoted to sport in tabloids and given the way they're known to sell papers, that actually in the hierarchy, in the pecking order of tabloid newspapers, sports journalists might be better regarded.

(Sidney)

Once again the broadsheet–tabloid split is invoked here as corresponding to the relative quality of sports journalism, although it is conceded that, in the more popular (or populist) newspapers, journalistic status may be determined by different values – commercial rather than aesthetic. Repeatedly in this study, a rather heroic picture of certain sports journalists emerged, which showed them to be capable of reaching beyond sport into the more universal and profound sphere of individual motivation, the 'human condition', the state of society, and so on. Here sports reporting becomes first sports writing and then writing which uses the subject of sport only as a literary pretext. So, by using sport as a vehicle for the exploration of wider subjects and themes rather than being 'consumed' by it, the 'art' of sports writing resists classification as just another product of the toy department of the news media. As in other forms of art, however, this quality tends to be attributed only to a few, unusually gifted individuals:

I also think somebody like McIlvanney is not only the best writer on the sports pages, he's probably the best writer on the paper. He has demonstrated that writing sports pages does not have to be inferior to writing the general news or being a foreign correspondent. There are very few writers who live up to those high standards but there are some. Ian Wooldridge I would say is probably the best writer on the *Daily Mail*, certainly one of the best. There's even the *Sun*, for example, although it does some deplorable things in its sports pages, you know, over-personalizing, vendettas against the England manager, and so on. There is some very good boxing writing in the *Sun* – very vivid. So I try to develop the idea that sports writing doesn't have to be downmarket simply because it's about sport, and that many a sporting experience can be as much a seriously deep psychological study of a man and a player and motivation. McIlvanney is probably the best example of that, particularly in boxing, where he reaches a very profound level, I think, in understanding what it is that drives sportsmen on to do what they do and why some sportsmen are greater than others.

(Darren)

This model of what has been acidly called the 'sports journalism is high literature of the Mailer-in-Esquire school' (Diamond 1994: 16) is especially prominent in the USA, with its stronger tradition of celebrity sports writers, for whom 'Sportswriting, at its best, is an art form accomplished with a work ethic' (Richman 1991: 337). However, it also threatens 'death' at its own hands in producing 'Sportswriting [which], at its worst, panders to the lowest tastes of readers, offering rumour instead of information, jokes instead of passion, opinion instead of insight' (Richman 1991: 337). For Darren, the approved or 'hardboiled' style of quality sportswriting is unusually extended to embrace some tabloid sports journalists but, as we have seen, sports journalism in general remains a highly stigmatized specialism.

The critiques quoted above of much current sports journalism and promotion of 'superior' writing are paralleled in the unfavourable comparison of the best textual material produced by the print media and the standard programming of the broadcast media, which are seen to be overly reliant on fact-based reporting and live coverage. Rivalry between sports media personnel is readily apparent, often over who gets priority access to sports performers after a game (usually the broadcast media; Rowe and Stevenson 1995) and over the appropriate job specifications in the sports media. As a British sports columnist asserted:

> There is a distinct shortage of investigative reporting on TV and radio. I'm hopeful that Radio 5 will commission some serious investigations. As you know some of these debates in sports are pretty fundamental stuff about the commercialization of sport, drugs in sport, many things that touch on serious social problems, and I think the sporting press generally has been slow to see that. I think newspapers are getting better but there was very little sign until very recently that television was prepared to do that. In fact, the point I made to the BBC the other day was that the number of actually scripted programmes about sport is minimal. Now I accept that live sport is live television, it's wonderful television, but there is also scope behind the scenes for doing much more, both on personalities and on issues relating to sport, than they're doing at the moment.
>
> (Darren)

Many sports journalists feel that there needs to be a more critical and enquiring approach to sport and, for the print journalists at least, this change of tack has been forced on them by the broadcast media's seizing of much of their traditional territory of describing sports events. Several print journalists argue that they need, in the age of live radio and television broadcasts and the Internet, to find a new role that enhances the media services already provided by the broadcast media. But some believe that the lack of an established culture of sceptical enquiry and distance from sources makes this transition difficult:

> but the greatest problem, far and away with Australian sports journalism, and I don't limit it to Australian sports journalism, is there is always a tendency towards sycophancy and biographies being hagiographies, and that whole line of Johnnie Bloggs was the greatest there ever was – and it doesn't matter that he's won five grand finals in a row now and can high jump ten metres, you never saw such a modest bloke who loves his wife! Look at him here with his two kids ... the great problem with sports journalism is there is way too much sycophancy.
>
> (Philip)

Philip notes, for example, that one leading sportsman (who cannot be named on grounds of defamation!) is regularly presented favourably in the press as a family man and 'nice guy', but that, 'If we had the world deadshit Olympics and I was a selector, I would send him'. He also describes the problem of being in the position (also commonly experienced by pop music and other entertainment journalists) of being granted an exclusive interview with a sporting superstar who is 'savvy about the media ways', and then feeling, as a sports journalist, inhibited by this privilege:

> the great man has agreed to speak to me. It is really something – the only print article he gave when he was out here and we did get on very well. It would have been, if I had really wanted to have a go at him, it's bloody difficult, he's given me twenty minutes and he ain't given anybody else twenty minutes.
>
> (Philip)

Such criticisms by sports journalists themselves that the print and broadcast media are not doing enough critical, investigative work are usually made in the name of their Fourth Estate function. It is argued that society – especially its vast cohort of sports fans – is being let down by lazy, compromised and trivial sports journalism.

This accusation (justified or not) of rampant sycophancy in sports journalism is widespread among other types of journalist and sports fans alike, meaning that contemporary sports journalism is caught in a critical pincer movement both from inside and outside the profession. The growth (at least in British soccer) of 'cottage industry' sports publications – 'fanzines' and now 'netzines' – is perhaps a symptom of the failure of sports journalists and other writers to serve and satisfy their audiences. In such cases (as is discussed in Chapter 4), sports fans have seized the means of cultural production by publishing amateur print texts and creating their own sports web pages and online magazines. Sports journalists generally do not see fan involvement in making media sports texts as a threat, with some of the more professional looking publications like the British football fanzine *When Saturday Comes* established as a hobby by professional journalists (in this case mutating into a proto-professional publication), and some contributing to them under a *nom de plume* (Shaw 1989; Boyle and Haynes 2000). Most (in my study, at least) have little interest in fanzines, as indicated by a tabloid sports journalist:

> *Calvin*: Yeah, one newspaper, the *Independent*, publishes a fanzine column, don't they? Maybe we could do that. I don't even bother to read it in the *Independent*. I don't know why, I just haven't got around to doing it.
> *D.R.*: So you've never been tempted to moonlight on a fanzine?
> *Calvin*: No [*laughing*], the only freelance stuff I do is a bit of broadcasting. But I'm basically lazy and I don't go looking for work.

This candid remark, made in jest, returns us (not accidentally) to the image of the indolent and complacent occupant of the toy department, enjoying life 'on a good wicket'. We have seen here the self-perceptions of sports journalists, as relayers and producers of sports information and analysis, oscillate between assurance and anxiety. Despite, then, its machine-like appearance, the media sports cultural complex does not always run smoothly and efficiently, pumping out sports stories with the ease of the Zybrainic Sportswriter. Some of the cogs in this machine have doubts.

Conclusion: hacks and hipsters

This chapter has examined closely several of the structures, principles and practices that shape, through sports journalism, the voluminous quantities of media sports texts that are available to us every day. In particular, by comparing external and internal opinions of the profession of journalism and its sports discipline, it was possible to see how culture is created out of a complex mix of diverse and multidirectional forces. For example, it might be expected, given the major importance of sports journalism as an attractor of audiences and as a supplier of content for print and broadcast media alike, that the sports specialism would have a status commensurate with its 'pulling power'. In fact, we saw that, despite the common impression of sports journalism as a comfortable and privileged enclave of white, middle-class men travelling the world watching games at other people's expense, many sports journalists felt professionally insecure and unappreciated. As in other parts of this book, these circumstances recalled the work of the sociologist Max Weber (1968), in this case his distinction between class and status. Just as for Weber it was possible for groups and individuals to wield considerable socio-economic power through class location but not be highly regarded by others (that is, be rich but with relatively low status), it is also often the case that the economic power of the sports department (in terms of the large number and handsome remuneration of personnel; importance for circulation, ratings, advertising revenue, and so on) is at variance with its cultural power (low professional reputation and esteem). For this reason, sports journalists often craved equal status with 'serious' journalists or even recognition of their writing as 'art'.

I observed that the economic power of sports journalism does seem, somewhat belatedly, to be raising its professional status, but that this improvement is at least as significantly due to sport being very much in vogue. Of course, the current fashionability of sport is in part related to its skilful promotion as a 'hip' cultural commodity – a phenomenon conspicuously evident in British soccer (Redhead 1991; Haynes 1995; Rowe 1995) and American basketball (McKay 1995; Andrews 1996; Boyd 1997). Such developments in the making and meaning of media sports texts reveal the impossibility of separating the different and interacting influences on sports culture. Hence, the economics of sport and media are deeply dependent on cultural dynamics – but no less than, as is addressed in the next chapter, media sports culture is profoundly influenced by economic imperatives.

Further reading

Brookes, R. (2002) *Representing Sport*. London: Arnold.

Creedon, P.J. (ed.) (1994) *Women, Media and Sport: Challenging Gender Values*. Thousand Oaks, CA: Sage.

Lowes, M.D. (1999) *Inside the Sports Pages: Work Routines, Professional Ideologies and the Manufacture of Sports News*. Toronto: University of Toronto Press.

3 | MONEY, MYTH AND THE BIG MATCH: THE POLITICAL ECONOMY OF THE SPORTS MEDIA

> The influence of television is felt in the ever increasing number of on-site advertising banners and logos and sponsorship tie-ins. Some athletes have become walking billboards for their multiple sponsors and equipment suppliers ... The commercialization of sports, even at amateur level, continues apace, justified by the constant need to bring in more money, and limited only by initial resistance from the public, which inevitably overcomes its outrage and learns to accept yet more blatant salesmanship in sport as a necessary evil which subsidizes the undertaking. If in junk sports, it's tough to separate the junk from the sports, then in all sports it's equally tough to separate the business from the sport.
>
> (Klatell and Marcus 1988: 21)

Introduction: valuing sport

I have delayed a fuller discussion of the economics of the sports media until the closing chapter of this first 'Making media sport' part of the book, but not because it is of any lesser importance than other influences on production – far from it, as the previous analysis has repeatedly shown. For example, in Chapter 2 we saw how developments in broadcast and print sports journalism are linked to the calculation of their economic value in increasing the size and broadening the base of media sports audiences. The discussion of sport and media economics leads into the second part of 'Unmaking the media sports text' for the slightly perverse reason that, just at the point where many other works in media and cultural studies tend to bracket off the rather unromantic 'business of business' and get down to the more freewheeling task of textual reading and interpretation, it is, I believe, all the more necessary to keep economic concerns to the fore. In this way, no artificial separation can be maintained between the 'light' sphere of culture and symbols and the 'heavy' world of economics and material objects. Instead, culture, social relations and economics can be seen – as is entirely appropriate under conditions where the economies and social structures of advanced capitalist societies are becoming increasingly dependent on cultural processes – to be inextricably linked in a manner that defies a simple equation involving arrows pointing in a single, determining direction. The sphere of culture is now more than ever where the key economic processes of production, distribution and exchange take place. At the same time, cultural production is always directly or indirectly, currently or potentially, connected to the world of making products, supplying services and generating profits.

I have argued here that the media are both the driving economic and cultural force in sport because they provide (or attract) most of the capital that in turn creates and disseminates the images and information, which then generate more capital and more sport, in an ascending spiral. Booms in capital accumulation are periodically subject to dramatic busts, as the 1987 Wall Street crash, the 1997 'meltdown' of the Asian 'tiger economies' and the 2000 'dot.bomb' demonstrate. There has been no such dramatic contraction of the media sports economy in general, but its seemingly unstoppable momentum slowed not long after the new century was born (and as the first edition of this book was published!). I will discuss below some of the latest twists and turns in media economics, but the chapter will inevitably reflect the extraordinary growth of media sport rather more than its current difficulties. As Toby Miller (1999: 115) has argued, expenditure on sport has heretofore seemed immune to 'conventional business cycles' and 'has grown through most recessions'. In recent memory, therefore, words like downswing and contraction have found little expression in the lexicon of the media sports cultural complex. It has been difficult, therefore, to question the 'article of faith for broadcasters that sports programming was a river of gold' (Maiden 2002: 33). But nothing undermines business faith more than the arrival of the receivers and the administrators, as has occurred in such high-profile media sport cases (discussed later in the chapter) as KirchMedia, XFL, C7 and ITV Digital.

The fortunes of individual sports and also of media companies can, in the ordinary course of things, shift rapidly in response to the involvement of sponsors, crowd attendance and TV ratings, broadcast rights, and so on. It is useful, then, to appraise the major forces in media sport, the ways in which they cooperate and conflict, and the consequences of this economic activity for sport and the wider society and culture. If no single party can be said to dominate the media sports cultural complex or to control its 'image bank', it can hardly be denied that the presence of major economic entities has resulted in far-reaching changes to the sport we see and read about, and to the culture in which it is located. To illustrate this point, we need only point to the cut-throat competition and multi-million dollar and pound investment involved in acquiring such mega media sports properties as the broadcast rights to the:

- Summer and Winter Olympics
- English Premier League soccer
- US National Football League

(Rowe and McKay 2003). That media sport involves serious money is obvious, but the cultural and economic consequences for media sports texts are less apparent. For this reason, we need to delve further into the place where economic and sporting muscles are flexed.

Sport, media and capital accumulation

In Chapter 1, I provided brief outlines of the intersecting development of sport and media, arguing that each institution had something that the other wanted – and with increasing urgency. The initial reluctance which both parties displayed in forming a deep alliance was, in part, due to the unprecedented nature of the economic and cultural relations that developed speedily from the late nineteenth century onwards (that is, consumer capitalism and national state-sanctioned media were 'feeling their way'), and partly because their initial economic base relied on direct exchange. So, when most of the revenue for sports enterprises stemmed from paying customers going through the turnstiles to watch sport in person in highly localized settings, not much in the way of mass marketing and promotion was needed. Word-of-mouth, wall posters and some rather staid newspaper advertisements were the major means of informing the paying public about forthcoming sports events, and the technological means did not exist (and when they did, were not initially welcomed) to record and transmit proceedings for those not present (Stoddart 1986; Whannel 1992; Boyle and Haynes 2000). Similarly, for newspapers more dependent on revenue from cover sales than on advertising, and interested more in the great events of state (as in the establishment press) or in scandal-mongering (the province of the 'yellow press'), sport had only limited appeal. With the development of national and international sporting competitions, the maturation of media advertising and the emergence of broadcast media for which there was no or limited direct payment by the 'consumer', new revenue streams and uses of the sports media were created. In this way, the media sports text became increasingly valorized, a commodity that could be produced, sold, exchanged and distributed. To understand precisely how the media sports text becomes such a valuable economic and cultural object, it is necessary to view it in terms of large-scale social, economic and cultural transformations (as occurred in Chapter 1), and also to appreciate the specific ways in which that object is desired or can be made to be or seem desirable.

Within the history of capitalist development, the sports media are not essential commodities: they are not vital for the maintenance of life like food, shelter and clothing, or 'consumer durables' that preserve food, wash clothes or transport whole families to work and school. Nobody has ever died as a direct result of media sport starvation, although passionate sports fans can do striking impressions of zombies during TV blackouts. Seen in this way, media sports texts are not very useful goods but they are, paradoxically, highly prized. This is so because they exist in an economic environment where, as many goods have become easier to mass produce and standardize, only a relatively small proportion of their total price is attributable to the cost of raw materials, labour and manufacture. Hence, the direct production cost of a compact disc or a dress or a child's toy can often be measured in pence and cents rather than in multiple pounds and dollars. Where, then, is the value added and capital accumulated? It is, increasingly, not in the material character of objects that can be reassuringly touched and used, but in the immaterial nature of symbolic goods (Hall 1989; Hesmondhalgh 2002). Value in this sense lies in design, appearance and in the capacity to connect different economic processes that exist in a complex interdependence (Hebdige 1989). An extensive and complex theoretical debate (that can only be addressed briefly and synoptically here) has been conducted since the late 1980s over the meaning of this development (see, for example, Harvey 1989; Hirst and Zeitlin 1989; Giddens 1991; Kellner 1995; Dunn 1998; Dandaneau 2001). This wide-ranging debate is over such far-reaching and difficult questions as:

- Are current circumstances an extension of the same 'logic' and process of modernity (which we might call 'advanced', 'late' or 'high') that brought industrialization, liberal democracy, humanism, and so on?
- Or have we moved on to a new 'condition' called **postmodernity** in which our social, economic, political and cultural life radically differs from its **modernist** predecessor?
- Has the mass production and consumption 'regime' pioneered by Henry Ford in the car industry (**Fordism**) changed a little (to **neo-Fordism**) or been replaced by a new, more targeted, smaller-scale and flexible way of producing and consuming goods and services (**post-Fordism**)?

Posing such questions requires a command of a rather daunting language in which terms like 'flexible specialization' and 'reflexive accumulation' compete for theoretical and conceptual supremacy. In the context of this book, it is necessary in the first instance only to be armed with the glossary of key terms provided and to follow the contours of the argument that media sport is at the leading edge of cultural and economic development. If cultural factors are emerging as central to economic processes – and most contemporary analyses suggest that they are – then sport and the sports media, as cultural goods *par excellence*, are clearly a central element in a larger process (or set of processes) that is reshaping society and culture (Throsby 2001).

Of course, goods have always had a cultural character (Hesmondhalgh 2002) – the 'respectable' appeal of a type of family sedan, the 'reliable' qualities of a brand of vacuum cleaner, and so on – but more and more commodities have nothing else to declare but their status as cultural goods with appropriately high levels of 'sign value' (Baudrillard 1981), as opposed to the more conventional Marxist concepts of use value (what something can do) and exchange value (what something is worth in a direct transaction). As Lash and Urry argue:

> [Yet] the objects in contemporary political economies are not just emptied out of symbolic content. They are also progressively emptied out of material content. What is increasingly being produced are not material objects, but signs. These signs are primarily of two types. Either they have a primarily cognitive content and thus are post-industrial or informational goods. Or they have primarily an aesthetic, in the broadest sense . . ., content and they are primarily postmodern goods (Eagleton 1989). This is occurring, not just in the proliferation of non-material objects which comprise a substantial aesthetic component (such as pop music, cinema, magazines, video, etc.), but also in the increasing component of sign value or image in *material* objects. This aestheticization of material objects can take place either in the production or in the circulation and consumption of such goods.
>
> (Lash and Urry 1994: 14–15)

If we consider this argument in relation to media sports texts, then they can be said to be particularly valuable not only because of their 'substantial aesthetic component' (the principal object of media sport is the aesthetics of bodies – their beauty, condition, size, effectiveness – in motion under specified conditions), but also because of their key role in the informational order (cognitive in only a limited sense in terms of 'patented' knowledge about training techniques and regimes, but certainly an informational sign given sport's major role in the news media). Media sports texts, with their almost unprecedented capacity to 'flow across and around these economies of signs and space' in both local and global contexts, their very high levels of 'sign-value', and with their intimate connection to all-pervasive *'information and communication structures'* (Lash and Urry 1994: 6), are almost perfect prototypes of signs in circulation, heavily loaded with symbolic value.

To develop this point a little further, Lash and Urry use the term 'reflexive accumulation' to describe a strengthening tendency in the processes of production and consumption of objects and images for the people involved to be in a position not just to be 'buried' in what they are doing, but to reflect on it, criticize it and adapt to it (Rowe and Lawrence 1998). In this way, human subjects can be partially disconnected from the social institutions, structures and identities (including class, gender, work, nation, locality and family) that they inhabit. Or, to put it another way, as the 'automatic' power of traditional social structures over individuals has weakened, new opportunities have emerged to behave, think and identify in less socially prescribed ways. This development, which is sometimes called 'postmodernity', may not be so very new and may still have much in common with 'modernity', but the existential and ideological fluidity of postmodern life is probably unprecedented. It has created, in one sense, a 'market' for collective identification, a vigorous competition between governments, business corporations and social movements for the 'soul' – and, not uncommonly, the discretionary income – of 'cultural citizens' (now described as 'postmodern subjects'; see Miller 1993, 1998a). In more obviously functionalist terms, perhaps a 'values vacuum' has been created whereby many people feel alienated, no longer believing deeply in anything, identifying with anyone, or feeling committed to any cause outside the immediate interests of themselves and their significant others. An opening exists, therefore, for enterprising parties to engage in the 'consciousness' trade (Enzensberger 1976), to help supply the meaning and commitment that rapid social change under late modernity or postmodernity have evacuated from many lives. But what phenomenon has the emotional force to bind symbolically the fragmenting constituents of society (evidenced, according to Enzensberger (1994) by proliferating civil wars from 'L.A. to Bosnia'), especially where there is abundant critical self-reflection, cynicism and a seeming 'exhaustion' of novelty? Not surprisingly, the answer in the context of this book is media sport.

There is a well known argument (e.g. Novak 1976) that sport is a secular religion, having taken over from the church as the primary place of collective and individual ritual, belief, ecstasy, and so on. When sports fans have their ashes spread on the 'hallowed turf' of their favourite sports stadium, the spiritual qualities of sport are very evident. When on occasion a sports team receives a blessing from a religious leader before a major sports event, it may appear that 'sacred sport' is supporting orthodox religion, rather than the other way round. If sport and religion have certain qualities in common, they also share an involvement with business, especially where the religion is, as Max Weber pointed out, the Calvinist form of Protestantism, which he argues supplied many of the values crucial to the formation of capitalism. Indeed, in one (unconsciously) prescient passage in *The Protestant Ethic and the Spirit of Capitalism*, Weber links all three institutions by stating that:

> In the field of its highest development, in the United States, the pursuit of wealth, stripped of its religious and ethical meaning, tends to become associated with purely mundane passions, which often actually give it the character of sport.
>
> (Weber 1930: 182)

If Weber's lifespan had stretched a few decades beyond the year of his death (1920), he would have seen not only 'the pursuit of wealth' in the USA and other capitalist nations given 'the character of sport', but also leisure pursuits like sport take on the character of the pursuit of wealth. He would also have seen sport appropriate many of the functions of established religion in increasingly secular societies dedicated to the worship of the god of conspicuous commodity consumption.

Irrespective of whether sport and its values are religious in the strict sense, in broad economic terms (concerned more with profits than prophets, to use a rather old pun) it is one of the key contemporary sites where the expression of strong emotions is translated into the generation of substantial capital. Or, more expansively, where (following Lash and Urry) aesthetic and informational signs meet popular emotion (which sometimes looks like mass hysteria) in a manner readily convertible into commodified pleasure. Media sport has, as we have seen, a proven capacity to bring potential consumers to the marketplace in numbers ranging from the respectable to the staggering. It is able at particular moments symbolically to reconstruct disparate human groups, to make them feel at one with each other (and perhaps, in the case of the Olympics and the World Cup of association football, the world). When contemporary advertising relies so heavily on making very similar items (such as sugared drinks, cars with shared components and 're-badged' computers) appear different, sport's capacity to stimulate emotional identification with people and things is priceless. Sport can connect the past, present and future, by turns trading on sepia-tinted nostalgia, the 'nowness' of 'live' action and the anticipation of things to come. Furthermore, even when our human sports 'subject' is being reflexively critical, rather than getting carried away by sporting affect, they can take an ironic, playfully postmodern approach to it, mocking the mangled language of sports commentators (like the satirical magazine *Private Eye*'s 'Colemanballs' section and book series), watching self-consciously bad-taste sports TV programmes (like Australian rugby league's *The Footy Show*) and buying sports newspapers that are parodies of 'straight' tabloid reporting (like Britain's *Sunday Sport*). This chameleonic capacity of contemporary media sport makes it a key aspect of the commodity cycle, its flexibility of form and use fitting perfectly contemporary requirements for speedy change and customization.

Media sports texts are perhaps, then, at the leading edge of this **culturalization** of economics: they cannot be eaten or worn yet billions of people desire them in a bewildering variety of types, and media corporations are willing to expend billions of units of currency to supply them, often 'free of charge', to the user. In return, as we have seen, invaluable access is given to audiences, on a global scale, which can be cashed in for large sums of money exchanged between sporting associations, clubs, officials and players, TV and sports management companies, sponsors, advertisers and governments. Media sports texts are particularly valuable assets because of their flexibility and inter-connectedness. A single sports 'live' TV broadcast can be shown in 'real time' and endlessly afterwards, and can be cut up and packaged in myriad ways, with its soundtrack separated from its visual images so that both can be continually manipulated and reproduced. The sports print media, both newspapers and magazines, can help stimulate interest before the event and 'keep it alive' for a lengthy period afterwards, aided and abetted by the celebrity status of elite sportspeople. In multi-media environments like the Internet, virtually any media sports text can be put to use in the virtual world. All manner of goods and services, from sports equipment and 'designer' leisurewear to beer, banking and tobacco, can invoke or be directly associated with media sports events, the associated messages adapted as necessary to the cultural sensitivities of different audience blocs around the globe (Rowe *et al*. 1994). It is for this reason that television broadcast rights to the major sports are often contested more fiercely than the sports events they are seeking to cover – even when those same media companies complain about how much money they lose by winning them. To understand this apparently economically irrational behaviour (which per-haps has turned out to be irrational after all) means delving further into the media sports cultural complex.

How to make money while losing it in sports television

Having set out the broad economic framework within which contemporary media sport operates, more precise explanations of why media corporations are prepared to expend huge sums on securing the rights to television sport are required. The Olympic Games constitutes a useful example of the economic appeal of broadcast sport and of the extent to which the rights pertaining to it are both protected and infringed. Detailing the statistics is not unlike recount-ing the latest world record time in the 100 metres sprint or the greatest number of points scored in the World Series, except that (at least until the early twenty-first century) more records have been broken more frequently in buying sports rights than in performing in sport. Taking the example of the USA's NBC television network, it transpires that in 1995 NBC won the US TV rights to the Sydney 2000 Olympics for US$715 million, as part of a deal in which it paid escalating fees of US$793 million and US$894 million for the 2004 and 2008 Olympics, respectively, to show the Games to American audiences in (then) unknown locations (which turned out to be, respectively, Athens and Beijing). Despite its capacity to sell subsidiary rights, charge vastly inflated advertising rates during key events, and make some other returns from various 'spin offs' (selling videos of Olympic highlights, for example), the cost of rights and of producing TV coverage ensured that NBC would lose large sums of money on the deal. But this does not mean that the NBC Board has suddenly become philanthropic, and is prepared to carry out a selfless task of public service by subsidizing the delivery of Olympics TV to the people of the United States of America and the rest of the world. It has a broader economic motive: the huge audiences for the Olympics raise the network's overall ratings, meaning that it is in a stronger position to negotiate advertising rights across its year-round, all-genre programming. The network also hopes for an Olympics 'spillover effect' – that viewers will be exposed to and stay with its other programmes or, even better, that it will 'get the habit' of switching on NBC first. Being the Olympics station brings with it a great deal of *kudos*, especially prima facie evidence (which might in practice be repudiated) that the network can handle with distinction one of the world's largest media events. In an image-saturated age where 'branded sign-value' is paramount, being known as the Olympic network – with all the brand recognition and prestige that the label entails – gives an important competitive advantage in the media industry. Securing the US broadcast rights to the Olympics also has a 'spoiler effect' – ambitious commercial rivals, such as Rupert Murdoch's Fox Network, can be thwarted (McKay and Rowe 1997) and induced to expend equally large sums of money on other broadcast rights on pain of being locked out of major TV sport altogether. They might also gain psychological ascendancy over other networks like CBS boasting a strong sporting culture who have lost out in the fight for key TV sport properties. All these justifications for paying out vast sums on broadcast rights for sport hold as long as it can be demonstrated that, by one means or another, over time benefits outweigh costs. As briefly noted above, and discussed in greater detail below, the orthodoxy that TV sport is more golden goose than dead duck has come under sharp challenge.

Historically, there is great symbolic and economic value to be gained from controlling the production and distribution of symbols and, in the case of Olympic sport, global images do not come any more desirable (Schaffer and

Smith 2000a). It is for this reason that there is so much antagonism between Olympic rights and non-rights holders, a struggle that also inevitably draws in sports organizations and even athletes. In Australia, for example, the zealous safeguarding of Seven Network's AUS$45 million television rights contract for the Sydney 2000 Olympics was the subject of considerable anxiety among its commercial and public rivals. At the earlier Atlanta Olympics, where Australian rights were also held by Seven, the Australian Olympic Committee (AOC) helped protect its 'investment' (that is, its opportunity to maximize rights revenue by guaranteeing exclusivity) by breaking up an interview between a non-rights holder (Network Ten) with two athletes, ejecting a Ten employee from an official function and, finally, by being instrumental in the withdrawal of the Network Ten staff's media accreditation (Moore 1997). For the Sydney 2000 Olympics, the AOC attempted to prevent the 'parasitical' behaviour of non-rights holders in making money out of athletes but not contributing to their upkeep by trading more liberal media access rules for a substantial subvention for its 2000 Olympic Medal Reward Scheme. In early colonial times bushrangers in Australia held up travellers on the open road, but in sport it is rights holders and official sponsors who are 'ambushed' in the various channels of the media. A diverting parallel game is thus played out, with non-rights holders trying to sneak as much sports coverage as possible, and unofficial sponsors seeking to associate their corporate logo as closely as legally permissible with major sports events. Their official counterparts, in true sporting style, do their best to stop them. If the sporting action is a little dull, especially in out-of-stadium events like cycling, the triathlon and marathon running, television viewers can search for 'ambush' corporate brand imagery strategically planted for the cameras.

By negotiating, honouring, helping police and strategically modifying broadcast rights, sports organizations and personnel become economic allies, even colleagues, of the media. Hence they need to be well versed in the arcane rules that govern rights, such as whether non-rights holders should be bound by the 'three by three by three' rule ('three minutes of Olympic footage three times a day in news programmes at least three hours apart') which has normally applied in countries like Australia, or by a stricter and more complicated variation of it which we could call the 'two by three minus eighteen minus two thirds rule' ('two minutes of coverage three times a day in established news programmes, but no events screened less than 18 hours after they took place', and no more than one-third of an event to be broadcast, even if it is the sub-ten seconds 100 metres final) as recommended by the IOC in Atlanta (Moore 1997: 4). Such deliberations also involve national broadcast policy priorities and the copyright laws with which any rights agreement must be in accord, and even whether the Olympics come under the rubric of 'news' (and, therefore, should be more fully reported on public interest grounds) or 'sport' (that is, more subject to broadcast restriction as just another form of entertainment). These issues continue to preoccupy the broadcast media and sports professionals because the entire economics of the media sports cultural complex turn on the careful rationing, packaging and sale of media sports texts in different markets. Hence, the idea of the global media sports spectacle is at its heart quite illusory: the images that appear to be so freely released have been subject to extraordinarily stringent pre-selection and control, and the sanctions taken against those who breach such arrangements (by, for example, implying official Olympic endorsement when it has not been negotiated and paid for) powerful indeed. High-end, especially 'live' broadcast sport appears to be in plentiful supply, but it is, in fact, subject to careful rationing and, as is discussed later in the chapter, would be controlled and harboured even more by highly concentrated commercial interests were it not for intervention by the state in the public interest.

The Summer and Winter Olympics, however, occur only over four-year cycles, which leaves large gaps between orgies of Olympic viewing, although after 1992 these were staggered at two-year intervals to ensure that the world did not have to wait so long for its Olympic television 'fix'. Other great media sports events – international tournaments like the soccer, rugby, and cricket World Cups, world championships in sports such as athletics and swimming, and major annual competitions with international involvement like Wimbledon in tennis or the US Masters in golf – have important places on the sports calendar, but they are by their nature intermittent and out of the ordinary. Filling television schedules is a constant task that cannot wait for the next global media sports spectacular. The 'bread and butter' of sports television, then, is annual competition within nations.

NBC had become accustomed to its position as the main sports network and, not coincidentally, the top rating network overall, having the rights to such major US sports as American football, basketball and baseball to supplement its Olympic fare. Yet in 1998 it found itself 'frozen out of football for the first time in 33 years' (Attwood 1998: 39). Given that American football is the most important television sport in the USA, with broadcast rights valued in 1998 at US$2.25 billion a season, the scramble for broadcast rights to it is vigorous to say the least. This contest takes place over rights to a game that is barely played, understood or watched in other countries (although not for want of trying; see Maguire 1999), thereby revealing the pre-eminence of the USA as a media sport market in its own right. As noted above, their direct economic value is almost overshadowed by the image of being a 'winner' (analogous to that of breaking a world record while winning an Olympic gold medal). As Attwood states:

Several morals can be drawn from this US price war. One is that, more than ever, sport is *the* most important commodity for TV. Another is that the desperation of grown men, most of whom have never played top-level sport themselves, to feel as if they are part of the game should never be underestimated.

(Attwood 1998: 39)

The struggle for television sport can be seen to be more than a fight for profit: it reveals the cultural power of sport, particularly in the higher ranks of large corporate enterprises, where aggressive, competitive masculinity is as evident in the boardrooms as in the locker rooms (McKay and Rowe 1997). For example, the loss by the CBS network of its rights to Sunday football in 1993 to a Fox network prepared to pay over three times the amount for them (US$1.58 billion as opposed to US$500 million), had a demoralizing impact on the entire network that went beyond the concomitant fall in ratings. As Attwood (1998: 39) goes on to say, the four networks which paid unprecedented sums for the right to televise American football into the early part of the twenty-first century 'regard football as so crucial to their credibility and programming that they are prepared to pay almost any price', and that this phenomenon is not confined to the boundaries of the United States, but 'demonstrates how crucial major sporting events are to networks, worldwide, in an increasingly competitive TV market'. Thus, as Singer (1998: 36) notes, 'today's rule of thumb mandates that any viable network must have sports to help raise the profile of its other properties'; here he means literally to 'have sports', listing the direct ownership of sports teams in the late 1990s by US media conglomerates, including Cablevision (the Knicks basketball and Rangers ice hockey franchises), Disney (the Angels in baseball and Mighty Ducks in hockey) and (the now AOL-merged) Time Warner (the Braves in baseball and Hawks in basketball). As Law *et al.* (2002) have demonstrated, media sport involves intricate 'supply chains' that go well beyond the 'usual suspects' (Disney, News Corp and AOL Time Warner) and the more obvious 'circuits of promotion' (Whitson 1998). While the cross-promotional possibilities of jointly owned media and sports enterprises are attractive, it is the cultural appeal of sport that ensures that old fears of club owners of 'oversaturation' and that '"giving away" the product on TV would kill the gate' are as 'misguided as Hollywood's fear of the VCR [video cassette recorder]' (Singer 1998: 36). Such popularity also allays the concerns of media proprietors in countries like the USA that sport is not worth the asking price:

There's good reason why sports is a TV staple: It's human drama at a base level, it's cheap to produce and it's live. One can't minimize the power of immediacy in this time-shifting era when sports are the last remaining live coast-to-coast events – the Oscars, the Emmys, even 'Saturday Night

Live' are tape delayed to the West Coast. Only sports has the nation, and sometimes the world, watching the same thing at the same time, and if you have a message, that's a potent messenger.

(Singer 1998: 36)

Once again, the power of sports television to create and connect nations fragmented by space, time and social difference is shown to be its crowning economic advantage. With this power, though, comes contest and even chaos.

The 'strategic chaos' of media sport

Network free-to-air television is, it should be noted, not the only player in the sports market. The fierce 'internal' competition between networks is replicated in the struggle between the network and pay television sectors. In some cases, as with Rupert Murdoch's News Corporation (which owns the Fox network and various pay satellite services like British-based BSkyB and the Hong Kong-based Star) or the Walt Disney Company (which owns both the ABC network and the leading sports cable channel ESPN), the enterprise is 'horizontally integrated' (that is, spread across different media and modes of delivery) and so is involved in both free-to-air and pay sports television. The continuing and accelerating realignment of organizations and convergence of technologies (as discussed in the Afterword) ensures that sports television will continue to be in a dynamic (which is often a euphemism for unstable) condition.

While it is premature to conclude that there is a single, integrated global sport or sports media market – for such a thing to exist much greater cultural homogeneity and economic rationalization would be necessary – there is a marked globalizing trend in media sport that makes it increasingly hard to insulate any aspect of sport and media in any particular country from external, disruptive forces (Maguire 1999; Roche 2000). Just how much power the media wield over sport can be seen through some brief case studies. In Australia, for example, a large country with a medium-sized population (now 19 million – as Turner (1990) has noted, a country with a land mass comparable to that of the USA and a population similar to that of Holland) some distance from the centres of power in media sport, there has been turmoil in sports television as the belated introduction of pay TV (in January 1995) precipitated a convulsion in the industry that is far from approaching a settled state. The intimidating presence in the free-to-air and pay TV market of Rupert Murdoch (who was born in Australia but gave up his citizenship to purchase key media assets in the USA) and his great commercial rival (and sometime strategic ally) Kerry Packer, owner of the top-rating Network Nine and (in)famous TV pioneer of one-day cricket, alongside a host of other 'players' like Telstra (the partially privatized national telecommunications company), Optus (whose major shareholder is the British-based communications company Cable & Wireless), the publicly funded ABC, Networks Seven (partially Murdoch-owned) and Ten (whose largest shareholder is the Canadian CanWest company) and many other interested organizations, has seen a story of almost medieval intrigue unfold. Notoriously, this epic narrative of communications and commerce involved, as is discussed below, unarmed combat over pay TV rights to the key Australian sport of rugby league that created a schism in the game from which it is yet to recover. Under circumstances in which a new conservative federal government was elected in 1996 on a platform that promised to reform the Australian system of media regulation (especially rules that restrict foreign ownership and prevent organizations having substantial holdings in both the print and the electronic media), sports television has been a cauldron of competing policy recipes and conflicting economic ingredients. Paul Sheehan, in surveying the global media sports scene, sees the Australia context as particularly chaotic and vulnerable to the domination of Rupert Murdoch:

> Strategic chaos is the one area where Australia is ahead of America. There has been a bloody insurrection against the old order financed by media money (Murdoch and Super League). There has been a horrendously expensive cable war (Murdoch/Foxtel v Optus) and there may be about to be a virtual merging of media and sport product if Seven and the AFL [Australian Football League] complete their mega deal [a free-to-air, cable, radio, Internet and foreign rights agreement until 2011].
> . . . In the biggest game of all, global TV sports, it is already game, set, match, Murdoch. Thank you, players, thank you, ball boys.
>
> (Sheehan 1998: 5)

In the ensuing shakedown of television ownership, control and regulation, Murdoch and Packer have both done well by cooperating rather than competing. Packer came to an accommodation with Murdoch over rugby league and took a stake in Foxtel. He (in cooperation with Ten) then successfully outbid Seven for the rights to Australian Rules Football. The failure of Seven's pay TV arm C7 (Eckersley and Benton 2002), the deep financial difficulties of the regional provider Austar and the capitulation in 2002 of Optus to Foxtel in the sharing of a common platform, ended significant pay TV competition in Australia. For all the political rhetoric concerning new players entering the media market, its two most powerful media barons retained and extended their influence. Sheehan's assessment of Murdoch's inevitable triumph in TV sport is not, however, universally shared – the *Los Angeles Times* in 1997, for example, described Murdoch's expensive attempt to control the sport of rugby league in Australia, Britain, France, New Zealand and the small number of other countries in which it is played as 'one of News Corp.'s bigger blunders' (quoted in Miller 1998b: 5). Expensive acquisition has, however, been a major part of News Corporation's global strategy (Andrews 2004). When a big financial player like Murdoch is sufficiently determined to make a major impact on a sport, the outcome is inevitably far-reaching, and the means by which that influence is exerted always involves media, especially television coverage. Thus, while Murdoch's strategy includes taking a stake not just in the sports media but in sport itself (hence his purchase of major stakes in rugby union and rugby league, and the ownership of individual sports outfits like the Los Angeles Dodgers baseball team), it is always the promise of wider TV coverage and cross-media exposure through his newspaper and magazine interests that forms part of the 'pitch'. Furthermore, when new forms of delivery involving sub-scription are involved, no media identity understands the importance of sport more than Rupert Murdoch. The turning around of his BSkyB satellite service in Britain (News Corporation is its 40 per cent majority shareholder) from a chronically loss-making to a highly profitable business entity can be traced directly to his securing of prime exclusive rights in 1992 to many of the most important games in Britain's national sport – soccer. In this task, he was given substantial encouragement by the more neo-classical economic elements of the Conservative Government of Margaret Thatcher, who disliked the public/private free-to-air duopoly of the BBC and ITV in free market terms almost as much as they loathed the BBC's news and current affairs on political grounds (Goodwin 1998). Since 1992, BSkyB has made several multi-million pound deals in sports like golf (including the Ryder Cup), cricket, rugby union and boxing, sometimes in association with the BBC and Channel 4. Not only have these contracts, with their strong elements of exclusive 'live' rights, had the effect of raising subscription levels, but also they have in some cases (including boxing and soccer) included a pay-per-view element, with its opportunities for the kind of direct economic exchange between sports provider (now via an intermediary) and sports spectator that once existed only at the turnstiles of sports stadia.

By turning the television set-top decoding box into an electronic turnstile, pay-per-view and subscription sport are, paradoxically, via new media delivery technology, recreating an older cash nexus. But now sports themselves are ceding to the media, for a handsome price, responsibility for the presentation of great sporting occasions to the largest component of the audience. The political implications of this shift are serious (as is argued more fully below), in that the new services – and many of the old ones – are now available only to those citizens with the capacity to pay. As Combe (1997) notes, BSkyB's premium, live and exclusive sports coverage enabled it, by 1996, to gain 5.1 per cent of channel share of audiences in Britain for its two sports channels alone. Combe argues that with free-to-air public broadcasters like the BBC restricted by the political imperative of holding down the licence fee, and their commercial counterparts required to compete in a more aggressive 'audience sale' market, BSkyB has been especially well placed to win broadcast rights auctions where the principal bargaining tool is the capacity to make an offer that is very hard to refuse, and which few if any competitors can match:

> BSkyB dominates the area of premium programmes with its strangle-hold on Hollywood films and sporting events . . . In terms of consumer welfare, the multi-channel industry structure diminishes consumer protection and undermines the fundamental concept of pluralism in a democratic society.
>
> (Combe 1997: 19)

The deleterious consequences for media companies and, ultimately, for sport, of the hyperinflation of broadcast rights have been noted already, but the impact of this exercise of economic power in sports television on viewers is also regarded by Combe as less than liberating:

> The stranglehold on sports rights enjoyed by BSkyB has changed the economics of broadcasting such events and transformed the organization of the events themselves to fit in with the criteria set by television. The continuing domination of BSkyB is as unsatisfactory as was the old BBC/ITV duopoly. Now, large numbers of viewers are excluded from seeing major events on purely economic grounds. The imminent arrival of digital television will set off another round of negotiations between broadcasters and sporting bodies with the OFT [Office of Fair Trading] casting an enquiring eye over the outcomes.
>
> (Combe 1997: 21)

Murdoch's £623 million bid in 1998 for Manchester United, the world's best known and richest football club, highlighted the economic desirability of simultaneously owning both broadcast rights to sport and the sports teams that are being broadcast (Brown and Walsh 1999). Despite enthusiastic support by Murdoch newspapers like *The Times* and *The Sun*, the bid was opposed by the Blair Labour Government (despite its warm relationship with Murdoch) and blocked 'in the public interest' by the (then) UK Monopolies and Mergers Commission. The grounds were that it would reduce competition in the broadcasting industry (Murdoch would be on both sides of the negotiating table in buying and selling TV rights) and that it would damage the already weakened fabric of English football by exacerbating the inequalities between the clubs in the Premier League and the rest. The Commission was unpersuaded by precedents in other European countries, such as French broadcaster Canal Plus's ownership of Paris St German and Italian Prime Minister Silvio Berlusconi's control of A.C. Milan, or Murdoch's ownership of the LA Dodgers. While the *institutions* of sport and media may have substantially merged or interpenetrated, their constituent *organizations* have in most cases remained formally distinct. For systematic, comprehensive organizational integration to occur in sport will not only be determined by state and suprastate industry regulation. The synergies that appear so attractive on corporate business plans may not materialize in practice given the added complexity of the operation, with the media, entertainment and sports industries providing several instances of public floats, acquisitions and mergers (including AOL Time Warner, English Premier League and Italian Serie A club flotations, and European pay TV operations in Germany and Italy) that have not performed as anticipated. Nonetheless, by 2002 Murdoch held stakes in English League clubs Manchester United, Leeds and Chelsea, and late in that year was expressing interest in the purchase of leading Serie A club Lazio from the Cirio food group (*The Australian* 2002: 29). The sport market, nevertheless, remains an uncertain one (Magee 2002; Wild 2002), as is graphically represented by the notorious 1995 incident (a photograph of which provides the cover image for Boyle and Haynes 2000) when Eric Cantona of Manchester United performed a flying kick on a spectator who was abusing him. The resultant bad publicity meant that 'more than £3m was wiped off Manchester United's share price', a 'minor fluctuation' that could be magnified many times by poor results on the field (Gardner 1998: 4).

The changing economics of broadcasting popular sports events – sometimes held in check as we have seen by public political values or by the desire of major sports organizations like the IOC to ensure maximum television exposure – nonetheless continually modify the conditions under which media sports texts are made. For example, the timing of 'live' sports broadcasts is now dictated by the need to stagger them over several days and nights, and/or to give a number of parties the opportunity to show whatever material to which they have gained access. Thus, while as recently as the 1970s most professional British soccer matches or Australian rugby league games started and ended on the same weekend day within 15 minutes of each other, the 'festival' of football now stretches over much of the week in the sports media equivalent of continuous process production. As seasons have extended and competitions proliferated in deference to the media hunger for sport – and to sport's appetite for media money – the prospect of creating a media sports cultural complex that defies the constraints of time and space – just as the first factory owners began to do in the eighteenth century – approaches closer. The difference, however, is that much of the population is now viewing the production process from the domestic sphere rather than participating within the factory walls. Watching, in this sense, is essential to complete the production cycle of relayed movement, meaning and imagery.

The constant availability of sport on television, though, is not necessarily coterminous with its popularity, even for some major sports events. This is because, despite occasional appearances to the contrary, even sports fans have to work, sleep, go to the supermarket, clean the toilet and offer emotional support to their families and friends. In other words, they have to make choices about when and what to view, in real time ('live') or otherwise. For this reason, the concept of prime time may have been stretched, but it has not been rendered meaningless. Grant Farred (2001: 3) makes this point about the Sydney 2000 Olympics, which he judges 'will be remembered as the Olympics that weren't' by East Coast American viewers at least. This comment would be something of a disappointment to the host broadcaster, the Sydney Olympic Broadcasting Organization (SOBO), which required some 3400 personnel, more people than were then (and since) 'employed by all the TV networks currently operating in Australia' (Gratton 1999: 122). Despite then IOC President Juan Antonio Samaranch declaring these to be 'the best Games ever' at its Closing Ceremony, various factors made it for Farred and others 'turn-off television'. These included: 'the fact that 15-hour tape delay (if you're on the East Coast) produces bad Nielsen ratings tells us not only that time-zone is everything, but that the old North–South economic paradigm is pivotal to culture' (Farred 2001: 3). It is suggested here that US TV sport viewers are accustomed to watching at convenient times and discomfited by too much distance from a land that, it should be recalled, describes its national domestic baseball competition as the World Series. Significantly, Farred argues that many viewers preferred the Internet's instantaneous provision of the 'pleasure of information' to the delayed 'pleasure of spectacle' (p. 4) offered by television. In such circumstances, television may attempt to be 'plausibly live', simulating events as if they are happening and shaping them into smoothly assimilated live narratives that are, in fact, recordings (Rivenburgh 2003). The Internet's developing capacity to marry informational and spectacular forms of pleasure threatens to reconfigure the economic structure of media sport, and is a strong motivation for the merging of media and Internet service providers, most spectacularly the (so far disastrous) 2000 merger of Time Warner and AOL (Hesmondhalgh 2002). The exciting prospect of radical vertical and horizontal integration of the Internet, media, sport and entertainment has faded somewhat, with AOL Time Warner reporting a US$98.7 billion loss for 2002, having a group debt in 2003 of US$26 billion (*Sydney Morning Herald* 2003: 33) and attempting to sell off various assets including its sports teams and events, which include:

The Atlanta Thrashers, the NHL's most recent expansion team . . . NBA [National Basketball Association] and MLB [Major League Baseball] teams in Atlanta, TNT Sports, the Goodwill Games, World Championship Wrestling, the CNN/SI sports network, *Time*, and *Sports Illustrated*, and is the NBA's cable partner.

(Miller *et al.* 2001: 66)

Irrespective of the state of the media, technology and information markets, however, computer users are yet to be allocated any more hours in the day and exemptions from work and family responsibilities than sports television viewers.

Irrespective of the logistical problems of bringing the viewer in front of the set, this economy of sports television is thoroughly representative of the newer 'economies of signs and space' discussed earlier, where power lies increasingly in the control of images and information by means of copyright and associated intellectual property rights, rather than by relying on the slower, more predictable processes of making goods or providing 'human' services. Of course, such exchanges do still go on and, somewhere and at some time, capital has to be exchanged. But following the 'money trail', as in contemporary tax and fraud investigations, is an ever more complex task. Television sport can, in strictly economic terms, be seen as a battlefield between media corporations seeking to generate revenue from all manner of sources – advertisers, sponsors, subscribing viewers and even from sports themselves (the more unfortunate ones who need TV exposure so much that they are prepared to pay for it). This state of affairs means that media mogul Rupert Murdoch frequently tops the *Sporting News*'s annual list of the most powerful people in sport rather than global sports celebrities like Michael Jordan, Tiger Woods, Serena Williams and David Beckham; powerful sports administrators like current IOC President Jacques Rogge or FIFA President Sepp Blatter (Rowe and McKay 2003); or sport and leisurewear entrepreneurs like Nike founder Phil Knight. Why such a person is at the centre of power in sport can be explained succinctly by the following opening paragraphs from a newspaper feature article on Rupert Murdoch as the 'champion of world sports':

Last month [January], American television networks spent [AUS]$26 billion on the broadcast rights for American football games for the next eight years. That is not a misprint. That's $26 *billion*. It works out to almost $1 billion for each of the 30 teams in the National Football League (NFL).

This stratospheric number is a foretaste of the revolution that is about to engulf television, and Rupert Murdoch's global sporting empire is playing a central role in that revolution. The revolution will occur on several fronts, all at the same time.

(Sheehan 1998: 4)

Given that, in 1980, NBC paid only US$72 million for the broadcast for the summer Olympics, the coming revolution in television has clearly already arrived. Perhaps, in Trotsky's (1969) famous formulation, it is in a state of 'permanent revolution'. Sheehan referred explicitly to the imminent techno-logical changes that are discussed here in greater detail in the Afterword, but even if we focus on the current 'Jurassic' period of television broadcasting (he refers to current TV networks as 'dinosaurs'), then the sports TV world has been in the grip of tumultuous 'climatic' change marked by a sharply rising temperature rather than a slow passage into a sportless ice age. What is con-fusing about these circumstances – and it is typical for the human sciences to have to confront a stubbornly reflexive complexity that is much less troubling for those in natural sciences like climatology – is that they often display counter-tendencies. Hence, for example, as Combe (1997) observes in his appraisal of statistics on channel share of audiences, in Britain between 1993 and 1996, when cable and satellite delivery really began to take hold (reaching over 15 per cent of all television households), the total terrestrial share was at the same level (69.9 per cent) at the end of this period, and the hard-pressed, publicly funded BBC1 channel actually increased its audience share (from 23.8 per cent to 24.1 per cent). There may, then, be a significant role in an even more differentiated broadcasting market for 'mass' public organizations like the BBC with proven brand identity and loyalty after the digital 'revolution'. Perhaps, though, the resurgence of some parts of public broadcasting will come at the expense, as occurred in the period 1993–96 in Britain under the old regime, of niche broadcasters (like the BBC's own second channel and the innovative commercial Channel 4) and of 'commercial public service' broadcasters aiming to appeal to wider audiences (like ITV), who lost ground both to general public broadcasters and to pay TV (Goodwin 1998).

From this British instance it can be seen that the global sports television market is, despite attempts to portray it as a single entity following predictable trends, a series of smaller national, regional and local markets occasionally linked by spectacular mega media events or by the more routine circulation of content from core markets to secondary ones. In fact, as O'Regan (1992: 76) points out, there is a tendency to exaggerate the extent to which television programmes, especially from the United States, flow freely around the world. He notes that while the USA was in 1989 responsible for some '71 per cent of the *international* trade' valued at US$1.7 billion in an estimated world tele-vision export market of US$2.4 billion (one which, it should be acknowledged, has expanded considerably since), it was in the same year estimated that television 'product' twenty-nine times greater in value (US$70 billion) stayed in its 'nation of origin'. Of course, such raw figures do not take into account other forms of 'cultural exchange' – such as the 'uncompensated' imitation of American programme genres like soap operas and quiz shows in many different countries – but they do indicate that judgements of a smoothly completed 'project' of economic and cultural globalization are seriously premature. Culture has continued to be a major sticking point in attempts to create an open global market for good services with, as Ann Capling (2001: 165) has pointed out, the 'the audiovisual sector, especially films, videos and television programs' being an 'extremely contentious' area in multilateral trade negotiations. There are few more highly charged areas of audiovisual culture than sport, with many nations intervening in the TV marketplace to protect the broadcast of listed events of national significance – almost all of them sporting (Rowe 2002). Cunningham and Jacka (1996: 40), furthermore, observe that most sports programming does not travel well in the global mediascape, so that 'Of the various genres of television . . . most are locally specific, and are not heavily traded', and genres like sport 'except for major international events like Grand Slam tennis, the Olympics, World Cup soccer, or Formula One Grand Prix motor racing . . . are usually entirely local in character'. The aforementioned example of American football is just such a game that has had little success in its attempts to 'export itself' as popular sports television (Maguire 1990, 1999; McKay and Miller 1991). However, as Hollywood film and US network television discovered many years ago, a successful if expensive-to-produce item in a domestic market is doubly successful when it can be distributed and promoted 'fully formed' in other markets.

For this reason, there is an unending search for new ways to exploit the same or partially modified economic goods and, as Cunningham and Jacka (1996: 40–1) recognize, 'under the pressure of burgeoning channel capacity and commercialization, new tradeable international formats are emerging', including those 'prompted by new forms of delivery like pay television', leading to the 'growth of specialist sports channels [which] will lead to the televising of sports not previously considered television fare, in order to fill the demand'. Sports like boxing have been quick to appreciate the international economic potential of 'pay-per-view' bouts involving heavyweight (in more than one sense) stars like Mike Tyson and Lennox Lewis, where all the resources of the broadcast and print media can be used, through staged pre-fight confrontations between the combatants and other devices, to stimulate an urge to pay to see the event on screen as it happens. That it tends to happen on US soil or in East Coast time zone friendly locations, or at times that are inconvenient for the boxers and ringside viewers but convenient for US TV viewers, reflects the aforementioned commercial clout of that country's television audience. Avid sports fans have been lured over time in respectable numbers to subscribe to pay TV, especially when the siphoning of their favourite live sports from free-to-air television means that they have no other home viewing option (as has occurred with rugby union in New Zealand). What is intriguing about much of the content of satellite and other pay TV delivered sport, however, is that there is no discernibly strong demand for it. Multiple 24-hour pay TV sports channels are as subject to the scarcity of 'good' (in the sense of 'good enough to pay for') content as are those devoted to film, comedy or drama. Apart from blue chip and some emerging sports (with what in the industry is called a cult following), the content of pay TV sport outside its core markets is often simply 'channel filler' – an alternative to the test pattern. In such cases, pay sports TV resembles what Raymond Williams (1974) describes in *Television: Technology and Cultural Form* as the prevailing conditions existing during the invention of television (and radio) in the first place – a technology looking for a use.

Sport as screen filler

In addressing questions of the uses and abuses of television sport, it is worth quoting the following well-known passage from Williams's book, not least because of the central place it gives to sport:

> Unlike all previous communications technologies, radio and television were *systems primarily devised for transmission and reception as abstract processes, with little or no definition of preceding content.* When the question of content was raised, it was resolved, in the main, parasitically. There were state occasions, public sporting events, theatres and so on, which would be communicatively distributed by these new technical means. *It is not only that the supply of broadcasting facilities preceded the demand: it is that the means of communication preceded their content.*
> (Williams 1974: 25, original emphasis)

When viewers, then, in one country switch on a 24-hour TV sports channel and encounter an obscure (to them) sport from another country (receiving the same broadcast, including commentary, as the citizens of that country), it is unlikely that they are receiving a service which they urgently demand. In such instances, it is not so much, as Cunningham and Jacka (1996) suggested earlier, a question of pay sports television growing to fill an emerging demand, but, somewhat curiously in economic terms, to supply the filler for what would otherwise be a newly created but empty space. Where sports are hoping to cultivate a new audience (and sometimes paying or subsidizing the broadcasters for the privilege), what is being offered for exchange is not TV sport for interested viewers but TV viewers for interested sports. The 'market' is constructed around the need to patch the holes created by technologically induced abundance; the opportunity to offer sports that cannot command huge broadcast rights revenue the chance to do so in the future by contacting some kind of television audience; and accommodation of those sports with more modest ambitions of receiving some valuable media coverage in the knowledge that some committed fans are willing to pay for it (Moore 1996). This form of sports TV delivery, unlike the networked free-to-air television that is heavily reliant on 'blockbuster', ratings-based viewing figures, is in principle amenable to smaller-scale, targeted, niche-marketed, post-Fordist sport (Giulianotti 1999), as is indicated by the development of a cable channel for golf in the United States and a women's sport TV network in Canada. But, at least in Britain and Australia, the pattern to date in satellite and cable sport has mainly involved broadcasting well-established national and international sports, accompanied by entertainment-based packaged segments that show snippets of sporting moments (triumphant and disastrous), novelty sports, 'extreme' sports (Reinehart 1998) and material relayed from one country to another for no other apparent reason than it is sport and there is a space in the schedule for it.

The 'bonanza' for minority sports promised by multi-channel pay TV has not yet eventuated, with claims of increased broadcast sports diversity more closely resembling political and marketing rhetoric than the actual practice of expanding the range of sports on television. As Crosswhite (1996: 58) has pointed out in the Australian context, for example, women's sports have often been required to pay broadcasters (both free-to-air and subscription) to get on screen, have come under pressure to be more 'watchable', and so have been forced to confront such questions as 'Should athletes go into Lycra outfits, or the sport alter the size of the playing area, or speed up the flow of the game, or change the venue, increase the crowd, etc?' Appleton (1995: 32), however, is less concerned by television changing sport than the need for sports organizations to cater better for television. This means for her mobilizing to secure greater genuine broadcast sports diversity rather than the 'resort to entertainment of the ilk of demolition derbies and mud wrestling rather than "real" sport'. My own research into questions of equity and diversity in Australian sports TV has found that, in a sample period of one month in 1999, only 5.8 per cent of sports programming on free-to-air TV was devoted to women's sport, but a tiny 0.71 per cent of all sport on pay TV was women's sport. One pay TV channel (Fox Sports 2) carried no women's sport in the sample period, but this was also the case with all three commercial free-to-air channels, leaving the two public channels (ABC and SBS) to carry almost 70 per cent of all women's sport. Such arguments and evidence indicate that (as will be discussed later in this chapter) the economics of sports television are inextricably bound up with questions of cultural politics. So, while a more complex mix of coexistent market forms of television sport does potentially exist, and is characterized by very different ways of creating and receiving media sports texts, the (full or partial) realization of that potential – or even its failure to materialize significantly at all – is dependent on political as well as economic factors.

Free-to-air mega sports events like the Olympics will continue to exist for the foreseeable future because, as the International Olympic Committee has recognized, their greatest economic (and cultural) asset is the massive popularity that can give billions of people the sense of simultaneously having the same sporting experience (Wilson 1998). On the other hand, smaller sports TV audiences can be catered for, targeted or (even if notionally) created through various forms of direct purchase. What Holger Preuss (2000: 122) calls 'match TV: A combination of free TV and pay-per-view' he believes to be 'the most probable variant for future Olympic coverage' given the globalization of television infrastructure. The delicate balance between these forms of delivery of sports TV will, however, be constantly under strain as commercial interests, governments and sports fans pursue their various and often contradictory inter-ests. Whatever the mode of delivery, and even if national public broadcasters manage to keep control over some 'hallmark' sports events, economic processes of varying scale and intensity are inevitably in play. This mutability of the production of broadcast media sports texts explains how they keep emerging, 'hydra-headed', despite some complaint that 'television has taken over sport'. It should be remembered, of course, that television is not the only means by which sports culture is framed, disseminated, peddled and circulated. Radio and print are also integral components of the media sports cultural complex, their products just as pervasive in the everyday world. Yet, while radio rights are contested for popular international and national sports; newspapers are com-mitting greater resources to the sports pages, expanding print and photographic coverage and headhunting their competitors' 'name' sports writers; and new general and specialist sports magazines are launched (and closed) every year, in sports television lies the most compelling expression of naked economic power in the media sports cultural complex. Accompanying this economic power to make media sports texts for vast audiences comes, as noted earlier, considerable political and cultural power. Because that arena is 'only sport', the extent and potential of this power is often underestimated, and it is important to draw out the political and cultural implications of the power to make media sports texts for the national and global citizenry.

Media sports policy, politics and myth

It is probable that many times a day, somewhere in the western world, a talk-back radio host or caller pronounces that 'sport and politics don't mix' or proclaims that 'politics should be kept out of sport'. Such comments are a little curious, given the many ways in which sport and politics interrelate. These include: deciding public spending priorities, such as allocations by national, state and regional governments to sporting organizations (Cashman and Hughes 1998) and by local governments for civic sports amenities (Mowbray 1993); anti-discrimination policies (such as Title IX section of the US Education Amendments Act of 1972, which denied 'federal financial assistance' to 'any education program or activity' that discriminated against any person 'on the basis of sex', and so had a substantial, positive impact on women's and girls' sport; see Guttmann 1991; Heywood 2000); and government restrictions on the advertising and sponsorship through sports such as Formula One motor racing and cricket of unhealthy products like tobacco and alcohol (Harris 1988). Sport and identity politics would also have to be for ever separated (Baker and Boyd 1997; Bloom 2000), and uncomfortable questions about, for example, the relationship between sport and violence against women suppressed (Benedict 1997). To be really vigilant about keeping sport and politics apart, it would be necessary to ban politicians from using sports metaphors like 'going the distance', 'levelling the playing field' and 'moving the goalpost after the game has started' in political speeches and interviews (Rowe 1995). The task of keeping sport and politics for ever separate is, then, not only difficult, but inherently futile. While the sphere of sport – as, among others, John Hargreaves (1982) has noted – can never be reduced to 'pure' politics, neither can it be entirely insulated from it. As a result, the sports media, which it was argued in Chapter 1 are always already implicated in the politics of communication, are necessarily embroiled in the politics of sport – and the 'sport' of politics.

The media, in various ways, are called upon to:

- provide good, wholesome family entertainment through sport;
- offer sensationally dramatic coverage that will attract healthy audiences (but perhaps for 'unhealthy' reasons);
- describe and show what happened to those who were not present or who want to see it again and differently;
- subject sport to intense scrutiny as part of the media's Fourth Estate function;
- support local, regional and national sporting efforts; and
- further the Olympian ideals of sport by transcending petty, partisan politics in the name of international peace and good will.

No single organ of the media can fulfil all of these expectations (some of which are seen as unfortunate obligations), just as different types of media sports text are better suited to the performance of some tasks than others. To develop this logic to its fullest extent absolves the sports media of any general responsibility for their actions beyond the minimal observance ('actionable', in any case) of the laws of defamation, obscenity, and so on. The sports public, it is claimed, is provided with what it wants from the media on orthodox, market principles – if a demand exists for a type of sports coverage, then the market will provide it. No single sports programme or publication, from this perspective, need feel responsible for what its competitors currently or might do. The different elements of the sports media, it plausibly follows, do what they do – until it is shown to be unprofitable or illegal to do otherwise. To take the sports media simply at their word and to accept this account of their motives, operations and effects would be as unwise as to confine analysis only to the surface properties of media sports texts. By pointing out the latent and sometimes manifest political significance of their practices, it is made more difficult for the sports media to evade the proposition that with cultural power comes political responsibility.

One major contention of this book is that, while the mythology of sport rests heavily on the belief that it is or should be free of the grubby workings of the political world, it cannot escape the less than glamorous struggle, both external and internal, for power and influence. In other words, sports culture – at least its official, 'legitimate' face – is highly romanticized. We have also seen that media have their own romantic myth – that of the fearless watchdog resisting the pressures of the state, capital and other powerful entities by exposing all and telling the truth. When isolated from each other, these two romantic dispositions pull in different directions; sporting mythology relies on the studied evasion of politics, while media mythology depends on a principled confrontation with it. The uneasy coming together of myths in making media sport helps explain the problems of professional practice and prestige for sports journalism analysed at some length in Chapter 2. An unsentimental take on how media sports texts are framed suggests that both sports and media mythologies – and so, inevitably, sports media mythologies – are mythological in a rather unfashionable, unspecialized sense. The 'lay' meaning of myth is that it is untrue or a mistaken impression (such as, 'it's a myth that watching too much sport on television makes you go blind'), whereas in most recent social and cultural theory, the term does not so much denote a lack of correspondence between what is said and what is 'real', but demonstrates the power of particular symbols and narratives in expressing widely, unconsciously and deeply held beliefs as 'natural' in any given society, irrespective of any burden of 'proof' (like the myths of romantic love, the 'perfectibility of man', of national cultural identity, and so on). The tension between these two meanings of mythology can be traced in media and cultural studies back to the seminal work of Roland Barthes (1973). It is being discussed in this section on political economy, and not in the 'usual place' where textual analysis happens, to demonstrate the indissolubility of the making and unmaking of media sports texts.

In *Mythologies*, Barthes (1973) attempts to deal with these different kinds of 'truth' – what is believed and what can be established theoretically, empirically and so politically (in terms of a class struggle and other forms of political action) as true. While in later works (such as Barthes 1978) he was somewhat less definitive about the clear division between truth/reality and falsehood/myth (Rojek 1985), the analytical and political dilemma has not gone away (Sugden and Tomlinson 2002). In particular, the ways in which myths can function to obscure objective judgement and cloak it in mystifying ideology is still troubling if the test of any 'truth claim' is reduced to a choice between available myths (Thwaites *et al.* 1994). In the light of the postmodern and post-structuralist assault on the enlightenment concept of 'truth' (see, for example, Norris 1993), how can we speak authoritatively about the way things 'really are' and so propose rational and progressive political values and actions? Rather than attempt to provide a simple answer to this question (which, if it existed, would mean that it need never be posed), it is preferable to develop and refine our understanding of the multiple phenomena and relationships that make the social world and its culture(s). Earlier in this chapter, for example, we saw the undeniable power of economic forces in the shaping of sport and of media sport, but it was also apparent that the mobilization of economic factors was dependent on cultural forces (including the popular appeal of sport in the first place). These symbolic and affective elements did not simply respond to economic imperatives but were critical in shaping economic possibilities (as shown, for example, by the stubborn lack of international 'transportability' of many sports no matter how slick the advertising and promotional campaign). An intellectually respectable political economy of the sports media, therefore, must seek to be aware of the many influences – strong and weak, constant and intermittent, predictable and unpredictable – on the making of media sports texts.

In illustrating this argument, it is useful to examine briefly some instances where the cultural politics of media sport are played out in contrasting ways. For example, in looking at the gender order in media sport above, it was clear that women have been subject to subordination and/or under-representation in two key organizational complexes – in media corporations as owners, senior executives and 'rank-and-file' professional personnel (Creedon 1994a,b) and in sporting organizations on governing bodies and as professional athletes (Jennifer Hargreaves 1994; McKay 1997). The intimate, longstanding linkage between sport and masculinity has helped secure the dominance of male sport in the media and of males employed to cover sport in the media. This is obviously not a simple question of capitalist logic in operation – male media proprietors and executives are drawn no less than other men to the expression of heroic, aggressive and competitive masculinity by associating themselves with the popular contact sports of which their fellows are so enamoured. In fact, there seems to be a strong streak of economic irrationalism in the desire for some businessmen to win at all costs in the boardroom as a form of compensation for not 'cutting it' at the highest level on the sporting field (McKay and Rowe 1997; Attwood 1998; Warren 2002). Yet, pressure to change this pattern of male predominance in media sport is coming from various sources. Sport is, somewhat belatedly, one of the important fronts on which battles for sexual equality are being waged, with both governments and feminist groups demanding an end to male exclusionism in sport (Jennifer Hargreaves 1994; Hall 1997). Women workers in the sports media have mobilized to improve their positions within media organizations (Cramer 1994), while women's sports organizations have demanded more air time and column inches, sponsorship and broadcast rights revenues (Crosswhite 1996). To a lesser extent, sport is also emerging as a site of contestation over gender and sexuality, with, for example, the Gay Games offering a challenge to the longstanding association of sport and 'hegemonic masculinity', Connell's (1987) conception of physically assertive, white male heterosexism that has historically dominated the institution of sport (Krane and Waldron 2000; Symons 2002).

These have not, however, all been external pressures: within the media sports cultural complex itself there has been a gradual realization that it is economically and otherwise senseless to alienate a large proportion of a market, which, if segregated too strictly on gender lines, would in the case of some sports (like the football codes) be close to saturation (Miller 2001). This is even without mentioning the key decision-making position of women in household consumption. Then there is the potential of new media technologies to provide more diverse sports fare, and the requirement for public and commercial broadcasters who have been outbid for sports broadcast rights by their rivals to make a virtue of necessity in 'signing up' some women's sports like basketball and netball. As a result, sports broadcast programmers and print editors have sought (with signal success in sports like soccer and rugby league) to attract substantial female audiences by adopting strategies such as overtly sexualizing sportsmen (see Chapter 5), explaining arcane rules to the uninitiated, giving greater and more sympathetic coverage of sportswomen, employing female sports commentators and writers, and so on (Miller 2001). In other words, commodity logic and cultural politics have interacted in new, intriguing ways – although not always with impeccably 'progressive' outcomes (as evidenced, for example, by the willingness of more women's sports and of individual sportswomen to emphasize sexual attractiveness as a marketing tool in pursuit of greater media, sponsor and advertiser attention). The issue of sex and gender equality in sport and media sport, and the ways in which it is confronted by governments and business enterprises, raises the wider question of the role of media sport in the whole domain of 'cultural citizenship'.

Fighting for the right to watch

The concept of cultural citizenship is a broadening of the traditional idea of the rights and responsibilities of states and citizens in recognition of the increased 'culturalization' of society. The outcome is a greater significance of culture and communication under 'postmodernity' in fostering the creation of informed, critically reflective persons capable of taking an active part both in their own lives and in those of the collectivities of various kinds – families, peers, pressure groups, political parties, and so on – in which they are involved. Just as, say, the idea of what constitutes a necessity and what a luxury has changed over many decades – possession of inside toilets, reticulated plumbing and domestic electrical power was, until well into the twentieth century, the exception rather than the norm for most of the population of the west (and still is in many non-western societies and in indigenous settlements in 'white settler' countries) – so what is considered to be an essential prerequisite for comprehensive participation in all of society's major institutions, debates and processes has been extended. In making informed choices, contemporary citizens need to have ready access to highly detailed information about the values, histories, performances and intentions of the various parties engaged in formal and informal political processes. Therefore, they must possess the means of ready communication in the public sphere (televisions, newspapers, radios, telephones, computers, and so on) and the appropriate educational means to decode, interpret, adjudicate on and respond to the messages that are circulating in that 'public sphere' (Murdock 1992, 1997; Golding and Murdock 2000).

As culture has become, across the past two centuries, industrially produced or provided and governed by the state (Bennett 1998), this entitlement to information for guidance in voting or family health, personal hygiene or even product choice (as applied both to commercial advertising and to state advice on safe and healthy consumer behaviour) has progressively expanded. It now involves the claimed right to certain kinds of cultural (including strictly entertainment) provision so that the citizen can take part fully in the cultural as well as the political life of the nation and even of humanity. Here a model of cultural heritage encompasses quite recent historical developments, like the twentieth-century practice of broadcasting major public events to the entire nation.

Because sports events have become the most important, regular manifestations of this national culture (Rowe *et al.* 1998), and despite the move towards their supply to the citizenry by commercial rather than by public broadcasters (Wilson 1998), media sport has become a major aspect of contemporary cultural heritage. Sport and television are, therefore, deeply implicated in debates about cultural citizenship in a way that would horrify cultural elitists (Tomlinson 1999).

Once, then, free-to-air television provided major national and international sports events at nominal direct expense to viewers, and these cultural items had been counted among the major rituals of national significance, they became incorporated into the citizen's cultural 'treasure house'. As a result, there would need to be compelling grounds indeed for the 'free list' of major television sport to be fully commodified, yet this is precisely what is threatened. The political value of (virtual) universal entitlement in the west has been challenged by market-based values, with the idea of abundant choice of television sports texts as the overriding imperative – a choice that involves a 'user pays' principle and one which positions sport as simply another commercialized entertainment option in an unforgiving and, ideally, unfettered cultural marketplace. The only rights that need to be safeguarded from this point of view, then, are those of sports media consumers from fraud, deception and other crimes of commercial practice, rather than in terms of any higher concept of the protection of significant cultural rights. The completed commodification of television sport would be consistent with its current direction, but would ultimately destroy the values associated with serving all citizens in favour of identifying, targeting and privileging affluent viewers. As Stan Correy puts it:

> Sporting tradition dictates that whatever the game, it was originally played for pure and honest motives. Money was the servant of the players not the master.
>
> In the 1990s, it's clear that sports tradition has lost out badly to commerce. The sports field is the battleground on which global TV corporations are fighting to test new television technology. The reward is not a gold-plated trophy but the traditional sports consumer. Profile: Male, 18–35, with enough disposable income to attract the sponsors with the big dollars.
>
> (Correy 1995: 80)

Debates about the rights and responsibilities in sports television are played out differently according to national context. In most European countries and various former British colonies, for example, broadcast sport was first dominated by public broadcasters, their control gradually loosened first by commercial free-to-air broadcasters and then by pay TV companies. In the

USA, with its much weaker commitment to non-commercial broadcasting, the sports media market developed much earlier (Wenner 1989), although this did not destroy network free-to-air sports television, which has survived and prospered through a combination of anti-trust legislation, broadcast synergies and the economic power of the networks deriving from television audiences captured for mass advertising rather than targeted for subscription and pay-per-view. There is, then, a complex intrication (that is, perplexing entanglement) of the economic, the political and the cultural in the determination of how televised sport is to be delivered and to whom.

In Australia, for example, the belated introduction of pay TV in 1995 enabled the (then Labour) national government to avoid what was seen as the folly of Britain's Conservative Thatcher regime, which (as was noted above) had allowed its political ally, Rupert Murdoch, to rescue his BSkyB satellite television venture by 'capturing' English Premier League soccer (Goodwin 1998). Australia embarked on what has been called 'the bravest effort at an effective anti-siphoning regime in the world' (Grainger 1996: 25) by amending in 1994 (just before the arrival of pay TV) Section 115 of its Broadcasting Services Act 1992. This law allowed the relevant minister (then for Communication and the Arts) to, in the words of the Act, 'by notice published in the Gazette, specify any event, or events of a kind, the televising of which, or the live televising of which, should, in the opinion of the minister, be available free to the general public'. Hence the Minister may list any event deemed to be of national importance or cultural significance that is usually broadcast on free-to-air television. The listed events exclusively involved sport, including horse and motor racing, soccer, tennis, basketball and golf, and covered events staged both in Australia and overseas. The provisions also allowed the minister to 'de-list' events if: 'satisfied that the national broadcasters and the commercial television broadcasting licensees have had a real opportunity to acquire, on a fair commercial basis, the right to televise the event live [and] that none of those persons has acquired that right within a reasonable time'.

This was a stronger regulatory regime than was devised in Britain, where the Blair government, elected in 1997, undertook to review and tighten up the weak anti-siphoning regulations of the Thatcher and Major regimes. The eventual framework of listed events created a hierarchy with full protection for 'A Level' sports events and diminished rights to watch sports events on the 'B' list 'live' and in full. In the European Union, a combination of general exemption and member state implementation has created a televisual patchwork of listed sports events (Roche 2000: 178–81; Rowe 2002). In all such cases there is direct intervention by the state in the workings of the sports television market, ostensibly in the interests of promoting the rights of cultural citizenship. As Law *et al.* (2002: 299–300) argue, without such 'national as well as international regulatory policy . . . sport spectacle consumers will remain . . . easy targets for those gradually filling in every moment of their attention'. In this case there is an assumed public right to watch major sports events free and 'live' as part of established national cultural heritage. This political determination, however, was not entirely immune from economic influences. The long-delayed intro-duction of pay TV in Australia has been attributed to the political influence of free-to-air broadcasters (Cunningham 1992), while the anti-siphoning regime may be seen as giving an unfair market advantage to the established free-to-air television sector over the fledgling pay sector. Indeed, criticisms of anti-competitive behaviour by government are not made only by pay TV broad-casters: netball, the only women's sport on the Australian list, quickly asked to be removed from the list because, as the National Executive Director of Australian Netball argued, 'it has not taken into account the fact that we have had to pay to get on free to air' (Smith 1996: 69), and pay TV held out the prospect, paradoxically, of being 'free' (even remunerable) for the sport and 'chargeable' for the viewer. As noted above, this has been a vain hope for most sports that were not already dominant. Furthermore, the Australian political apparatus did little more than watch from the sidelines while the sport of rugby league (as discussed above) disintegrated in the mid-1990s as Australia's two most powerful media barons, Rupert Murdoch and Kerry Packer, fought over free-to-air and pay TV rights to the sport.

Throughout the struggle (which ended in a truce in 1998 after two years of hugely expensive court action, a massively inflated and unsustainable rise in players', coaches' and referees' salaries, and a disastrous split competition in 1997) each side tried to win the mythological war, with the Packer camp stressing class, loyalty, tradition, nationalism and 'blokeish' masculinity, and the Murdoch camp promoting values of upward mobility, flexibility, pro-gressive change, globalism and a more sophisticated, even glamorous appeal (McKay and Rowe 1997). Broadcast and print journalists and presenters charged with the responsibility of reporting these events with objectivity and fairness tended, if employed by the contending parties, to report from behind their own battlelines (Packer TV versus the Murdoch press, with the rival Fairfax newspaper company revelling in the role of 'neutral' umpire and honest broker). The tragi-comedy (Rowe 1997b) dragged on for several more years, though, with the iconic South Sydney Club (the 'Rabbitohs') being first expelled in a blaze of anti-Murdoch publicity from the new National Rugby League competition on economic grounds, and then re-admitted after a court decision that their treatment had been unfair (Moller 2002). News Corporation was legally vindicated in 2003, but the 'Rabbitohs' club stayed in the league. The 'Super League' saga lost the various combatants a great deal of money – an estimated AUS$600 million for News Corporation alone (Eckersley and Benton

2002: 20). It presaged a development that many in media sport could barely imagine – the end of the TV rights party.

When sports television fails

In recent decades, there has been a long boom in media sport. As noted above, sports desks and the pages that they create have greatly expanded (Tunstall 1996), and sports magazines have appeared and folded with signal frequency. Some inroads have been made by sports Internet services, with Rod Brookes (2002: 46) observing that 'whereas a number of household names on the Internet are only expected to be profitable in the long term, Internet companies producing sports content are already generating significant revenue'. For print and the Internet, technological innovations, convergence strategies, shifts in advertising revenue, changes in audience patterns, and the 'shake-down' from the 'dot.bomb' collapse of information technology stocks and investment, have all created a dynamic media sport environment. But, as we have seen, the major driving force of media sport has been television, which has injected funds in 'telephone book numbers' into sport in pursuit of broadcast rights. In parallel with the information technology boom (Shiller 2000), television sport has been deeply involved in a frenzied inflationery round of purchasing desirable business 'properties', in this case broadcast rights and, preferably, the entities that wholly or partially own those rights. Also in com-mon with the bizarre billion-dollar venture capital purchase of startup Internet companies was the belief that the rise in the market would never end, that a 'new economy' had replaced the old one that was so chronically subject to a cycle of boom and bust, and that this investment could be used as a platform on which to increase revenue streams created by organizational synergies and emerging consumer needs.

The 'iron laws' of capital accumulation, however, are not so easily set aside, although the sports industry did for some time seem weightless (Miller 1999). At some point, investment, expenditure and revenue must be brought into the same ballpark (to use an appropriate sporting metaphor). In the early twenty-first century, it became apparent that television sport, for all its *fin de siècle* success, had in many cases over-reached itself. There has followed a retrench-ment that is increasingly registering as a 'red needle' across the media sports cultural complex, with several instances of companies folding, advertising revenues shrinking, subscription numbers stagnating, broadcast rights deals contracting, sportspeople's incomes falling and TV screens fading to black. It is uncertain whether this is a temporary market correction or will have longstanding ramifications, but there is no doubt that television sport has experienced a sobering challenge to its belief in its own invincibility. As two commentators note:

> It is widely acknowledged that the modern sports era began ten years ago [1992], when Foxtel Chairman, Sam Chisholm, then Chief Executive of Rupert Murdoch's satellite broadcaster BSkyB, was given approval by Murdoch to outbid BSkyB's rivals for the television rights to the new English Premier League.
>
> BSkyB ended up paying what at the time seemed the enormous sum of £304 million for the four-year deal . . . Until this year [2002], television rights payments for major sports continued to be ratcheted up each time they came up for grabs. In 1993, Murdoch's US Fox Network virtually doubled what rival television networks had been paying for National Football League rights packages; and then went on to invest in ice hockey, college football and baseball. When the English Premier League's television rights next came up for negotiation, in 1996, BSkyB retained them in the face of spirited bidding, for £674 million, or £168.5 million a season, a rise of 121% and in June 2000, BSkyB won them for a further three years for £1.11 billion, another 120% jump.
>
> (Eckersley and Benton 2002: 20)

While some English soccer clubs claimed that the initial broadcast rights were originally undervalued, and that Murdoch quickly recouped his investment, there is no doubt that revenues to broadcasters would have to be spectacular indeed to match this escalating level of cost. They were not. Ironically, Murdoch, who famously told his shareholders in 1996 that he would 'use sports as a battering ram and a lead offering in all our pay television operations' (quoted in Millar 1998: 3), and was willing to acquire broadcast sports rights at almost any price, now complained that 'prices being paid to sport and sporting bodies have got beyond an economic level' (quoted in Eckersley and Benton 2002: 20). Sport, as noted above in the case of Super League, is crucial to the development of new broadcast services, and to converging telecommunications and computing services. As a result, it becomes (usually willingly) entangled with major corporate strategies, gambles and power plays. In this case, it was 'News's plans for a global pay TV network' that came unstuck 'when its bid to buy the DirecTV satellite pay TV operation from General Motors was rejected' (Maiden 2002: 33). The value of the broadcast rights fell, therefore, as the promise of fully globalized subscription services receded once more, leaving Murdoch's 'chief lieutenant, Peter Chernin, [to] put it even more bluntly, saying "clearly, you would have to say we've overpaid"' (Maiden 2002: 33). Compounding the problem was the post-recession and September 11th fall in advertising revenue, with Murdoch describing the advertising market as 'anaemic', but one finance journalist using more dramatic language in judging it to be the 'worst fall-off in overall ad spending since World War II' (McCarthy 2002: 2A). In discussing intense competition for advertising revenue between the 2002 Winter Olympics in Salt Lake City and Super Bowl XXXVI in New Orleans (the latter having been put back to just five days before the start of the former because of the assault on the Twin Towers), there is some surprise that there is seemingly not enough room in the huge American media sport market for two such prime events to flourish. Media sport seems now to be subject to orthodox laws of supply and demand, with Tony Ponturo, vice president of global media and sports marketing for the major brewer Anheuser-Busch, the biggest advertiser at the 2002 Super Bowl and Olympic sponsor, stating 'The U.S. media market is glutted with more sports and entertainment properties than there is ad money to go round' (McCarthy 2002: 2B). Ironically, on the same page, *USA Today* advertises its online coverage of the Winter Olympics, thereby illustrating the 'glutted' condition of the US media market.

The result has been a US$3 billion dollar write-down of US sports rights alone, about a third of which is accounted for by News Corporation (Chenoweth and O'Riordan 2002). This is not just an American problem, although the combination in the United States of over-production, cultural protectionism and sporting introversion has exacerbated and accelerated the decline of the media sports market (Miller *et al*. 2003). Competition in that market has also led to such desperate initiatives as the formation in 2001 of XFL, an American football tournament launched by the World Wrestling Federation and broadcast by the once dominant in sport, now eclipsed network NBC. The rationale was to offer a spiced up version of gridiron that borrowed from the hyped, parodic presentational techniques of the 'pseudo sport' of wrestling. XFL did not see another football or TV season, having 'delivered the lowest prime-time ratings of any of the four networks' and 'lost XFL and NBC [US]$35m each' (Brookes 2002: 14). NBC, locked out of broadcasting the major sports leagues by exorbitant rights, tried again in 2003 when it covered the Arena Football League, 'a hybrid sport that is much quicker and higher-scoring than the NFL' that has existed for 17 seasons (Rubino 2003), albeit promoting it in a more restrained manner than XFL (Sandomir 2003: 4). The establishment of such new sports competitions by media companies and sports is a sign not of the health of media sport, but of the unsustainable contractual arrangements that currently exist. Morgan Stanley has predicted that total major US TV network losses on sport in the period 2002–6 will be US$1.3 billion (Miller *et al*. 2003).

The shock to the sporting system that there can be such a thing as 'negative growth' (the expression used by economists when they can't bring themselves to say something straightforward like 'shriveling wealth') has now registered across the globe. The business pages of newspapers, by 2002, began to speak of media sport calamities and, for the first time, that sport had become the 'sick man' of the cultural industries in articles such as the following:

> Suddenly, it seems, the business of sport is in serious trouble. The looming shake-out is likely to affect everyone from media to clubs, players and the fans. The warning flags have been flying for months, now the sirens are blaring. Sport is in real trouble around the world, and some large codes are on life support. The drama that is unfolding this weekend in dressing rooms and club boardrooms is like nothing the sport industry has seen before.
>
> (Chenoweth and O'Riordan 2002: 21)

The cause of the crisis, given the co-dependent relationship of sport and television, lies with the failure of the media to match revenue to expenditure, a problem that they, in turn, pass on to the sports that they have enriched. The extent of the problem in television sport is revealed when it is recognized that the 'weekend' referred to immediately above occurred during probably its greatest global festival – the World Cup of association football, staged in Japan and Korea but reaching out to the four corners of the earth. It is extraordinary to talk of the crisis of media sport when, in the wake of the World Cup, FIFA issued the following press release containing information that trumpeted the global success of the tournament. Given that global audience figures for mega-media sports events have tended to be based on 'guesstimates' and marketing (de Moragas Spà *et al.* 1995), FIFA took a more cautious and rigorous approach to audience measurement, but still produced extraordinary figures:

> Television coverage reached 213 countries, virtually every country in the world, with over 41,100 hours of dedicated programming. This represents a 38% increase in coverage over the 1998 event and sets a new record for a single sporting event. Contrary to some expectations, live audiences were not affected by the time zone differences for viewers in Europe and Central and South America. In fact, the cumulative live audience showed an overall increase on the 1998 figures.
>
> Although the overall global audience was down on France 98, this decline was entirely due to the introduction of audited audience measurement in China for the first time, which allows for more accurate reporting . . .
>
> The cumulative audience over the 25 match days of the 2002 event reached a total of 28.8 billion viewers. The corresponding audience for France 98, with unaudited viewing figures for China, reported 33.4 billion. However, if China is excluded from the statistics for both events, the totals show an increase of 431.7 million viewers (+2%) this year.

These impressive figures make the 2002 FIFA World Cup Korea/Japan™ the most extensively covered and viewed event in television history. Despite the time difference between Asia and the major football continents of Europe and South America, record audiences and market shares were reached in many countries . . .

Viewers the world over demonstrated their willingness to trade sleep for soccer and change their viewing habits and daily routine in order to watch the FIFA World Cup™. In terms of viewer hours, calculated as the total number of hours watched by all viewers, this year's tournament set a new record for a sports event of 49.2 billion worldwide . . .

Out-of-home viewing contributed to the 2002 Final being the most viewed match in FIFA World Cup™ history, with 1.1 billion individuals watching this game . . .

Soccer has long been seen as the perfect vehicle for sponsors to deliver messages to the dream male demographic, but statistics for the 2002 FIFA World Cup™ indicate that women's interest in the tournament is growing rapidly. For example in Japan, the audience split for the whole of the tournament was virtually even, at 51% men, 49% women. The FIFA World Cup™ attracts audiences outside the typically male-dominated arena of sports broadcasting . . .

Excluding China, the total global audience has increased by 431 million viewers over France 98.

(FIFA 2002)

These statistics show vast numbers of men and women coming together before the television screens in their homes, commercial premises and public sites to watch football. Of the many figures produced, my personal favourite is the 94.2 per cent market share gained by Brazil's TV Globo when covering the England versus Brazil match (46 million viewers and a 30.2 per cent rating). The game took place at 3.30 am local time (FIFA 2002). It is important for international sporting bodies like FIFA to capture and promote these impressive numbers as they represent a massively lucrative lure for the purchase of broadcast and sponsorship rights and a powerful statement that they do, indeed, control 'the world game'. The IOC, as operators of rival mega-media sports spectacles, make similar claims to the global status of Summer and Winter Olympics. There is, consequently, a strong incentive to massage and inflate the 'guesstimate' figures that are spread around the world and become authoritative through repetition. Thus, for example, it has been claimed that 1 billion people watched the Opening Ceremony of the 1988 Seoul Olympics, then the 'largest television audience in history' (Rogers 1993: xiii) until exceeded by the Opening Ceremonies of the 1992 Barcelona and 1996 Atlanta Olympics, with their estimated global viewing audiences of 3.5 billion (Gordon and Sibson 1998: 209). When, for example, de Moragas Spà *et al.* (1995: 207) sceptically examined the claim of '3.5 billion people simultaneously watching the Barcelona Opening Ceremony' in 1992, they considered such factors as access to TV sets in developing countries, levels of interest in sport, viewing alternatives and time zone variations. The authors concluded that, even based on an optimistic estimate of a 'potential world television audience [of] 2.3 billion . . . the highest possible audience for a single event, such as the Opening Ceremony, must be estimated to be between 700 million and one billion' (p. 215). This is still a striking statistic, but one that at worst is only one-fifth of the original estimate. The International Olympic Committee (2002) estimated that the Sydney 2000 Olympic Games, broadcast in 220 countries, were 'the most watched sports event ever', with over '3.7 billion people tuned in to watch . . . representing a 20% increase over the 1996 Atlanta Olympic Games four years before'. Total viewer hours were estimated at 36.1 billion and 'Nine out of every 10 individuals on the planet with access to television watched some part of the Olympics'. Important for arguments above concerning access and cultural citizenship was the claim that '90% of coverage broadcast on channels available to the entire population of each country'. The economic significance of these audience ratings is clearly reflected in the statement on the revenue generated by the Sydney 2000 Olympic Games, with the value of broadcast rights recorded at US$1331 million, 45 per cent of total revenues of approximately US$3 billion. These far exceeded any other source of income with, for example, tickets to venues generating only US$551 million or 19 per cent of total revenue (IOC 2002).

Much of the attention that has been given to media sport, especially when dramatic simultaneous world viewing statistics are circulated by the very media who benefit from them, has involved analysing its relationship to the wider process of globalization, of which it can be seen as both significant expression and engine (Maguire 1999; Bairner 2001; Miller *et al.* 2001). While the globalization of sport has been judged to be, in various ways, uneven, inconsistent and subject to resistance and some market failure, it has been in the context of continuing expansion of the media sport industry. Only recently, therefore, has it been necessary to ponder the consequences of global recession. There are several disastrous post-millennial stories around the world in which the next great leap forward in media sport has resulted in a career-threatening hamstring injury. One of the most spectacular examples of these is Germany's KirchMedia, who seemed to hit paydirt in 1996 when FIFA sold them the broadcast rights to the 2002 and 2006 World Cups. The Kirch group bought the rights for a reported record 3.3 billion Swiss Francs (2.3 billion Euro; Bunn 1999: 5) as part of a consortium with Swiss sports marketing group ISL. But the cost of the investment and the delay in recouping it led to ISL's bankruptcy in May 2001, with Kirch acquiring the worldwide TV rights to the World Cup (Milmo 2001). KirchMedia had great difficulty in selling the rights at the inflated prices necessary to make its original investment profitable. Ambitions to sell high-priced fees to pay TV companies were in conflict with legislation in most European nations protecting free-to-air broadcast of listed events of national significance (as discussed above). European rights had previously been sold through the European Broadcasting Union (EBU), a group of mostly public service free-to-air broadcasters (some of whom, curiously, are in North Africa and the Middle East). National broadcasters, when required to negotiate individually, baulked at the higher broadcast rights fees. The BBC, for example, refused to pay for the 2002 World Cup a fee that it claimed was 70 times the figure for the 1998 World Cup (BBC Sport Online 2001). A game of 'brink-personship' ensued across various media markets, in which the unthinkable possibility emerged that the Korea/Japan World Cup would not be seen in countries where football was the dominant denomination in the secular religion of sport. This did not happen because Kirch was forced to accept much lower broadcast rights fees for the World Cup than it anticipated, precipitating its own collapse and the bizarre outcome of the German federal government having to underwrite the cost of broadcast infrastructure so that Germany, the host country for the 2006 World Cup, could watch the previous tournament. The disastrous collapse of Kirch was not, though, just the tragic tale of one company and one mega-media sports event (Rowe 2002). It also involved the collapse of Kirch's pay TV arm, Premiere, and resulted in a dispute over the buy-back of a £1 billion investment by News Corporation (Gibson 2002a). It caused problems for Formula One motor racing, for which Kirch also held broadcast rights and in which it had a significant financial stake. As income from Kirch was also of major importance to German football clubs, many of these now faced bankruptcy.

The TV sport picture was darkening. In the same year, the UK's ITV Digital went into administration with debts of £178 million, leaving several of the smaller clubs in the Nationwide League in dire financial straits. ITV also admitted that it had paid too much – £183 million for a three-year deal – for Premier League highlights, with its in-season weekly Saturday night highlights programme estimated to be losing £750,000 per week in 2002 (Milmo 2002). In Italy, the two pay TV companies that had invested huge sums in the rights to football, the French Telepiu and News Corporation's Stream, were forced to merge (Chenoweth and O'Riordan 2002). Across the world, C7, the pay TV sport channel of Australia's Seven Network, lost Australian rules football coverage to a higher bid by a Foxtel-led consortium and folded. In summary, predictions of the emergence of a global, sports-led pay TV and interactive services industry have proven to be wildly optimistic, and many nation states (and some sports organizations like the IOC) remain stubbornly opposed to the exclusive capture of the prime sports content that would force a massive rise in subscription numbers. By 2003, the World Broadcasting Unions (WBU) organization and its constituent members like the EBU, the Asia-Pacific Broadcasting Union (ABU) and the Arab States Broadcasting Union (ASBU), mounted a strong counter-attack in defence of open public broadcasting of sport. One Japanese broadcaster, for example, argued for a change to broadcasting arrangements that led to the sudden fading from Japanese consciousness of the World Cup that they had co-hosted. This state of affairs, its representative argued, was caused by the exclusive control of post-World Cup images by pay TV (Fujiwara 2003: 24). An Arab broadcaster, similarly, argued that sports federations should 'rehabilitate the role of broadcasting unions to ensure that sport does not only become the privilege of those rich enough to afford it' (Harguem 2003: 23). There is, of course, a strong element of self-interest in such arguments, but they mark a detectable turning of the tide in the affairs of sports TV after several years of discursive dominance by neoclassical economic philosophy wedded to in-practice commercial oligopoly.

These developments might be the source of a little ironic pleasure in witnessing the puncturing of *hubris* and give comfort that television sport is still afforded some protection from complete commodification. But these positive feelings are mitigated by their disruptive impact on sport, which has become dependent on the television drip feed. Many sports organizations took the unsustainable amounts of media money and spent it on equally unsustainable player payments, which have often absorbed 75 per cent of total revenues. As clubs and teams concentrated their efforts on poaching each others' elite athletes, and caring little for smaller sports organizations or the long-term infrastructure of the game (such as 'bringing on' young sportspeople), many have accumulated huge debts. Having mortgaged their futures, sports teams bloated by force-fed TV funds now face severe cutbacks and even insolvency. In the case of UK soccer, for example, a boom has been proclaimed and validated by the signing of leading players from other countries (facilitated by international sports labour market de-regulation and lured by multi-million pound contracts; see Miller *et al.* 2001; Magee 2002; Magee and Sugden 2002; McGovern 2002). But there is now a strong sense of impending doom:

> The British football industry is in financial crisis. Any other business might be pronounced dead and buried but this sector is different: when it comes to the people's game, the heart still very much rules the head.
>
> Despite the financial turmoil – wiser heads might say reality – that has crashed down on the sport over the past 12 months, the hopes of fans,

players and investors continue to require clubs to wield the cheque book even when the coffers are empty.

And it seems that all those who should know better – from banks to investors to the finance directors of the clubs themselves – appear happy for this suspension of credibility to continue . . .

As a result, most League clubs are in hock to two competing interests – their bank and Sky TV. As one football finance expert puts it: 'The sport has sold its soul to television'.

(Wild 2002: 15)

Such analyses suggest that the full price of the sport's Mephistophelian compact with television is now being exacted. The dependency of clubs on television, with 'Only Murdoch's millions stand[ing] between many clubs and financial ruin' (Wild 2002: 15), is marked for the smaller clubs by both the trauma of the loss of ITV Digital funds and an almost pathetic gratitude for receiving very occasional appearance fees. For example, an FA Cup replay between non-league Dagenham and Redbridge and Second Division Plymouth Argyle was broadcast 'live' by BSkyB in early 2003. This game was reflective of the 'romance' of a competition that pits full-time professionals against part-time players, and was therefore of some televisual interest. Although Plymouth had failed to beat their junior opponents in the first match, the additional income from BSkyB made this poor performance profitable, with the club's Chairman stating:

'If you'd asked before the game would I take a draw and get £265,000 in TV money for a replay, I would have said "yes" '.

'For a club like ourselves the FA Cup is all about maximizing your revenue'.

(Errington 2003: 40)

The game was duly broadcast 'live' and Plymouth Argyle lost, with their manager describing the unaccustomed experience of appearing on national television (also broadcast, in fact, in other countries; see Afterword) and being humiliated: ' "The whole of the nation has seen us having a poor performance and that hurts as much as anything else" ' (Errington 2003: 43). The 'sport may have sold its soul to television', but the pain of loss on the field of play is still felt as keenly as on the balance sheet.

The evidence is clearly that the trade in sporting souls is a cross-border one. The 2002 football season was said to be 'getting off to a shaky start with the grim state of the television business resulting in growing doubts about the future of lucrative broadcasting deals and concerns over the finances of several major clubs' (McCathie 2002: 20). The commencement of the Italian season was, in fact, postponed because of disagreements over TV rights, with Italian public broadcaster RAI offering 'to pay the nation's football league only half the EUR88 million (AU$157 million) it paid last year to show highlights of matches' (McCathie 2002: 20). The result has been stagnation in the player market as:

> Worries about the balance sheets shredded by years of over-spending on players and fears the television-rights bubble is about to burst, mean club chairmen now tell their coaches a player's price matters as much as his quality.
>
> (Huggins 2003: 30)

Television executives like the Chief Executive of the Australian Nine Network, Ian Johnson, are now repeating minor variations on the mantra that:

> 'Sport is so expensive, the networks just cannot afford to be paying what we have in the past. Any sporting body that has been the recipient of huge sporting-rights fees should be putting it in the bank and thanking their lucky stars they signed those deals when they did, because it won't be happening again'.
>
> (in Eckersley and Benton 2002: 20)

There is no doubt that the broadcast sports rights contracts being (re)negotiated in the wake of the recession in sports television will be, for the foreseeable future, rather less favourable for peak sports organizations and clubs, and that there will be a negative economic impact on coaches, elite athletes, and so on given the prime importance of media capital to sport. As noted earlier, many major sports have been 'loss leaders' for converged media corporations, but the principle of the 'loss leader' is that what is lost in the direct transaction is more than matched by the income from other sources that it stimulates. This balance has been, at least temporarily in many cases, lost. The recession in TV sport has also led to a round of collapses and mergers, creating a number of TV monopolies and quasi-monopolies. This has placed television in a stronger bargaining position with sport.

It is always dangerous to commit the sin of 'presentism', the belief that what currently holds will be for ever thus. Observers of the hi-tech Nasdaq stock market index will grasp this point well, and if they are investors will now have a visceral understanding of it. When the first edition of this book was written in the late 1990s, there was little sign of the wreckage in TV sport ahead. It might be that, in a further five years, circumstances will have again changed dramatically, and a new cohort of TV and sports executives, sportspeople and viewers will be afflicted with the amnesia that turns so much of contemporary life into a blur of buzzwords, beliefs and fantasies. In the English Premier

League in 2003, for example, the Russian oil billioniaire Roman Abramovich has bought and paid millions of pounds into the ailing Chelsea – or 'Chelski' as the tabloids now describe the club. But whatever the economic trials and tribulations of media sport, its public visibility is undiminished and, if anything, enhanced. This is because although 'live' TV sport is the bedrock of the economy of sport, it is gossip and scandal that keep it in perpetual view both in and outside the formal framework of the sports media.

Sport as school for scandal

It is worthwhile to look briefly at media sports scandals because they reveal how the political economy of media sport extends far beyond the production, distribution and consumption of sports reports and live television. We have noted how sport has notable popular appeal for large (especially male) sections of the population, and that media sports texts take many forms, from 'hard' objective reporting to the 'soft' news of gossip, background and 'colour' (Andrews and Jackson 2001; Whannel 2001a). However, sport's cultural prominence and the visibility of its celebrities make it a useful vehicle for carrying news stories 'outside' itself and its routine audiences. Some of these stories are positive in nature, drawing, for example, after success in major international competitions like the Olympics, on the nationalist impulse that can be activated in many citizens, irrespective of their usual involvement in sports spectatorship (Miller *et al.* 2001). But scandals are particularly instructive because their inherently transgressive quality raises the possibility of 'contagion' or, as John B. Thompson (1997: 59) puts it, 'a corrosive impact on the forms of trust which underpin social relations and institutions'. As we have seen, sport for its adherents is the bearer of strong mythologies of nobility and fair competition, while even those who are not sports fans are of necessity aware of the material success and high standing of sports stars. Media sports scandals like those involving, for example, Ben Johnson's disqualification after winning the 100 metres at the 1988 Seoul Olympics for taking performance-enhancing drugs, or the trial of iceskater Tonya Harding for conspiring to injure her US teammate and rival Nancy Kerrigan, or Mike Tyson snacking on the ear of an opponent, directly transgress the 'fair play' values of sport. In other words, the contradictory mythological structure at the heart of sport – ennobling physical contest and benevolent universal values versus 'base' competition and cynical exploitation – is ripe for the periodic production of scandals that explode through the media sports cultural complex with firestorm intensity. These may be exhausted or dowsed, but the embers of sports scandal glow perpetually, with the media providing the perfect accelerant.

A 'scandal' can be created even out of fairly routine occurrences in a sporting event of great significance, like the public pillorying of the English soccer 'golden boy' and then Spice Girl fiancé (now husband) David Beckham for being sent off for kicking an opponent (admittedly in a rather innocuous manner) in a 1998 World Cup match against Argentina (Miller 2001: 8; Whannel 2001b: 140). The case of Beckham is especially instructive in revealing the volatility of sport celebrity and scandal, with an ever-changing cast of heroes and villains in a constantly shifting pattern of deification, celebration, demonization, punishment, damnation, rehabilitation and redemption of Biblical proportions. The speed at which these shifts occur can be bewildering, with Beckham re-installed in enhanced form as English masculine exemplar in the space of a few years (Whannel 2001a,b) and, as will be seen in Chapter 6, is even potently if mutely manifest in the successful feature film *Bend It Like Beckham*. The most sublime moment of his restoration came during the 2002 Korea/Japan World Cup, when, as England captain, Beckham confronted his fate and scored a crucial penalty against his nemesis – Argentina. The press that had abused him in 1998, describing Beckham as 'One Stupid Boy' and 'an over-coiffed terp' (quoted in Brookes 2002: 98–9), now loved him to death. Beckham's 'moment' was now ecstatically shared and almost no inhabitant of the UK could have missed the banner headlines plastered across media space. Among these many texts the clichéd statement that 'When Beckham scored with that penalty it was better than sex' (Ridley 2002: 5) in a British tabloid paper captured the temper of the times that had seen Beckham transmute from whipping boy to Love God. The figure of Beckham could also be scrutinized by academics in sociology, media and cultural studies for signs that he embodies a positive shift towards a less ideologically constricted masculinity and sporting celebrity (Cashmore 2002). With Beckham constructed so improbably (perhaps impossibly), the potential for a fall from grace is ever-present. Thus, in the political economy of media sport, male celebrity figures like David Beckham, Michael Jordan and Tiger Woods (and, to a lesser extent, high-profile sportswomen like Serena Williams, Anna Kournikova and Marion Jones, who nonetheless have to contend with sport's unequal gender order) function simultaneously as popular weather vanes for the exploration of social trends and ideologies, and as priming agents ensuring the cultural ubiquity of sport.

To qualify as media sports scandals, the transgressive behaviour does not, in fact, have to occur in the pursuit of sport. The Corinthian status of elite sportspeople means that, as in the case of the O.J. Simpson murder trial, a retired footballer turned sports commentator and film actor is still associated predominantly with his exploits on the field of play (McKay and Smith 1995), while the prosecution of boxer Mike Tyson for rape is directly connected in the media to his performance in the ring (not to mention his identity as an African American male; see Sloop 1997). In the case of high-profile HIV-positive athletes like Earvin 'Magic' Johnson and Greg Louganis, the stuff of scandal is provided by the positioning of sexuality within elite sports culture. The mere fact of being gay can be scandalous within this culture, as Justin Fashanu, the first soccer star to 'come out' and the first million-pound black footballer in Britain, discovered to his cost. He hanged himself in May 1998, largely ostracized by his footballing peers and facing allegations in the USA of the sexual molestation of a minor.

An especially striking case that illustrates how off-field behaviour can be massively newsworthy is that of Wayne Carey, the most famous Australian Rules footballer of his generation, who resigned from the North Melbourne club that he captained in 2002 after the public revelation of his affair with Kelli Stevens, the wife of his vice-captain, Anthony. This 'Downfall of a King' (*Who Weekly* 2002: 27) represented a double transgression, a 'betrayal' of both marital vows (Carey was also married) and of the compact between club-mates (the expression is used advisedly, given the strong male bonding in team contact sports). In a city where 'footy talk' dominates discourse in season (and not uncommonly outside it), this resulted in more 'morning after' stories in one Melbourne newspaper devoted to the Carey scandal than to the 11 September 2001 destruction of the World Trade Center (Robinson 2002). The Carey case also revealed something of the temporal rhythm of the sports scandal – in the space of a few weeks, coverage of Carey in Australian newspapers went from low-key (the scandal broke just before the start of the football season) to ubiquitous and then quickly subsided (Robinson 2002). This effervescence of scandal is obviously temporary, but all the 'data' generated by it is a cultural resource that can be quickly recalled and redeployed, as occurred in February 2003 when Carey, now reconciled with his wife Sally (as Stephens was to his) and playing for a new club in a new city (Adelaide), found himself embroiled in a scandal involving a 'luxury' hotel room, a party, various women to whom he was not related by marriage, and a spa. After a few days of intense media coverage of the incident, a young woman withdrew allegations made on radio that she had photographed Carey falling off a bed, drunk and naked except for a T-shirt, and that she had seen him kissing a blonde woman (McGuire 2003: 3). Her story and retraction were told to *New Idea* magazine, which had 'reportedly paid Sally Carey AUS$150,000 for an exclusive interview that appeared in the previous week's edition' (McClure 2003: 8). At this point the story petered out – until the next opportunity to reactivate the scandalous potential of the sports celebrity.

In general terms, scandal cannot be contained within the sports world even where it emanates directly from sporting activity, nor can the heroic mythology of sport be protected from scandal when the 'extra-curricular' behaviour of sportspeople brings it into disrepute by association. As Thompson (1997: 58) argues, scandals have wider social ramifications than is often acknowledged, being 'consequential not just for the lives and reputations of the individuals immediately affected by them'. In the case of sport, they do not merely damage the 'forms of trust' on which the institution relies, but also permit the use of a powerful and popular institution for the exploration and contestation of significant contemporary social issues. In the cases briefly cited above, these include: matters of resort to unethical means in the pursuit of approved goals; normative conceptions of the body and the use of drugs; private ambition versus the collective good; norms of conduct among women; the relationship between aggressive sporting masculinity and a propensity to violence; physical and other forms of abuse of women by men both inside and outside marriage; the racialized nature of the justice system; the stigmatization of homosexuality and celebration of male heterosexual promiscuity; gender inequality in sports fandom, and so on (Rowe 1997a).

In coming to an understanding of the political economy of the media sports scandal, it is, therefore, necessary to appreciate how the hunger for content, the power of celebrity, and the ready transportability of images and information within and across media, create the conditions for a full-blown media phenomenon, but that to prosper they must articulate with social questions that are of importance to media audiences and 'moral entrepreneurs' (Cohen 1980) alike. Media sport scandals, then, service the cultural economy by comprehensively connecting sport, economics and the wider socio-cultural order. They operate in the zone that the social anthropologist Victor Turner (1990) calls the 'liminoid', where social conventions become frayed at the edges, and the consequences of their transgression unpredictable, even subversive. Recurrent media sports scandals are, ultimately, no more than spectacular instances of the everyday product of the sports media. As grist for the media mill, keeping sport to the forefront of formal news coverage, celebrity gossip and everyday conversation, media sport scandals are structured into its systems of production rather than bizarre disruptions to them. Every fragment of sports report, snatch of commentary, still shot and flickering image, and all other elements of sports discourse, are couched in visual and verbal languages whose grammar and syntax, vocabulary and framing, carry within them a kind of politics. These need not be overt, clear or consistent, but they represent a politics of the popular that is pumped out unreflectively every day in the name of sport. As Barthes (1973) has famously noted, it is not when politics is close to the surface and easily recognizable that it is at its most popularly powerful, but when it is strongly present but apparently absent, allowing myths to do their work on the emotions, and ideologies to represent the interests of the privileged few as the natural order for the many. We underestimate the political economic weight of the media sports cultural complex at our peril.

Conclusion: media sport lost and found

In their programme for a revitalized and critical political economy of communications set out in the early 1990s, Golding and Murdock (1991: 17) are critical of the 'romantic celebration of subversive consumption' and the loss of interest in 'the way the mass media operate ideologically, to sustain and support prevailing relations of domination' that they see as marking the work of 'new populist' cultural studies theorists like Fiske (1989a,b). They go on to argue that even if it is conceded that there is value in focusing on 'the moment of exchange when the meanings carried by texts meet the meanings that readers bring to them', it leaves out far too much of the overall story:

> But even if this wider perspective is restored there is still the problem that cultural studies offers an analysis of the ways the cultural industries work that has little or nothing to say about how they actually operate as industries, and how their economic organization impinges on the production and circulation of meaning. Nor does it examine the ways in which people's consumption choices are structured by their position in the wider economic formation.
>
> (Golding and Murdock 1991: 17)

In this first part of the book, I have taken seriously the question of how the cultural industries work *qua* industries and their consequent impact on the meanings that we derive from media sport, in the process acknowledging (although not deeply analysing) their position in the wider economic and social formations (such as, respectively, the informational economy and the media sports gender order). This chapter has engaged with the political economy of the sports media, addressing and/or anticipating the 'three core tasks' of political economy 'in practice' proposed by Golding and Murdock (1991: 22), analysing the production of cultural goods alongside the political economies of texts and of cultural consumption. In the following section of the book, 'Unmaking the media sports text', the conditions of media sports text production and the properties and uses of those same texts will be simultaneously borne in mind. It is thereby hoped to avoid analytical amnesia concerning pivotal components of an integrated approach to the study of sport, culture and the media. In the light of the emphasis given to sports television so far, it might be expected that we would first turn to sport on screen – but before the cathode ray tube came the word and the voice of sport.

Further reading

Maguire, J. (1999) *Global Sport: Identities, Societies, Civilizations*. Cambridge: Polity.

Martin, R. and Miller, T. (eds) (1999) *SportCult*. Minneapolis, MN: University of Minnesota Press.

Miller, T., Lawrence, G., McKay, J. and Rowe, D. (2001) *Globalization and Sport: Playing the World*. London: Sage.

Roche, M. (2000) *Mega-Events and Modernity: Olympics and Expos in the Growth of Global Culture*. London: Routledge.

Sugden, J. and Tomlinson, A. (eds) (2002) *Power Games: A Critical Sociology of Sport*. London: Routledge.

Part II
UNMAKING THE MEDIA SPORTS TEXT

TAKING US THROUGH IT: THE 'ART' OF SPORTS COMMENTATING AND WRITING

Some work in Britain analysing sports writing in the Sunday newspapers and the language used to report on football matches and football hooliganism, points to its lexical and conceptual poverty. With some exceptions the language, even when compared with usage in the rest of the media, is notoriously stereotyped.

(John Hargreaves 1986: 151)

Introduction: the world of sports speak

In Part I, most attention was paid to the question of how media sports texts get made, by whom and under what conditions. Suitably equipped with an appreciation of the forces and processes of varying magnitude that go to produce media sports culture, it is important also to understand something of how its texts are structured, the forms that they adopt, and the ways in which those texts work in connecting sport's producers and audiences. This task involves the alternately pleasing and infuriating process of deeply interrogating the wild allusions, frantic imprecations, melodramatic narratives and hysterical outpourings that comprise much of the dauntingly extensive and intense culture of media sport. Of course, there is no 'typical' sports text as such, but rather a jumble of genres and subjects that can be said to fit under the rubric of sport because they have some connection (often tenuous) with its mythologies, organizations and personnel. Such texts are visual and aural, printed and spoken, taking the form of 'live' commentary on television, radio and the Internet, structured segments of news bulletins, brief 'updates', lengthy newspaper feature articles, descriptive reports of games, 'insider' slices of gossip, serious novels and 'cheapskate' (auto)biographies, and so on in bewildering variety and profusion. Each media sports text creates and adheres to its own rules of

sub-genre and textual relations, representing the sports world and situating it within the wider world with which, often reluctantly, it must deal.

Media sports texts sometimes take on the quality of sub-cultural 'anti-language' (Montgomery 1986), a lexicon and syntax that is an offshoot of the 'tabloid-speak' that selects aspects of popular speech. It then takes such liberties with that speech it becomes *sui generis* – that is, unrecognizable as anything other than itself (Chippindale and Horrie 1990). This specialist form of sports discourse binds producer, reader and text by the force of its own conventions and rules, but other textual forms are centrifugal rather than centripetal, opening themselves and readers to matters somewhat wider than results, injuries and transfers. There is a need, then, to analyse the ways in which sports mythologies 'leech out' into wider domains and are used to invest other subjects with popularly digestible meaning, and also the manner in which the discourse of sport incorporates elements of external discourses in interpreting events in the sports world. In this way, sports texts and social ideologies, mediated through different institutions and discourses, can be seen to be in constant interaction, each appropriating and relinquishing imagery and language in the unending process of representing the social world. Given the cacophonic nature of 'sportuguese', it is difficult to find a quiet, ordered space from which this somewhat abstract project can be commenced. For this reason, we shall go straight to the most overheated, parodied and reviled sports text of all, the 'live' sports commentary.

Live commentary, dead language

There is no other media sports text that is subject to greater ridicule than the live broadcast (especially television) commentary, which describes for viewers what they are seeing. There are some obvious reasons for this phenomenon: sports fans who are skilled in 'reading' what is unfolding before them on the screen resent intrusive, inexpert and mistake-ridden commentary. Yet, much commentary is not aimed at committed television sports fans – they will watch 'the match' whatever happens. Some turn the television volume down to the point of inaudibility and just watch the images, while others will choose their audio commentary and switch media. Committed cricket fans, for example, commonly mute the TV audio in favour of the more sedate radio commentary (in the case of commercial free-to-air television avoiding loud advertising announcements in the process). Some of the more hyped-up commentaries are intended for those 'unconverted' viewers whose interest has to be stimulated by communicating a sense of high drama in the events on screen. If television sports commentators, then, are irritating a core audience while trying to lure a peripheral one (sometimes with the kind of elementary explanation of rules and moves that is almost guaranteed to infuriate the *aficionado*), then it is hardly surprising that they are so often subject to hostile commentary themselves. Live sports commentators are in any case especially easy targets because, however much they 'bone up' on sports statistics and player profiles, and irrespective of the degree to which they rehearse their patter, if their commentary is going to air at the same time as the broadcast, then they have little opportunity to correct errors and avoid asinine remarks. In this sense, live television sports commentators resemble the athletes and officials whose performances they are describing and assessing. Just as association footballers have found, to their deep sadness, that own goals and sending-offs cannot be re-shot for live TV, the inanities and infelicities of live commentators are for ever. This is a rare working condition in the contemporary mass media, where scripting, pre- and re-recording, drafting, editing, spell-checking, and so on limit the error count of the final textual product. It is this performance element that in live television commentary invites critical assessment by laying bare the organized chaos that lies hidden behind much television production. Of course, such commentary (as noted earlier) is also a staple of radio sport, but it is a little less subject to vigorous criticism, perhaps because the listener does not usually have the 'corroborative' evidence of their own eyes possessed by their viewing counterparts. One technique developed in the 1990s by US networks like NBC has helped spare the blushes of live sports commentators. During multi-sport events like the Olympic Games or when telecasts have been delayed by such exigencies as time zone differences, 'plausibly live' broadcasts are shown to viewers. These are cleaned up in advance of the broadcasts and made to appear more seamless, consistently exciting and error-free than they would otherwise have been if shown live (Silk *et al.* 2000). This is an ethically questionably practice, but a godsend to inept producers, camera operators and commentators.

One former TV sports commentator (whose most famous words are discussed later) argues that, in British soccer at least, the art of commentating is in long-term decline, giving way to the 'age of the summarizer', a 'craze' now 'rampant throughout the game' (Wolstenholme 1998: 184). His diagnosis is that commentary has been infected by non-professionals since the early 1970s:

Managers, players, former players were brought in to pontificate on the box and trot out their favourite clichés, such meaningless gems as 'they've got it all to do' or 'they'll be desperate to get a result'. Television commentators picked up such remarks and before you could say, 'They must keep it tight at the back', you had television newspeak long before the days of 'do I not like that'. Viewers were given tactical lessons, they had opinions thrust at them – and not all the comments were accurate.

> . . . the studios were crowded with people only too willing to give their opinions, to analyse what they had seen and to argue about anything and everything. Sometimes they were left with egg on their faces.
>
> (Wolstenholme 1998: 184)

No doubt, these sport-specific terms could be substituted for those of other sports, and their followers would similarly complain of the linguistic aridity of their sport's 'television newspeak'. Here the 'craft' of professional sports commentating is felt to be threatened by the untrained practitioner just as the sports journalists quoted in Chapter 2 believed that their occupational credentials were being compromised by the ghosted columns of ex-players. That 'the studios were crowded with people', however, reflects the expansion of TV sport in terms of the time devoted to it and its audience reach. The aforementioned film *Bend It Like Beckham* (see Chapter 6), it might be observed, opens with a scene involving real-life television sports 'pundits' that affirms the place of this growing cast of cliché-spouting 'summarizers' in the popular interpretation and articulation of sports culture.

It could be argued, however, that making fun of television sports commentators (who are not usually print journalists by profession) has itself become a popular sport. As mentioned in Chapter 3, the London-based satirical magazine *Private Eye* for many years ran a 'Colemanballs' column and anthology book series named after the veteran television sports commentator David Coleman, but covering the solecisms of other sports commentators. In 'postmodern' fashion the main 'offenders' may become cult heroes, with, for example, the British motor sport commentator Murray Walker having his own dedicated 'Quotes' page of 'walkerisms' on the Internet, containing many examples of deathless prose by means of which 'he often entertains viewers not by describing the drama on the track, but by his litany of literal backfires. Few other sports callers are so renowned, and yet so acclaimed for their mouth running in sixth gear while their brain remains in reverse' (Jellie 1998: 3). By selecting some entries in the Murray Walker Quotes Page, the pleasurable appeal of recording errors can be discovered. For example:

1. Mansell is slowing down, taking it easy. OH NO HE ISN'T! It's a lap record.
2. And that just shows you how important the car is in Formula One racing.
3. I know it's an old cliché, but you can cut the atmosphere with a cricket stump.
4. As you can see, visually, with your eyes.

In this short catalogue of mistakes, there is a gross miscalculation of performance (1), an unfortunately banal summation (2), a curious malapropism (3) and a 'virtuoso' double tautology (4). Recording and circulating them is not only, as here, a 'cyber parlour game'. Comedians find rich material for parody, as in the case of the Australian radio show *This Sporting Life* and its television offshoot (a series of which was broadcast by British regional television), hosted by the spoof sports commentators 'Rampaging' Roy Slaven and H.G. Nelson, while British television shows like *They Think It's All Over* are named after and pick over fragments of sports commentary. Novelists (and part-time sports writers) like Martin Amis also apply their dialogically attuned ears to the synthetic speech of sports commentary, as in the case of the 'sportuguese' monologue by the protagonist Keith in *London Fields*, who, when asked in a pub to recall a recent football match, immediately falls into familiar, received speech patterns in 'incanting' sentences like, 'A draw looked the most likely result until a disputed penalty broke the deadlock five minutes from the final whistle' (Amis 1989: 91). That a section from Amis's novel was reproduced in the *Faber Book of Soccer* dedicated to the documentation of 'good soccer writing' (Hamilton 1992: 2) indicates the degree to which caricatured media sports texts now flow freely out of the mouths of broadcast commentators through the patter of comedians and popular speech onto the pages of newspapers and blackly satirical novels. On occasions, television sports commentators like Murray Walker engage in self-parody (like 'I don't make mistakes, I make prophecies which immediately turn out to be wrong', quoted in Jellie 1998: 3) in an increasingly elaborate self-referencing and reproducing system of quotation and caricature.

Ultimately, parody tips over into pastiche, as it becomes increasingly difficult to establish the 'original' that is the source of all the fun. Media 'sports speak' admirably qualifies, then, as a premier instance of what Baudrillard (1983) calls 'simulacra' (copies of copies whose 'master' was long since lost in a blizzard of reproductions) or of what Jameson (1984) describes as the postmodern product of the 'logic of late capitalism' (an endlessly playful dissolution and recombination of the boundaries of genre and style). Media sports texts can be seen in this way as reflective and partially productive of a wider shift towards what can be called, in rather ugly neologisms, the 'ironization' of culture and the **mediatization** of advanced capitalist, postmodernized societies. To put it more plainly, the media sports cultural complex generates texts which, while they may be intended initially to be serious and focused on a sporting phenomenon, can be rapidly appropriated and used for quite different purposes. Further evidence of this trend is presented in the following discussion of sports print texts, with renditions (straight or warped) of media sports speak appearing not only in the professional media, but also in the amateur and semi-professional sports fanzines (especially emanating from British soccer; see Chapter 2) published by supporters.

Media sports speak also reappears as a comic component in everyday speech. It is common, for example, for 'park' footballers to give their own imagined, imitated and exaggerated sports commentary when scoring goals or tries, liberally sprinkled with ironic sports clichés about being 'over the moon', 'gutted' and 'sick as a parrot'. By lampooning sports commentators, other media professionals assert their technical, communicative superiority and sports fans present their credentials as experts in decoding games. Just as is the case with the print sports journalists discussed in Chapter 2, live television and radio sports commentators are constantly required to justify if not their existence (although there are many fans who wish that they would find a more useful occupation, like selling second-hand motor vehicles), then certainly their qualifications for taking up such a prominent place in sport. What is required of the sports commentator, then, is to enhance the experience of watching by various means – through poetic powers of description and evocation (as is often said of highly regarded cricket commentators like the late John Arlott); to provide supplementary information (as in the case of Murray Walker's 'encyclopaedic knowledge of the sport'; Jellie 1998: 3); or to supply the kind of 'insider', expert knowledge that is gained by playing sport at the highest levels (hence the aforementioned movement of retired and even currently practising professional sportspeople into the media). Each form of commentary is equally open to critique – the poetic regarded as self-indulgent ('pseuds corner'), the informational as 'trivial pursuit' or 'anorak' knowledge, the insider as inarticulate and untrained. The live broadcast sports commentator is subject to exacting demands by fellow viewers and listeners because they (usually he) are in broad terms doing the same thing, and for a separation to be maintained between paid commentator and unpaid media spectator requires a demonstration of the superior (or at least the enhancing) quality of the professional's observations.

One way in which this potential for adverse or ridiculing response from those exposed to sports commentary may be avoided is through unobtrusiveness (low-key description and analysis with plenty of space left for the action to speak for itself – a task rather easier in television than on radio). Good sports commentators may, like efficient assassins, be most effective when not drawing attention to themselves. Another tactic is to attempt to bridge the gap between commentator and viewer by symbolically merging them. In much the same way as, for example, politicians regularly deploy the rhetoric of unity to represent themselves as being 'of the people' by using the pronoun 'we', so sports commentators often attempt to install themselves as the eyes, ears and voice of the media sports spectating public. This identification between commentators, viewers and listeners is particularly effective in international sport, where an 'us' and 'them' framework can be easily established. In covering, certainly as national broadcasters, sports competitions between citizens, cities or teams from the same country, commentators are usually expected to display at least a notional impartiality, but when a readily recognizable 'Other' exists in the shape of the representatives of other nation-states (or if covering a 'hometown team'), the broadcast commentator is licensed to dispense with any pretence of objectivity.

McHoul (1997) notes, in reflecting (from the perspective of ethno-methodology and conversational analysis) on the mode of address of sport's television, how the practice of 'doing "we's" ' (the selection and deployment of a pronoun) implies significant types of relation between sportspeople, coaches, officials, broadcasters and viewers. The example he uses from the 1988 Summer Olympics in Seoul is not, strictly, of a television commentator but is, in fact, of a swimming coach at the time who subsequently became a commentator. Nonetheless, the mode of address and behaviour of Lawrie Lawrence are much adopted by 'live' broadcast commentators in a state of high, patriotic excitement. His antics are described by Miller (1990: 92) alongside those of the Australian Channel Ten television commentator who, as Lawrence's 'coachee' Duncan Armstrong won the 200 metres freestyle in world record time, expostulated 'Oh my God, Oh my God!' in the manner of Meg Ryan in the much imitated simulated orgasm scene from the film *When Harry Met Sally*. In analysing who are the 'we' when Lawrence shouted, 'We won! We won!', McHoul (1997) argues, following Sacks (1992), that there are two types of 'we' – a specific 'list' (say a named group of swimmers or runners) and a vaguer 'category' (say of men or women). How, he asks, can disparate individuals with very different histories become 'we'?

> there's always the possibility that nonswimmers such as coach, crew, and even family can get, as it were, on the list. Or else there can be categorical 'we's' available to team fans, or indeed (particularly in the case of the Olympics) to any person with the same nationality as the swimmer.
>
> (McHoul 1997: 319)

At rare dramatic moments there is an unforgettable coming together of live TV sport event and its commentary, making it impossible to disentangle what happened from what was said. The Australian sports commentator Norman May (1984: 116), for example, describes his much replayed words in the closing moments of the men's 4 × 100 metres medley in the 1980 Moscow Olympics, '5 metres, 4, 3, 2, 1 – Gold, Gold to Australia, Gold', as 'my best known single commentary in 27 years as a broadcaster'. At such times, sports commentator and audience also seem to become one, united in the ecstasy of victory.

Live TV sports commentators, therefore, have highlights reels to match sportspeople's. These do not always involve high-pitched, emotional expression. The aforementioned British comedy programme, *They Think It's All Over*, takes its name from a cool piece of improvisation by Kenneth Wolstenholme, who commentated for the BBC in its coverage of the 1966 World Cup Final (the only time to date, it is my melancholy duty to report, that England has won the Jules Rimet Trophy). In the final moments of the game its result was in doubt, with only a single goal separating England and (then West) Germany until a last-minute England goal made the outcome certain. As the goal was scored, Wolstenholme's memorable words were 'Some people are on the pitch. They think it's all over ... it is now'. The cool detachment and thespian timing of Wolstenholme's comment enhanced the sporting moment, although his own reflections attest both to the multiplicity of its uses and its unconscious genesis:

> ... fourteen words which have stuck to me ever since. I have even described them as my pension because they have been used so many times by so many people, yet quite honestly I cannot remember ever saying them. But then, the excitement of an occasion can do strange things to the memory ...
>
> (Wolstenholme 1998: 128)

The 'art' of sports commentating may, then, be as mysterious as Ian Wooldridge's (1998: 8) claim that Wolstenholme 'ad-libbed five words into a microphone at Wembley that were destined to be re-broadcast more times than Winston Churchill's "We shall fight on the beaches" exhortation'. By such means sports commentary can become part of the national estate, with the former Director-General of the BBC, John Birt, giving a suitably preservationist justification for the revival of the commentary by stating that 'he wanted to bring the famous words to the notice of the younger generation' (quoted in Wolstenholme 1998: 186). The commentator himself has felt his most famous statement to be 'Sadly ... over used' (p. 186), but the media sports cultural complex has logged his words for deployment on-demand in numerous, diverse contexts.

McHoul, May, Birt, Wooldridge and Wolstenhome are all describing the extraordinary power of sport – one which would be unique were it not for some instances of intense national identification in times of war or disaster – to encourage a literal identification between 'actors' and 'non-actors'. More even than in the cases of 'subcultural' music or 'projection fantasy' film, the performances of sportspeople are appropriated by sports fans as 'ours'. Live broadcast commentary on major international sporting events is consummately aware of this power, and in this way media sports texts can be seen to be actively engaged in the task of recruiting audiences (especially for advertisers) by first 'signing them up' as on the same 'team'. This well-established theoretical notion of 'interpellation' – what Althusser (1971) calls 'hailing' subjects in much the same way as people in the street automatically turn around when someone calls out 'Hey, you!' (appropriately here we might add the line from the Madness song *One Step Beyond*, 'Don't watch dat! Watch dis!') – is more than a matter of technical communication. It is also a question of ideology. If media sports texts have the power to unite, temporarily or in the long term, symbolically or materially, disparate audiences into relatively coherent groups of patriots or consumers, then they are potentially deliverable, as Golding and Murdock (1991: 17) noted in Chapter 3, to those who wish to 'sustain and support prevailing relations of domination'. For example, the patriotic fervour generated by Argentina's winning of the soccer World Cup in 1978 (at least temporarily) assisted the fortunes of the oppressive military *junta* whose slogan was '25 Million Argentinians Will Play in the World Cup' (quoted in Kuper 1994: 174). From the mouths of sports commentators can come social ideologies in the guise of innocently hysterical descriptions of play.

Ideologies and Olympic extravaganzas

Live sports broadcasts (over which, of course, commentators exert only partial control; see Chapter 6) do not have to be rampantly xenophobic to be the bearers of ideology. Gordon and Sibson (1998), for example, note how the absence of commentary on some of the smaller and more marginal national teams during the television broadcast of the opening ceremony of the 1996 Atlanta Summer Olympics had the effect of further marginalizing those nations. Tomlinson (1996), similarly, in his analysis of the commentary at Olympic opening ceremonies, argues that at the 1984 Los Angeles Summer Olympics, the aforementioned (and much lampooned) BBC commentator David Coleman's:

> welcome to the Coliseum mixed history, myth and politics: 'in the sunshine of this Californian afternoon, ancient Greek rites, Hollywood fantasy and the reality of life in 1984 will find common ground. . .' (Transcription from BBC broadcast). There were more nations and more competitors than ever before at LA (despite Soviet bloc boycotts), welcomed by a showbiz style of 'pure Hollywood extravaganza on a gigantic scale', as Coleman put it. 'The show must go on'.
>
> (Tomlinson 1996: 590)

In hosting on behalf of a national television audience a ceremony which, during the 1992 Barcelona Summer Olympics, Coleman described as being watched by 'half the world's population' (quoted in Tomlinson 1996: 595), commentators, with their combination of scripted and spontaneous utterances, are able to call on the grandest myths of all – those which pertain to universal humanity, and the capacity of the Olympics to promote global 'peace, harmony and progress' (the theme of the 1988 Seoul Olympic opening ceremony). Yet, as we have seen, commentators are also in the business of making sure that their audiences differentiate between their compatriots and the other branches of the great human family whom they fervently hope will lose. This universalist–partisan balancing act is a difficult one to perform, and helps to explain the somewhat schizophrenic quality of much media sports discourse, as live commentators try to temper their often hysterical and 'one-eyed' support for an individual or team with a more even-handed appreciation of the skills of their opposition. To return briefly to McHoul's reflection on Lawrie Lawrence, the cry 'We won! We won!' could be all-inclusive only if every potential division was denied, leaving us with the heartwarming but improbable meaning that 'humankind' was the winner. Such sentiments are, in fact, rarely heard outside the more platitudinous pronouncements of commentators during mammoth broadcasts for major sports events. Or beyond the utterances of sports officials like the IOC's Juan Antonio Samaranch, whom Tomlinson (1996: 597) quotes as describing the 1992 opening ceremony in his native Barcelona as 'the greatest festival of our contemporary society'. We should also not forget the transparently disengenuous claim by commentators that sport or a particular sport 'was the winner today' when made after an unsatisfactory result in a sports contest. Solace after a major sporting loss can be found, then, by retreating to the universal and high-minded values that much of the time are discarded in the search for passionate, loyal media audiences. For an English fan, for example, tennis is always the winner at Wimbledon, because almost certain loss awaits their country's players.

Broadcast commentators, however, get criticized not only for their technical failings and banalities, but also for bringing political issues (usually inadvertently) to the surface. For example, when in January 1998 the British television soccer commentator John Motson remarked in an interview that he sometimes had difficulty differentiating between black players when clustered on the pitch, there were angry allegations that this was a 'replay' of the old racist saying that 'they all look the same to me'. The sheer, relentless availability of media sports texts like live television and radio commentary, as in the case of the sports celebrity scandals discussed in Chapter 3, also facilitates often heated debates about racial and ethnic stereotyping, gendered denigration and exclusion, the celebration of violence and aggression, discrimination against those who are elderly or not able bodied, and so on. The riposte during such popular debates is often that too much is being read into an offhand or joking remark, or that an injudicious word was chosen in the heat of the moment in the same way that most 'live' broadcasts are littered with errors of grammar and expression, and replete with *non sequiturs* and 'spoonerisms'. Certainly, few live commentators with the primary responsibility of accurately describing great media sports events wish or are permitted to be socially provocative, although their fellow studio 'summarizers' usually have greater rhetorical licence. Setting aside the methodologically opaque question of intention (Silverman 1993), what is said or written can be subjected to detailed analysis to reveal which views of the world, couched in the language of sport, are being given an airing. As Blain and Boyle argue:

> And, since being a television or newspaper journalist or editor is a position of privilege, we should bear in mind that the ideologies the mainstream media produce or reproduce when giving us accounts of sports-related matters will tend to be those of socially dominant groups rather than those who may be disempowered: we are more likely to find out what men think about women than the other way round; more likely in Italy or France to find out what Whites think about Blacks than vice versa; more likely on British television networks to find out the English view of the next World Cup than the Welsh or Scottish expectations. Conversely, the accounts which we do *not* hear tell us a lot about the groups denied a voice on TV and radio or the press.
>
> (Blain and Boyle 1998: 371; original emphasis)

The circulation of discourses of dominance in media sports texts, then, occurs as part of the overall flow of ideologies and mythologies in and out of the media sports cultural complex and the social structures, large and small, to which it is linked. These texts can be especially effective bearers of ideology because they seem so innocuous and can be decoded in such habituated fashion because of their repetitiveness and familiarity. The nasty sting of racism (Carrington and McDonald 2001), (hetero)sexism (Hemphill and Symons 2002), and so on, may not be felt on the surface but can nevertheless efficiently enter the ideological circulation system by means of sport. While, as Blain and Boyle suggest, there is an obvious tendency for powerful forces to protect their own interests (and sport, even when it is not wedded to the media, has an institutional disposition towards deep conservatism; see Brohm 1978), this cultural system is not as functionally self-reproductive as it may appear. One of the protections against any powerful group entirely or even substantially 'sewing up' sports meanings is (as I have argued above) a quite deep-seated suspicion of (sometimes even contempt for) the sports media by audience members. The frequent refusal to give high levels of professional respect to many producers of media sports texts (like broadcast commentators and journalists) is, as we saw in Chapter 2, galling for them and often rather unfair (especially when journalistic colleagues take an unduly snobbish view of the 'toy department'). Ironically, though, public scepticism about the sports media is also a buffer against those media exercising undue ideological power. This is not to argue that all media sports texts are 'reactionary' and all criticisms of them 'progressive', but rather that resistance to the cult of the sports media expert is also something of an assertion of popular power against one of the most efficient and extensive factories of meaning and value yet devised. If the sports television commentary gabbled by the man (usually) with the bad hair, the pocket vocabulary and the messy private life (reported with much glee by his news journalist colleagues) is hard to take altogether seriously as an efficient vector of dominant ideology, so, too, is much of what appears under the banner of print sports journalism. Which is not, of course, to say that sports writers lack a large (sometimes compulsive) readership or that what they produce is not also a source of pleasure (sometimes cruel) for what it informs about sport and disfigures in language.

On the page, off the air

Sports texts, as I have argued, have many forms, functions and readerships (see also Rowe 1992). The traditional sports report is intended to bear witness to what has occurred for those who were not present. At the most basic, denotative level this is an uncontroversial (if, depending on the result, by turns exhilarating and depressing for those who care) statement that, for example, Crewe Alexandra drew 0–0 with Burnley in Division Three of the English Football League at the Gresty Road Ground before a crowd of 2816 cold, wet masochists. Not much human intervention is needed here: a few units of data are 'sent down the wire' or entered into a computer database, producing a text that has little more cultural resonance than the shipping or stock market reports (hence the invention of the Zybrainic Sportswriter discussed in Chapter 2). Except that, just as those anonymous units of information have much greater importance and depth of meaning for the seafarers and 'desk jockeys' who depend on them for their livelihood, the relevant sports fan will not only invest these facts (which must be unimpeachably accurate) with significance, but also expect more information. Thus it is unlikely that many followers of sport will be satisfied for long with a simple news digest format.

Beyond the bare outline of what occurred lie questions that break down and elaborate what is known in summary form. How exactly did it happen? Which were the pivotal moments? Who should be exalted/demonized? What was the atmosphere like? The written sports report text, therefore, unlike the more immediate audiovisual form (which, nonetheless, is also moulded by producers, commentators, camera operators, and so on), is reliant above all else on connotation, evocation, elaboration, embellishment and interpretation. As was also noted in Chapter 2, the electronic media have had a very serious influence on the status of the print sports text. Once the reader had to take the word of the writer concerning the veracity and accuracy of what was written or, at least, the journalist could be challenged only by the relatively small number of people present. Now it is expected that the report will be produced at high speed and then must be reconciled with the perceptions of a potentially huge audience that has been exposed to the event in sparkling sound and vision. McGuane (1992), in the introduction to a collection of *The Best American Sports Writing 1992* (a work chosen more or less at random from that part of my personal library devoted to remaindered books picked up in sales – which may or not be significant for my argument), makes clear just how exacting can be the demand of the reader of the print sports text, especially when access has already been gained to the moving media sports text:

> The reader of sports writing is a strict, occasionally cruel individual. There has never been a modernist period in sports writing, much less a post-modernist spell. Anything beyond telling the sports fan what actually happened requires the heart of a lion, a jeweler's eye. Otherwise, one risks being tossed out by the reader himself [*sic*]. The sports page of any newspaper is truly an impact zone where writers and readers compare impressions of something they often have both seen. No one is taking anyone's word for anything. Opinions are truly earned. Fancy sports writing is some of the worst writing of any kind.
>
> (McGuane 1992: xv)

McGuane is reflecting a very traditional view of sports writing which, it seems, is being superseded in the television (and even the post-television) age. The contributions to *The Best American Sports Writing 1992* are by no means confined to the objective style of 'realist' sports reporting, despite his claim that 'what is shared, foremost, is the event' (McGuane 1992: xv). Among the twenty-five contributions (only three of which are by women, which indicates the existence of traditionalism of a different kind) drawn from a pool of 'more than 350 national, regional, and specialty publications' (according to the back cover) including the *Washington Post*, *Sports Illustrated*, *Los Angeles Times* and *Yale Review*, there are not only elaborate reports of sports events. The collection also contains biographical profiles of sportspeople like boxers Mohammed Ali (Gildea 1992) and Sonny Liston (Nack 1992), and more provocative essays like Barry's (1992) 'Why the NBA isn't as offensive as you think'. Some of this writing is, indeed, 'fancy', seeming to aspire, like the 'name' sports journalists mentioned in Chapter 2, to the status of literary art. It is not, then, altogether accidental that the first piece of writing mentioned in the foreword to *The Best American Sports Writing 1992* is a poem by David Rein called 'A Baseball Player Looks at a Poet', which likens the criticism of sports performances to that applied to 'the act of writing' (Stout 1992: ix).

In the absence of the capacity to give the direct sense of 'having been there' offered by television and still photography, the reader is presented with a meaning frame which, in the language of economics, adds value (in this case cultural) to the primary text (at its most basic, the statistical result of a game contest) through secondary texts that occupy the infinite discursive space of debate and analysis of what is known and what might be revealed. Print sports texts, then, are not limited to accounts and treatments, however extended, of formal sports events. Apart from what is generally available for scrutiny and open to description is what is open to speculation and revelation. The revelatory print sports text moves in the opposite direction to the 'evidentiary'. Instead of taking what is (at least in technical terms) publicly on view and, via the mediation of the journalist, 'translating' it for consumption in the private sphere, it takes what is hidden and then, again after being mediated, makes this 'privileged' information public and so available for private digestion. A further form of print sports text is aware of the politics of sport, taking the sports world as a sphere with its own relatively autonomous politics or relating its internal politics to the wider domain of politics either directly (as in the state's involvement in sport) or indirectly (by seeing sport as a metaphor for politics). Sports writing moves beyond straight reportage and insider gossip in this instance and takes on a campaigning or petitioning role. The final mode of print sports text I shall examine here may be conscious of its own position and so reflexively aware that it is part of what is being discussed. Here the lived experience of sport meets the aesthetics of sports writing. The text is about sport but it is also a thing in itself – sports writing becomes literature and sport becomes physical culture, even art.

These different modes of sports writing (there are no doubt other forms and hybrids) can only briefly be illustrated and analysed here, but constitute a rich vein for textual enquiry across different sites in the media sports cultural complex. Working from the short digest form of print text upwards it is apparent that, even within very strict word limitations, the text is set in play in a manner that never allows it to be tied to the 'bare facts'. If we take two fairly random recent examples from very different newspapers – the much scorned British tabloid *The Sun* and the highly prestigious *New York Times* – it is clear that similar devices are used to attract the interest of readers and to provide an 'angle' for the interpretation of the sports event. In 'Super Goals', a 24-page Monday *Sun* soccer supplement (sponsored by Ford), there are sports stories of varying length and type: manager profiles, features on significant weekend games, a 'where are they now?' section, a 'lifestyle' segment (asking traditional questions of players like their favourite foods, although now with some less traditional answers than 'steak and chips'), and so on. For many lower division games, there are snippets (sometimes without by-lines) like the report of a match, with the punning headline, 'CHIP OFF THE OLD BECK', between Cambridge United and Chester:

> GRANT BREBNER showed David Beckham is not the only Manchester United man capable of hitting long-range stunners.
> On loan with Cambridge United, Brebner got two drives on target only to see Chester keeper Ronnie Sinclair produce two great saves.
> Brebner said: 'I couldn't believe he stopped them'.
> Stuart Rimmer scored Chester's first before Paul Wilson equalised, but Rob McDonald sealed City's win in the final seconds.
>
> (*Sun Super Goals*, 26 January 1998: 17)

This is a report of a game lasting a minimum of 90 minutes involving 28 players (including substitutes), various team staff and match officials, and a crowd (admittedly not of epic proportions) of 2473 – all in just 66 words. But in that small print media space, room is found for mentions of an elite team and of a footballer who, as is discussed in Chapter 3, was 'exclusively' interviewed and pictured in the same issue of the newspaper on the occasion of his engagement to a Spice Girl (so enabling a little word play on the '*Sun*-speak' word 'stunner'). Apart from this celebrity association, a theme of thwarted ambition is introduced and the opportunity taken for verbatim comment from the story's main subject, while the final paragraph is a condensed account of the identities of the goal scorers, the order of scoring, and the dramatic resolution to the narrative 'in the final seconds'. In other words, this 'cameo' print news story operates as precisely that – a narrativized account that introduces character, conflict and the passage of events. Yet much of the information contained in it (which teams and players were involved, who scored and when) is provided only four pages away (p. 21) in the Soccer Results Service section. This duplication of the spare, summary data of match statistics operates as narrative supplementation which contextualizes and elaborates on the sports event. This is a technique that is used just as routinely in august broadsheet newspapers as in tabloids.

The following report (supplied by the Associated Press news agency) with the headline 'Bourque Out, Pens Win' of a National Hockey League game in the *New York Times Sports Friday* Scoreboard section is one such example from the broadsheets:

Jaromir Jagr got Ray Bourque kicked out of the game and then assisted on one of Kevin Hatcher's two goals as the Pittsburgh Penguins beat the host Boston Bruins, 4–2, last night.

Ron Francis became the 11th player in National Hockey League history with 1,400 career points when he assisted on Stu Barnes's goal to make it 1–0 with 7.2 seconds left in the first period. The goal came during a five-minute power play after Bourque checked Jagr from behind, sending him head-first into the boards behind the net.

Bourque also received a game misconduct for the first hit – the first ejection in his 19-year career. Without their top defenseman, the Bruins couldn't hold on, and Tom Barrasso stopped 29 shots to keep the Penguins unbeaten in their last six games (4–0–2).

(*New York Times Sports Friday*, 30 January 1998: C6)

Allowing for some variations in the nature of the two reports – the latter is twice as long (133 words), covers a much more elite sports contest and does not involve direct interview – there are remarkable similarities in approach between two very different newspapers. The *New York Times*'s sports section, like *The Sun*'s, contains more elaborate stories than those reproduced above, including several that are not reports of specific sports events. Yet both provide summary data of what occurred (in the case of the *New York Times* directly below the report) accompanied by brief stories that highlight the roles of the main 'actors', the key individual contests, the pivotal moments in the game, statistical patterns, and so on – and all in three paragraphs.

Such news story formats can be regarded as international print sports media genres (or sub-genres) that accommodate both the sporting preoccupation with statistics and results and the deep concern with the mythological status of sportspeople as heroes and villains, champions and battlers, engaged in an eternal contest for supremacy on the field of play. Some of these abiding concerns of sports culture are shared with other elements in the wider media in obeying, as Galtung and Ruge (1970, 1973) have influentially proposed, the dictates of particular 'news values' which signal the presence of 'newsworthiness' (see also Schudson 1991; Palmer 1998). Several of the dominant criteria for newsworthiness – the principles according to which only a few of the billions of daily events are selected for media coverage and, of that tiny proportion, only a minute number are given any sustained attention, with a few matters receiving saturation coverage – are observed in the small sports stories I have presented.

This does not mean that the stories are self-evidently worthy of attention, but that they are constructed in a manner that ensures that they respect the usual rules of news media text production and presentation. The pressure to reproduce the professional ideologies that govern practice is not just felt in the basement of sports journalism. As, for example, Alina Bernstein (2000) has shown in her study of newspaper coverage of the 1992 Barcelona Olympics, journalists are required to entertain, simultaneously, both localist (how's our team going?) and 'global' considerations (who won the glamorous Olympic events dominated by somebody else?). Deborah Stevenson (2002), in a rather different context, has analysed the ways in which the print media juggled sexuality, gender and nation as 'angles' in the 1999 Australian Tennis Open. The rules that have to be taken into account include 'personification' (the reduction of large-scale, perhaps abstract events to the actions and motives of recognizable people), 'elite status' (the use of celebrity and, when it is not present, connections made to it), 'consonance' (the events and their treatment are easily fitted into readers' everyday frameworks and expectations when confronting a sports news story) and 'negativity' (the established media wisdom that, on balance, bad news is more newsworthy than good – in our examples frustration at having shots saved in a minor game instead of playing for Manchester United and marrying a Spice Girl; and getting 'kicked out of the game' for the first time in a '19-year career'). Thus, even brief, formulaic and modest print media sports texts are surprisingly effective in reaching beyond themselves to other games, people, issues and myths. All texts are **inter-textual** in that, to be effective, they must make connections with other phenomena and stories. Yet the degree of intertextuality is limited by the amount of media space allotted (it is hard to be too expansive in sixty-six words, although some sports writers achieve an economy of style to rival Ernest Hemingway) and the tasks that have to be performed in particular types of stories (giving the score, the time of scoring, the identity of the scorer, and so on). Once the print coverage of sport is severed from any requirement to report actual, public events to people who have often seen and experienced them in some way, then the opportunities to 'free' the text from its stricter obligations proliferate. Thus, for example, a sports journalist can liken, in quasi-poetic language, an Australian cricket captain to one of the greatest minds of the twentieth century. Of Steve Waugh (nicknamed Tugga) it can be said that 'There are silken fibres within Tugga's tough exterior and an Einstein lurking inside his shaggy baggy green cap' (Meher-Homji 2002: 90). Pronouncing on the intellectual prowess of elite sportspeople, however, has its news value limitations. More newsworthy is the kind of text that is ostensibly generated by news media resources unavailable to ordinary citizens, whereby sources can be tapped and interviews gained in producing new knowledge.

Revelations, exclusives and 'bungs'

The revelatory print sports text affords greater licence to its creator because it trades on information that is obscured from the public gaze. It relies on privileged access to the sports world that enables it to generate gossip, information that would be mundane if it did not concern sports stars, and unattributed statements and knowledge about the inner workings of sports organizations. A story in the sports pages of a British tabloid newspaper, the *Daily Mirror*, demonstrates how revelatory sports texts work. Entitled 'I PLAY IN THE BIG LEAGUE ... GAZZA DISNEY! Says LES FERDINAND', its main hook involves a reported ' "goofy" exchange' between the English soccer internationals Les Ferdinand and Paul Gascoigne 'as the England players gathered for last summer's European Championship' (Wiechula 1997: 42). It enables readers to eavesdrop on a conversation between two prominent sportsmen in a place inaccessible to the sports public, although it transpires that the conversation has already been recounted in 'the latest issue of Total Sport magazine' and also involves an interview with one of the interlocutors. Thus the story is patched together with a combination of recycled information about a publicized private conversation and direct access to one of the personalities involved (the one who has 'spilled the beans'), made especially newsworthy by its impugning of the standards of Scottish football. The revelatory, controversial tone, reinforced by the tabloid trademark bolded type face and a 'doctored' photographic image of Gascoigne complete with Mickey Mouse ears, nose and whiskers, is central to the attention-grabbing pitch of the story:

> **Les Ferdinand has amazingly told Paul Gascoigne he's 'just playing in Eurodisney' in Scotland.**
> The Newcastle and England international responded tongue-in-cheek after Gazza took the 'mickey mouse' over the Magpies' title collapse last year.
>
> Strike ace Ferdy revealed that while Manchester United's double-winning England contingent hadn't rubbed it in before Euro '96, Gascoigne took the p*** a little bit.
>
> **Medals**
> 'He kept on saying, "Aaarrgh, you lot blew it, you lot s*** yourselves, look at my medals".
>
> 'But, as I said to him, "It's alright for you playing up in Eurodisney".
>
> 'I said I could go to Eurosdisney, score 40 a season and get myself a few medals too'.
>
> (Wiechula 1997: 42)

This snippet from the story contains key elements of the genre in its familiar use of dramatic words ('amazingly', 'revealed'), nicknames ('Gazza', 'Magpies', 'Ferdy'), compressed media sports speak ('Strike ace', 'title collapse'), puns ('took the "mickey mouse" ') and authentic seeming – although coyly presented – swearing ('took the p***', 's*** yourselves'). The headline also plays on differences in accent, with Disney echoing the Scottish way of saying 'does not' as 'disnae'. The critical comments about Scottish soccer (likely to appeal to the principally English readership), the inter-textual reference to Disney, and the feeling of being privy to elite football banter, all obey those orthodox principles of news value that promote controversy, celebrity and revelation.

This format can be varied: some stories carry the tag 'exclusive', relaying information that has been captured by or leaked to the sports journalist, like the following opening to a small item from the sports pages of the British tabloid newspaper *Daily Star*:

ALBION WANT ROYLE

EXCLUSIVE: By Ralph Ellis

Joe Royle is poised to bounce back into football as West Brom boss.

The 48-year-old has leapt to the top of the Hawthorns wanted list in the search to replace Ray Harford.

I understand Albion officials have made checks with Royle's old club Everton to make sure all his contractual ties at Goodison Park have been severed.

(Ellis 1997: 42)

What Ellis 'understands' is unattributed information that he has gained on the sports round – later in the story we are told that 'Royle has told friends he's ready to go back to work'. The sources are mysterious – unnamed friends and club officials – but the story has the authority of insider knowledge to which, by its nature, the readership cannot be privy. Another variation is the interview that generates the highly detailed information that only a dedicated sports fan would be interested in, but which the sports journalist has access to through the interview process and by collating and analysing data. For example, an interview-based story on the Yankees' baseball catcher Jorge Posada in the *New York Times Sports Wednesday* is packed with statistical minutiae like 'He said he was leaner after reducing body fat percentage to 6 percent, stronger after adding 15 pounds of muscle and quicker after thousands of sprints and agility drills' and 'Posada (.250 average, 6 homers and 25 r.b.i. in 1997)' (Curry 1998: C2). Such stories, however, stop well short of critique, concentrating instead on the unashamed entertainment functions of the sports media. Others, however, take up the press's more serious, campaigning role, as in the back-page exposé by Harry Harris (1997) entitled 'TOP SECRET – SOCCER BUNG DOSSIER', which appeared in the same edition of the *Daily Mirror* as Gazza and Mickey Mouse.

This type of 'exclusive' affirms and celebrates the media's Fourth Estate role, applauding its own part by breaking a story that exposes the inner, illicit workings of sport. In this instance, *Mirror Sport* claimed to be instrumental in prompting a Football Association inquiry which found that, in contravention of its own rules, hidden payments ('bungs') were paid to various parties in the transfer of players between soccer clubs. Over three pages, the '3 YEAR BUNG PROBE' is described, an interview is conducted with the 'FA'S BUNG BUSTER', readers are told 'HOW WE TRACKED DOWN THE CASH' and the newspaper's role in the scandal is chronicled under the heading 'VICTORY FOR *The Mirror*'. Here, the insider knowledge of the sports world (signified by the use of the slang term 'bung') is used in a crusading manner, seeking to 'clean up' sport on behalf of a public suffering from the corrupt use of sports funds. If the *Daily Mirror*'s self-mythologizing seems somewhat excessive, it is perhaps because of over-compensation by sports journalists whose professional and ethical standards are routinely denigrated. Such exposés transform, if only temporarily, the toy department of the news media into something more adult and serious – like the furniture section. At its most ambitious it produces de-mythologizing journalistic books on sport like Simson and Jennings's (1992) *The Lords of the Rings: Power, Money and Drugs in the Modern Olympics*, although the authors are at pains to stress that 'We are not sports journalists. We are not part of a circuit where too many reporters have preferred to keep their gaze fixed on the sporting action and ignore the way sport has been destroyed by greed and ambition' (p. x). Here, again, the emphasis is on revelation and disclosure. As they state in their introduction:

> This book discloses what you are not allowed to see on TV and what the newspapers do not tell you about the Olympics and world sport. For the last four years we have sought to discover who controls sport, where the money goes and why what a decade ago was seen as a source of beauty and purity is now tacky, anti-democratic, drug ridden and auctioned off as a marketing tool of the world's multinational companies.
>
> (Simson and Jennings 1992: ix)

Such critiques of the inner workings of major sporting phenomena like the Olympics are usually highly populist in nature. Simson and Jennings (1992: 271), for example, want to remove the 'perks' of the IOC so that 'we might bring sport back down from this wasteful Mount Olympus and into the hands of the ordinary people'. As the Atlanta Olympics approached, Jennings's (1996: 1) *The New Lords of the Rings: Olympic Corruption and How to Buy Gold*

Medals opened with a call to 'Save the Olympics, Before It's Too Late'. Within two years, the breaking of the Salt Lake City Winter Olympics corruption scandal (Guttmann 2002) provided multiple opportunities for sports and other journalists to expose the often-sordid inner workings of the Olympic 'family'. But, while performing a no doubt valuable and traditional media role, those engaged in sporting exposés tend to confine themselves to problems in sport that need to be fixed according to highly idealized standards (sport as 'a source of beauty and purity'), to leave the relationships between the sporting and other worlds relatively unexplored, and to take a rather unreflexive and unself-critical view of the activity of writing about sport. The final type of sports writing and text to be discussed display a more acute consciousness of the cultural (re)production and change in which they are implicated. They also have a propensity to extrapolate from the experience of sport to wider human experience. At this point, sports journalism enters the more refined realm of sports literature.

Literary moments

These 'aesthetic' texts deploy the full toolbox of literary devices to invest sport with new meaning and sports writing with new status. They can be found in the newspapers and magazines that tolerate or promote literary style, in novels, poems and short stories that take the subject of sport as a point of departure for the exploration of 'existential' themes. It is this form of writing that is usually to be found in edited sports anthologies (like Aymar 1994; Coleman and Hornby 1996). Matthew Engel's (1986) *The Guardian Book of Cricket*, for example, selects articles published in that newspaper since 1826, describing the ebbs and flows in their quality in the same manner as literary critics characterize the fortunes of literary movements:

> And it seems to me that soon after 1968 *Guardian* cricket writing may have entered a second golden age. There was some vintage stuff in the paper in the early 70s: Arlott in his pomp, Cardus firmly back in the fold for his last years, wit and craftmanship from Eric Todd and Brian Chapman, the young Blofeld and the first brilliant flashes of Keating. After Cardus died, Ian Peebles, for all too short a period before his own death, contributed a series of quite scintillating essays. The paper had a good war during Packer, just as it did during D'Oliveira – and bodyline.
>
> (Engel 1986: 15)

This 'great tradition' of English cricket writers, it is pointed out above, had handled some of the major sporting controversies of their day that also touched on important social issues: the Packer 'war' with its assertion of the power of television and the commodification of leisure; the 1968 D'Oliveira affair and its bearing on international reactions to South African apartheid (both of which are discussed in Cashmore 2000); and the 'bodyline' cricket series of 1932–33, where 'Cricket's imperial significance, the fragility of Anglo-Australian relations, and the social ravages of the economic depression combined to give the on-field events a sharper edge than might normally have been the case' (Stoddart 1979: 142). In attending to questions that stylishly link sporting and social phenomena, Engel (1986: 15) notes that these sports writers are given 'an intellectual freedom that you sign away in exchange for the pay cheque just about everywhere else in the business'.

If we compare the language and form of the following two passages with those quoted earlier from other types of sports writing, it can be seen – even allowing for the elapse of time, changes of style and the expansion of the sports pages to encompass multiple modes of writing – that this type of print media sports text does not sit easily with a highly formulaic and circumscribed approach:

> News of sport is, in general, news only inside the small world of sport. When it bursts into the outer world by the weight of its own importance it invariably tends to appear in false perspectives. The vehemence of the protest against the omission of Basil D'Oliveira from the MCC team for South Africa has amazed the close little world of cricket; and its amazement has, in turn, amazed those who live outside it.
>
> (Arlott, 11 September 1968, in Engel 1986: 168)

Here, in an understated and sophisticated way, John Arlott is addressing the relationship between the intersecting worlds of sport and politics without reliance on 'exclusives', 'bungs' – or anyone being told to 'p*** off'. But not all such writing need have such serious intent. As the following nostalgia-tinged opening paragraph of a Neville Cardus article reveals:

Kent v. Lancashire

The distance from Lord's to the Dover cricket field is farther than the crow flies or even than the train travels. Here we find a different habitation than cosmopolitan Lord's: here is Kent and real England. The Dover field is tucked away in hills along which Lear must have wandered on his way to the cliffs. There are green lawns and terraces rising high behind the little pavilion, and you can sit here and look down on the play and see the cricketers all tiny and compact. In such a green and pleasant land as this, with June sunlight everywhere, slow cricket by Lancashire has not seemed quite so wearisome as usually it does. The absence of animated play has gone well in tune with the day's midsummer ease and generous warmth. We have been free to watch the game idly and give ourselves up with lazy delight to the June charm and flavours of a field all gay with tents and waving colours; and we have been free to observe the delicious changes in the passing hour – the full flight of noon, the soft, silent fall to mellow.

(Cardus, 1, 2 and 3 July 1926, in Engel 1986: 84)

This pastoral, anti-metropolitan view of 'real England', with its allusions to the Williams Shakespeare and Blake, provides a pre-television 'word picture' of a sports event, fleshing out the descriptions of play by communicating ambience. Cardus's prose brings to the fore the 'Arcadian backdrop to Englishness' (Bracewell 1997: 8) rather than the modernist, performative details of bowling and batting averages. Its lush vocabulary and almost exaggeratedly laidback tone separates it not only from the more upbeat contemporary writing, but also from the plainer prose and more hectic description of much of the sports writing from its own period. This type of sports journalism has the 'feel' of fiction and, indeed, problematizes the distinction between the fictional and the factual, which, from the viewpoint of postmodernity, looks somewhat less secure than it once did. As Foley (1992) has argued in reflecting on his ethnographic study of youth and sport, positivist social science and realist journalism both deploy 'narrative devices' borrowed from fiction in representing their subject, selecting disparate events and weaving them into a coherent story. Their naivety and lack of reflexiveness, he argues, leads them to believe that the texts they construct to describe reality do not also to a degree mediate and transform it (because a representation can never absolutely correspond or stand for 'the thing itself'). This is a postmodern recognition of the pivotal role of textual relations in which both writer and reader 'produce' the text in a social context not entirely of their making. Here the print media sports text does not stand alone as an 'omniscient' account of reality produced by a God-like authorial figure with total vision but without the usual human failings. It is distinct from 'the naive realism of new [and, no doubt, old style] journalism and the conscious fictionalization of literature' (Foley 1992: 47). Indeed, the blurring of conventional academic and fictive techniques has also become a feature of some research-based writing on sport (Denison and Markula 2003).

Print media sports texts which 'play off' notions of the non-fictional and the fictional, the objective and the subjective, the universal and the particular, the real and the artificial, simultaneously take on the character of social science (at least its cultural studies 'wing') and the form of literature sometimes described as 'faction'. A work like Don DeLillo's (1997) novel *Underworld*, for example, takes a real historical but heavily mythologized event, the 'Shot Heard Round the World' in the dramatic 1951 New York baseball game between the Giants and the Dodgers (an event that coincided with the Soviet Union's second-ever nuclear test). It weaves into its narrative a close, journalistic description of the play and an aestheticized observation of the setting, using real people (like Frank Sinatra, Jackie Gleason and J. Edgar Hoover) and invented characters, melding the fictional and the non-fictional in a manner that threatens to make the distinction redundant. This approach is demonstrated by the following passage:

> Not a good pitch to hit, up and in, but Thomson swings and tomahawks the ball and everybody, everybody watches. Except for Gleason who is bent over in his seat, hands locked behind his neck, a creamy strand of slime swinging from his lips.
> Russ says, 'There's a long drive'.
> His voice has a burst in it, a charge of expectation.
> He says, 'It's gonna be'.
> There's a pause all around him. Pafko racing toward the left-field corner.
> He says, 'I believe'.
>
> (DeLillo 1997: 42)

This short extract from a very long American novel evokes the excitement of the spectator (who is a radio journalist) and could be an orthodox sports report were it not for some extraneous elements that signify it as literary (such as the description of Gleason's condition). This 'factional' piece, nonetheless, indicates how many sports reports do, indeed, resemble fiction in their selective assemblage of facts, invention of quotations and setting of the scene.

I make this point in closing the section to avoid too neat a taxonomy of the print media sports text. We have examined various examples of modes of sports writing located in different 'organs' of the media, and it is clear that rigid constraints of content, form, function and length exist which govern the production and reception of many such texts. The presentation of highly technical information, use of formal and informal language that only the initiated can easily decode, and a repetitive, easily recognizable style make the reception of sports stories into an habituated pairing of the familiar author (the sports 'hack') and the implied reader (the sports 'nut'). In Chapter 2, we noted criticisms by some sports journalists themselves of the rather limited scope of sports texts and various attempts to break out of this writing strait-jacket. But there are also elements of sports culture that can be found in places which are not acknowledged as sporting – for example, in what might be called 'secondary media sports texts' where the language of sport as metaphors and similes permeates non-sporting discourses (including politics and business). Hence, when a political reporter describes a minister as having 'a safe pair of hands' or a business reporter represents an attempted company takeover as a 'race' involving 'hurdles', then elements of sports language and culture are being insinuated into other texts, with the meanings and mythologies of sport invoked. Some print media sports texts – 'amateur' or 'semi-professional' fanzines – are now in circulation that (also as noted in Chapter 2) make few claims to technical excellence. Stapled publications like *What's the Story, England's Glory!* (dedicated to the English national soccer team), *Come in No. 7 Your Time is Up* (Bristol City), *Rub of the Greens* (Plymouth Argyle) and *Up the Arse!* ('Arsenal's Premier Spurs-Bashin' Fanzine') have small circulations, poor production values and (to be kind) uneven writing quality, but they form a not insignificant part of a print media sports text 'scene' (Haynes 1995; Rowe 1995) characterized by multiple modes and expanding spaces – and with spoken live sports commentary for satirical inspiration.

Conclusion: from script to still

In this chapter, I have analysed elements of the sports spoken and written word in attempting to understand something of their formal properties and the types of textual relations that they generate. Live broadcast sports commentary, for all the enthusiastic lampooning to which it is subjected, is a potentially powerful instrument for the symbolic unification and denigration of nations and peoples at moments of high sporting excitement. Print media sports texts, however, have greater flexibility of form – from a 'straight' results service to shrill 'tabloid speak exclusives' to tranquil poetic reflection – if less immediacy of impact. Broadcast commentaries and print stories devote much time and space to description of events and places that cannot be or have not been seen, or are seeking to enhance what has been or is simultaneously being seen. The next chapter examines, then, the visual aspects of media sports texts, turning first to the memorable image frozen in time – the still sports photograph.

Further reading

Coleman, N. and Hornby, N. (eds) (1996) *The Picador Book of Sportswriting*. London: Picador.

Denison, J. and Markula, P. (eds) (2003) '*Moving Writing': Crafting Movement in Sport Research*. New York: Peter Lang.

McGimpsey, D. (2000) *Imagining Baseball: America's Pastime and Popular Culture*. Bloomington, IN: Indiana University Press.

Reilly, R. and Stout, G. (eds) (2002) *The Best American Sports Writing 2002*. Boston, MA: Houghton Mifflin.

FRAMED AND MOUNTED: SPORT THROUGH THE PHOTOGRAPHIC EYE

The chapter number 5 is in an oval on the left.

In newspapers and magazines images of sportsmen in action proliferate, but we constantly see symbols of sportswomen's femininity (and particularly images that are saturated with sexuality), rather than pictures of female athleticism ... For example, a female athlete posing with a male athlete where he has a dominant stance and she a submissive one; photographs of male athletes surrounded by female admirers; photographs of female athletes crying with elation or embraced by husbands or boyfriends; in situations and poses that have no apparent connection with sport; in domestic contexts, pregnant or with children; and photographs of female athletes highlighting hairdos, make-up, and clothing.

(Jennifer Hargreaves 1993b: 62)

Introduction: still sport

The epic moments of sport, for all the ready availability of prose, poetry and the moving image, are most memorably captured by still photography. The 'frozen in time' sight of the instant of a famous victory or gesture is perhaps the most potent of all media sports texts, able to convey historical weight, emotion and a sense of the unique. One of the most memorable is the 'black power' protest by Tommie Smith and John Carlos on the victory dais at the 1968 Mexico Olympics (Given 1995; Johnson and Roediger 2000; Guttmann 2002), which, by the 1990s, had become incorporated into corporate leisurewear marketing campaigns as images of funky black radical chic (McKay 1995). Like all media texts, sports photographs work through a particular ordering of signs and codes that are part aesthetic, part ideological. They are not innocent records of events – through selection, composition and manipulation (cropping, 'burning', 'brushing', and so on in traditional photography and computer commands in digital photography), sports photographs offer up an account of how the world is (or how the photographer thinks it should be). The most important object in sports photography is sport's prime instrument, the human body. The bodies of sportspeople are closely observed through striking images that draw their power not merely from the drama of action, but also by connecting the imaged body to wider social issues and identities. Hence the body in sports photography is always invested with a wider representational role as sexualized, gendered, racialized, and so on.

It is necessary in pursuit of the task of 'unveiling' the media sports text to analyse the 'rules' of sports photography, the kinds of social relations and characteristics offered to the viewer as normal or abnormal, remarkable or banal. Given that the photograph is also usually accompanied by headlines and captions that help 'anchor and relay' the 'photographic message' (Barthes 1977), the text needs to be examined in its totality (it should not be assumed in advance, however, that image, headline, caption and text together form a consistent communicative 'fit'). As with the written sports media, still photographs can be classified according to genres and sub-genres, each with different qualities, motives and implied viewerships. 'Secondary' still photographic sports texts can also be found through the use of images and visual metaphors (such as in advertising) that set popular knowledge of and feeling for sport to work for another purpose. It is the 'primary' still photographic sports text of the captured sporting moment, though, that first commands our attention – the image that transfixes the reader as they go to turn the page through its sheer visual and emotional power, its capacity to make us wish that we were there – and, even if we were, that we, too, had seen it that way.

Caught in the act

Still photography is, as observed above, a form of communication that relies on the notion of 'capture' – frozen for all time is a gesture, an expression, incident or landscape. It is conducted like any other communicative act through processes of selection; many 'snaps' may be taken but only one shot selected out of the multiple variations of angle, focus, composition and light. Even when the image is caught, it can be altered in many ways to improve its impact. Fiske (1982: 109) notes, for example, how a newspaper's picture editor cropped and shaped an incident from a 'riot' in London's Notting Hill to enhance a concentrated sense of confrontation by cutting out 'extraneous' details of houses, trees and bystanders. He quotes the approving comments of the editor of another newspaper, Harold Evans, that the picture 'was the result of perceptive picture editing as well as of resourceful photography' (Fiske 1982: 110) by eradicating signs of domesticity, nature and other such manifestations of 'normalcy'. Holland states that the truth claims of such 'photo-journalism' rely on the concepts of 'neutrality and objectivity', which, if handled in a dubious way, may provoke suspicions of viewer manipulation and textual fabrication and to the asking of questions like:

> Was that starving baby separated from its mother so that it looked even more forlorn in the picture? Was that man waving a stick really shouting at the policeman or simply telling the photographer to get out of the way? Was there help at hand for those desperate people just beyond the edge of the frame?
>
> (Holland 1998: 418)

This is not to argue that there is no correspondence between what the camera caught and what was happening at that moment, but merely that many techniques are available to photographers that are ethically dubious and, whatever the motives of the photographer, a framed, two-dimensional image can never be 'the thing itself'. However realistic a photograph might be in style and effective in delivering a feeling of 'having been there', then, it is, like all other media texts, a manufactured representation of the real. Furthermore, as Becker argues, the picture itself is only one component of the text:

> Photographs attain meaning only in relation to the settings in which they are encountered. These settings include ... the historically constructed discourses in which specific topics and styles of photography are linked to particular tasks or patterns of practice (Sekula 1984: 3–5). The photograph's setting also includes the concrete, specific place it appears and how it is presented. In the newspaper, photographs have no meaning independent of their relationship to the words, graphic elements and other factors in the display which surround and penetrate them.
>
> (Becker 1992: 144)

In 'taking in' a photograph, then, we are also exposed to the caption, headline, the positioning of the item in relation to other items, the reputation of the publication and, importantly, we respond to the subjects with which they deal according to our own 'reading positions' as male or female, black or white, young or old, working class or bourgeois, and so on. When looking at a sports photograph, our response to an image of a despondent athlete will be largely conditioned by our relationship to them, encouraging sympathy, hostility, indifference or glee according to our sporting affiliations and loyalties. In this way, looking at a photograph can be regarded as one social construction coming into contact with another in a perpetual cycle of producing, modifying and circulating meaning. It is necessary to make these brief, preliminary comments because the 'action' sports photograph works through seeking to

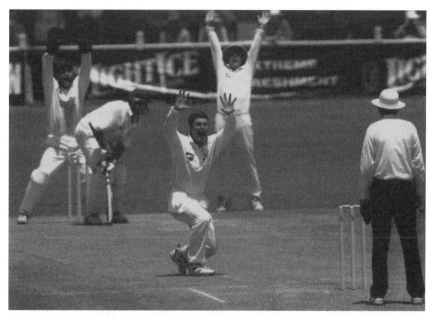

Frozen in time: action appeal and the judgement of history
Picture by Darren Pateman, courtesy of the *Newcastle Herald*

screen out all these reminders of the conditions of its production. The viewer impact sought is to instil a feeling that the sports event can be accessed directly through the photograph by its presentation of a pivotal moment in determining the result (who won and why) or in conveying the atmosphere of the event (what it felt like to be there). The latter type of sports photograph tends to be more self-consciously aesthetic, sometimes making a claim to be taken more seriously as an art object. But it is the action shot that is the staple of sports photography, reinforcing and conferring status on the elite sporting body by showing it doing the extraordinary things that so many people admire and envy.

If the action sports photograph is the premium sports image, and a considerable degree of cultural power attaches to being conspicuous in the sports media, then we might ask who gets to be shown 'doing the business'. It is here that ideology, power and media representation connect. Issues of visibility and invisibility, and images of domination and subordination, are always central to the reading of the media sports text. Understanding the politics of the still photographic image requires an analysis of what is seen and what is obscured, and of the seemingly natural hierarchies that are routinely offered for consumption. Most current studies of gender and media sport are of television (such as

Messner *et al.* 2000, 2003; Higgs *et al.* 2003), and those addressing print are mainly concerned with text (e.g. Markula 2001). Nevertheless, there is a good deal of accumulated empirical research on sports photography arguing that it is heavily gender biased in that we see sportsmen much more than sportswomen, and that they are often shown doing different things in a manner that confers greater prestige on male than on female athletes. Kane and Greendorfer (1994), in surveying research on gender and sports photography, discover a pattern of, first, 'underrepresentation and symbolic annihilation', and second, of a type of coverage they call 'caricatured femininity'. In terms of the former, they find that 'The overwhelming evidence from this literature is that women continue to be severely underrepresented in the highly prestigious world of sport' (Kane and Greendorfer 1994: 36). In coming to this conclusion, they cite a study of the covers of *Sports Illustrated* magazine between 1954 and 1978 in which sportswomen received only 5 per cent of coverage (Boutilier and SanGiovanni 1983). Similarly, of photographs in *Young Athlete* magazine between 1975 and 1982, less than 33 per cent included female athletes (Rintala and Birrell 1984). If these studies are thought to represent the 'bad old days' before more enlightened attitudes to gender took hold, the authors point out that 'Several of the most recent studies [such as Lumpkin and Williams 1991 and Duncan *et al.* 1991] have replicated findings from earlier research' (Kane and Greendorfer 1994: 35). Lest, again, it is objected that these data are from the USA, similar findings have emerged from studies in countries like Australia (Brown 1996) and Britain (Jennifer Hargreaves 1994).

But the quantity of images is only one aspect of power in the sports media. There is also the second issue raised by Kane and Greendorfer of their quality, and in this regard they conclude that 'the literature suggests that even when sportswomen are depicted in the media, they are consistently trivialized and marginalized through the type of coverage they receive' (Kane and Greendorfer 1994: 36). In supporting this conclusion, they cite such studies as the analysis of the 1979 *Sports Illustrated* Silver Anniversary issue, which found that 60 per cent of all photographs of sportswomen showed them in 'passive, non-athletic roles' compared with only 44 per cent of all photographs of sportsmen (Boutilier and SanGiovanni 1983). If this finding appears to be somewhat surprisingly close in the proportions of males and females shown to be 'inactive' in sports photographs, there are many other quantitative and qualitative studies that produce a starker contrast in the 'gendering' of sports photography. Stoddart (1994a: 5), for example, found that quantity was not the main problem, in that 'Photographs of sportswomen are plentiful in newspaper sporting sections. It is noticeable, however, that the representations are not necessarily about sport and frequently show women as passive rather than active participants'. Duncan (1990), in an analysis of 186 photographs from the

1984 and 1988 Olympic Games, notes the frequently close similarity of images of women in sport and in soft pornography.

There is also a dependent relational element in many images of sportswomen, with an emphasis on male coaches as authority figures, emotional attachments to partners and, if applicable, children (whereupon the mother is frequently turned into a 'supermum'; McKay 1992). In other words, the 'pure' power of the action sports photograph can be diffused by distracting attention from the pristine sporting moment and stressing other characteristics of the female photographic sports subject, such as their parental role, how they look after their hair or manage to perform in sport at the highest level while staying 'feminine' and 'sexy'. Empirical findings, of course, vary according to place, media and sports covered. Paul M. Pedersen's (2002) content analysis of photographs of interscholatic athletics in Florida newspapers, for example, found that females received only a third of total photographic coverage of athletics, and that photographs of them were less well positioned in the newspapers and more likely to be black and white than photographs of male athletes. However, there was no significant gender difference in photograph type, such as in the proportions of action, still, 'mug' and posed shots. It can also be suggested that there is nothing inherently wrong with a link between sport and sex. There is something improbable about paying massive attention to the sporting body as an athletic instrument but then rigorously suppressing any notion that it might be or do something else. The image of the sporting body may, then, also be an erotic or aesthetic image, as much concerned with the athletic body as 'sex machine' as the efficient engine of sports accomplishment. We might first canvass possible responses to the sports text in which the photographic subject challenges the viewer with Rod Stewart's pop refrain, 'Do Ya [perhaps, Dare Ya] Think I'm Sexy?'

Sports bodies: hot and hard

In the section above, I introduced the action sports photograph in newspapers, and the detected tendency for them to carry hidden ideologies of gendered power through the disproportionate quantity and quality of images of active, ruggedly individual men and passive, dependent women. Action sports photography concentrates on the 'motivated' body: it is doing something to itself and to other bodies. Acres of print are devoted every day to tracking the sports body in motion as it is invested with multiple meanings – the triumphant body, the dejected body, the endangered body, and so on. There is another area of photography that focuses on the body that has a less respectable profile than sports photography. It is called pornography and is dedicated to the sexual excitation of the viewer. It might be suggested, taking the earlier point further, that there are many parallels between sports photography and pornography, and it is fruitful to pursue questions of the extent to which many sports photographs adopt a direct or indirect mode of sexual address akin to the pornographic, and the ways in which the active/passive dichotomy is played out in both sport and photography. By following this line of argument, I shall not attempt an analytical separation of the erotic and the pornographic. In *The Erotic in Sports*, Guttmann (1996: 179) concludes that 'the best way out of the definitional *cul de sac* seems to be the frank acceptance of subjectivity' – that is, that one person's 'smut' is another's 'thing of beauty', and vice versa. It is still, though, worth probing the question of the power of both photographic subjects and viewers in the sphere of sexuality. All texts, after all, can be differentially interpreted, but all also have structural properties that invite particular decodings and deter others. That sport and sexuality have a long association is indisputable, as Guttmann points out in the opening passage of his book on the erotic aspects of sport:

> When Greek men and boys journeyed to Olympia to compete in the great panhellenic festival that honored Zeus, when Greek girls ran races at the same site for an olive branch and a portion of sacrificial cow, everyone seems to have understood that physically trained bodies, observed in motion or at rest, can be sexually attractive.
>
> (Guttmann 1996: 1)

Dutton (1995), similarly, notes the erotic dimensions of ancient artistic representations of the sporting body in sculpture and painting. So, if sport and sex have been constant companions for millennia, the opportunity afforded by the modern mass media (which, according to Cohen and Taylor (1976: 106) included the emergence of an industry devoted to the 'hobby' of masturbation) to develop this relationship must involve some linkage between the photographed sporting and sexualized bodies. Both sports photography and pornography are fixated on the body, minutely examining its performative possibilities and special qualities. Both are concerned with arousal – either of the photographic subject straining to perform at their best or of the viewer in deriving pleasurable excitement from the image before them.

Pornographic images tend to take two forms. In 'hard core' pornography there is plenty of action – a person or persons is doing something to another person or persons. It might be suggested that there is a precise equivalent in sports photography of what is called in hard core pornography (both moving and still) the 'money' or 'cum' shot (L. Williams 1989) – the visible male ejaculation that is the culmination of male-oriented pornography, which parallels the 'ecstatic' captured moment (as discussed in Chapter 4) when a winning goal is scored or a decisive play is made (Miller 1990, 2001). Sometimes

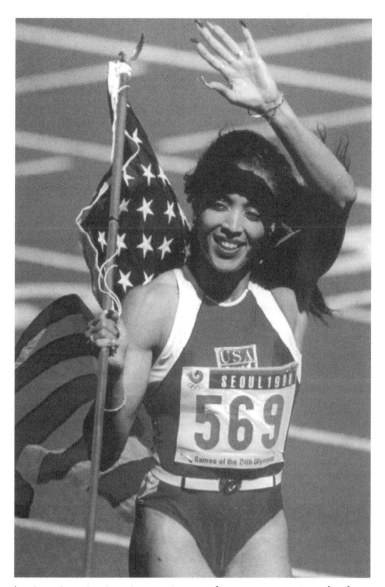

A win–win–win situation: an image of a temporary triumph of identities of nation, gender and race
Associated Press

(as in the case of most representations of male–female intercourse) the active/ aggressive male(s) is represented as exerting power over the passive/responsive female(s), while at other times (such as in the case of fellatio) it is the passive/ responsive male who seems to be exerting power over the active/compliant female. In the case of 'hyper' close-ups in hard core pornography (where the viewer 'possesses' the very pores of the bodily object viewed) and in more muted form in 'soft core' pornography, the power relationship is between the passive recipient of the gaze and the 'controlling' gazer (usually female and male, respectively, in the case of heterosexual imagery). These issues of power in and of the photographic image apply both in pornographic and sports images. Who is being shown as active and in control, and who is just being 'operated on'? Who is projecting a strong image to the viewer, and who is merely allowing themselves to be ogled?

The main feminist critique of both pornography and sports photography is that women are usually positioned as subordinate in all such tableaux. The image of women in the media is already a heavily sexualized one (van Zoonen 1991), meaning that whatever activity a woman is shown to be engaged in is likely to present her as sexual being first and foremost. The sexuality and appearance of sportswomen of the 1980s and 1990s like the late Florence Griffith-Joyner, Katarina Witt, Gabriela Sabatini and Mary Pierce have often obscured their elite sporting status (Williams *et al.* 1986; Heaven and Rowe 1990). In the new century, the politics of gender image are a little more complicated by both the increasing sexualization of sportsmen that is discussed later (Miller 2001), and the carefully calculated and marketed style innovations and projections of female sports celebrities like Serena Williams and Anna Kournikova (Evans 2001). Often, sportswomen are seen to be performing gender roles rather than sporting ones, and sometimes, as in the case of 'Flo-Jo' (whose early death in September 1998 from a heart attack at the age of 38 was allegedly caused by her taking large quantities of the performance-enhancing drugs whose masculinizing, physical effects might have been partially masked by her 'hyper-feminine' appearance), are happy to capitalize on the commercial advantages that follow a highly sexualized profile. Inevitable controversies flow from trying to draw a line between what is seen as the 'legitimate' expression of sexuality in sport and what is judged to be an ultimately repressive and short-sighted exploitation of sex that colludes with those patriarchal forces that seek to reduce women to their subordinated sexuality. In the case of Anna Kournikova, for example, a sportswoman can be seen to be doing extraordinarily well with regard to material wealth and celebrity visibility, despite an indifferent performance in her chosen sport (in this case tennis). Kournikova's earnings from sponsorship and endorsements exceeded US$10 million per year while she was still in her teens, while the women who were winning recognized tennis tournaments on the international circuit gained rather less income and attention (Evans 2001; Miller 2001; Brookes 2002). A content analysis of two British tabloid newspapers around Wimbledon fortnight found that female-related articles/photographs accounted for only 5.9 per cent of total sports coverage and discourses of masculinity/femininity were highly traditional – which is to say patriarchal (Harris and Clayton 2002). The study found that Kournikova appeared in over a third of all coverage of women, two-thirds of which was outside the immediate context of tennis. These statistics are even more remarkable given her familiar early exit from the tournament. When sportswomen explicitly play the role of soft pornographic subject on the covers of sports magazines, in newspapers, calendars, posters and publicity shots (in Kournikova's case, no London 'tube' traveller could have avoided her lingerie-clad image during the media-sampled Wimbledon tournament mentioned above), intense debates quickly ensue. These hinge mostly on traditional feminist condemnations of sexual objectification as opposed to a more pragmatic and libertarian approach (some of it postmodern or post-feminist) that emphasizes individual choice and agency (Davis 1997; Schaffer and Smith 2000b).

Probably the best known example of the overt photographic sexualization of the sporting female body (perhaps more accurately described as the sexualized presentation of the female body in a sports-licensed context) has been the annual *Sports Illustrated* swimsuit issue that has secured much attention (much of it negative) since its first appearance in 1964. Laurel Davis's (1997) book length study of the production, meaning and reception of the swimsuit issue considers the extent to which sport is male dominated and a sports magazine like *Sports Illustrated* is a *de facto* men's magazine akin to early *Esquire* and *Playboy*. The swimsuit issue sells about 5 million copies compared with its regular 3.3 million sales, an increase of over 50 per cent and a tenfold increase on newsstand sales (Davis 1997: 17). It can be safely assumed that this large 'spike' in readership is not caused by a short-lived, annual upsurge of interest in sport. Davis explains its success using Connell's (1987) concept of 'hegemonic masculinity' (briefly described in Chapter 3), seeing in the swimsuit issue a malign alliance of consumer capitalism and the reproduction of a range of power relations:

The problem with *Sports Illustrated*'s practice of securing a large audience of men by creating an atmosphere of hegemonic masculinity is that on the way to the bank it tramples over women, gays/lesbians, people of colour, and people from the (post)colonialized world. Hegemonic masculinity itself is defined as the antithesis of these others, and thus is built on the backs of these others.

(Davis 1997: 120)

Davis's analysis opens up, then, to embrace wider dimensions of power than those simply based on sex and gender, arguing that each is intricated in a complex and sometimes contradictory manner. This is contested theoretical terrain, and the conceptual reach and efficacy of hegemonic masculinity can be challenged (*International Review for the Sociology of Sport* 1998; Miller 2001). Pursuing the gendered image of sports photography further, though, it is apparent that the use of scantily clad 'proto-sporting' women (that is, models wearing something skimpy that is vaguely associated with sport or leisure) on the cover is a standard promotional strategy of sports magazines like the Australian edition of *Inside Sport*. A representative example (April 1997) is of a model in a leather bikini holding a crossbow, while inside she is featured in various poses and with equipment associated with the pursuits of swimming, diving, archery, roller hockey, baseball, soccer, cycling, skateboarding, water skiing and boxing. In none of these sporting activities is a brief black-and-white two-piece swimsuit the usual apparel. In the same issue there is a '16-page bonus' of the best Australian sports photography, in which it is claimed that 'Australia isn't only producing world-class athletes. We're turning out the world's best sports photographers too. Here's proof' (*Inside Sport* 1997: 40). It is instructive to look more closely than is usual at this popular imagery, and also at the photographs published in the previous year in the *Carlton and United Breweries Best Australian Sports Writing and Photography 1996*. The analysis is a little inexact in that only the principal subjects have been counted in those photographs where there are large numbers of (mostly out of focus) spectators and some other media personnel. The 'findings' of this quick content analysis (which can be conducted easily by any viewer of sports photography with, I suggest, similar results in most cases) are presented in Table 5.1.

Table 5.1 Analysis of two examples of 'best' Australian sports photography

	Photos	Action no. (%)	Non-action no. (%)	Main subjects no. (%)		Photographers no. (%)	
				Male	Female	Male	Female
Inside Sport	21	20 (95)	1 (5)	37 (100)	0 (0)	11 (100)	0 (0)
Carlton 1996	17	13 (76)	4 (24)	23 (77)	7 (23)	13 (93)	1 (7)

The data in Table 5.1, the analysis of which makes no claim to sophisticated statistical representativeness, are instructive in highlighting the gendered nature of the sports photographic text. In the case of the *Inside Sport* feature, not a single sportswoman appears, while almost every shot features action of a mostly dramatic, often violent kind. Most of the images, when examined further, are close-ups or medium close-ups, allowing the viewer to see the strained expressions of the sporting combatant. None of the pictured sports – basketball, athletics, sea- and wind-surfing, sailboarding, swimming, cycling, cricket and the football codes – features a performer in a leather bikini. In the rest of the magazine there is negligible coverage of women's sport, thereby creating a deep split between 'serious' sports photographs involving professional sportsmen and 'decorative' sports photographs involving models pretending to be professional sportswomen. Hence, sports magazines like *Inside Sport* (which, in this case, is part of a publisher's roster that includes 'girlie' magazines) take their place alongside young male-oriented media organs (the term is used advisedly) like *Loaded* and *Ralph* in sedulously resisting (as Davis found in her case study of *Sports Illustrated*) what they see as the unwarranted incursions of feminism. *Inside Sport*'s self-proclaimed 'biggest issue ever', on the eve of the Sydney Olympics (September 2000), had on its cover two models in patriotic body paint swimsuits (a 'trailer' for a photo spread inside that did interesting things with flags) and a photofeature of Ali, 'our 1999 Sportsmodel of the Year', on a tropical island that functioned as 'the ideal pre-Games training venue for *our* preparation' (*Inside Sport* 2000: 106, 109) As Stoddart (1994a: 8) points out, *Inside Sport*'s 'editors openly admit to using sexual images to sell copy to male readers', by which, of course, he means only 'straight' male readers (possibly with some gay women as niche readership). Short of successfully persuading such publications to change their target marketing strategy to include women and gay men, the only immediate mainstream alternative is to follow the rather troubled path of women-oriented sports magazines in the USA (Creedon 1994b).

In the case of the *Carlton and United Breweries Best Australian Sports Writing and Photography 1996*, there is a little more variation in what is taken to be a good sports photograph. There are more non-action shots and a small number of women featured but, while there is less reliance on close-ups, it is also the case that all but one of the women (the Australian Aboriginal runner Cathy Freeman, with captioned name mis-spelt 'Kathy') who appear are filmed at long distance. Not coincidental, perhaps, given the paucity of images of women, is the absence of any expressive sexuality and eroticism in the photographs. Little in the way of sexual projection occurs in the action shots, as viewers are encouraged to concentrate on what is being done rather than on how appealing the athlete might look in doing it (although allowance should be made for the full and unpredictable repertoire of human desire, which might, for example, extend to finding bloodied faces and painful expressions sexually arousing). There is nothing altogether surprising about this observation given the active repression of homosexual desire in male sport (Pronger 1990; Messner 1992). Thus, the 'alibi' for men gazing on other men in sports photographic texts is admiration of their sporting achievements rather than of their musculature (Miller 1998c). Yet there are two images of sportsmen in the *Carlton and United Breweries Best Australian Sports Writing and Photography 1996* collection that do have a sexual quality. In each, the sportsman is not active but is receiving and/or returning the gaze. One shot of the Olympic swimmer Kieren Perkins floating in a pool has a faintly voyeuristic quality (he cannot see the camera), while another posed shot of the face of 'pin-up' rugby league player Andrew Ettingshausen with shower water pouring down can be read as a 'smouldering' return of the voyeuristic gaze (a photograph of Cathy Freeman, in a similar style and by the same photographic team, has less water, is in extreme close-up and has a more androgynous quality).

These latter images introduce an important question and development. We may wonder what happens to the image of the sportsman when positioned as the recipient of the gaze in a similar fashion to that of the traditional objectification of the female body. Of course, male bodies have long been gazed at as objects of desire (for both homosexual men and heterosexual women) with varying licence to do so, ranging from 'secretive' viewing of men's sports magazines by gay men (see Miller 1998c) to the open if often sanitized appreciation of male bodies in pop culture. Until recently, there has been a reluctance to objectify sexually the male sports body. This was left to the female sports body, which (as noted above) has tended to be regarded as only tangentially sporting. The gradual freeing up of fixed socio-sexual identities, the influence of feminism, and the increasingly overt sexualization of culture and commercialization of sexuality have resulted in a strengthening trend of openly sexualizing sportsmen. Thus, just as some female athletes have allowed themselves to be represented in traditional soft core poses in calendars like the Golden Girls of Athletics and the Matildas soccer team (in Australia), so the Men of (Rugby) League Calendar (Rowe 1997c) offered up images of the male sporting body to the sexualizing gaze (Lynch 1993). It even became possible for sportsmen like Andrew Ettingshausen, as we shall discuss below, to feel 'violated' by intrusive cameras in a manner not dissimilar to that of many celebrity women.

Politics and portraits

The increasing eroticization (making sexy) and aestheticization (making beautiful) of the male athletic body does potentially change the gendered dynamics of cultural power that I have analysed in this chapter. For example, *Black + White Magazine*'s (1996) 'The Atlanta Dream Issue' consists of 170 nude portraits of Australian Olympians bound for Atlanta in a non-sexually segregated media context (that is, containing still photographic images of both male and female athletic bodies). Can it be proposed that this is an instance of significant change in the differential imaging of sportsmen and sportswomen? It is useful to examine this case of bringing sports photography out of the sports pages through the 'art' publication to the popular magazine in some detail. A selection of the images was carried in the Australian edition of the popular 'gossip' magazine *Who Weekly* (June 1996) under the front-page banner 'TOP ATHLETES BARE ALL IN A CONTROVERSIAL ALBUM' (the magazine helped to generate part of this controversy by being banned from some super-market chains). Of the four images presented on page 1, two were of men and two of women, only one of which was an action shot (a male sprinter). Of the three non-action shots, the men's were of torso and head, but the women's involved the whole body (that is, breasts, thighs, and so on). In the contents page, nude images of a female athlete (one in silhouette) were used, alongside an inset of four (clothed) women from Leni Riefenstahl's famous film of the 1936 'Nazi Olympics', *Olympia*. Riefenstahl's work is discussed in a short accompanying article entitled 'The Athletic Aesthetic', presumably to demon-strate that naked athletes have been filmed for many decades (in the case of this story, the only nude still images shown are of four distant men). Yet, of the twelve naked athletes selected for the 'photospread', eight are women. The only 'full frontal' shots (although by no means a majority of total images) are of women, with men being carefully posed or cropped, or using the traditional recourse to a strategically placed object interposed between viewer and penis – here a pair of oars in one shot and a large fish in another. Most athletes (male and female) are not shown in motion (although there is a spectacular shot of a female beach volleyballer hanging from a rope above a waterfall), but all the males are standing – only women are shown in reclining positions, with one of a woman water polo player closely resembling 'soft-core style'. Only one image – of two female divers – features any person-to-person contact, in this case with one on top of the other in a manner that connotes lesbian imagery (another soft and hardcore pornographic staple).

In reading, then, this selection for popular consumption of nude images taken from a self-consciously artistic publication, it can be suggested that there are persistent differences (probably largely unconscious) in representation of sportsmen and sportswomen that carry over even into areas of apparently equal treatment. The text that surrounds the *Black + White/Who Weekly* photospread stressed sympathetically that 'Posing nude is not something these athletes do every day – training relentlessly for the Atlanta Olympics in July is more their speed. And with an impressive list of victories behind them, these champions are ready to take on all their equally pumped peers' (p. 30). Yet, while seeming to try to 'do the right thing' in terms of gender equality, more attention is paid to the misgivings of female athletes about posing naked, informing the reader that 'Swimmer Samantha Riley took her mother and boyfriend, Norwegian skater Johan Koss, along for support' and quoting the photographer that 'Sam was nervous . . . I'd do a polaroid and she'd have a look at it and then show her mum and decide if it was OK or not' (p. 20). Even the small inset photographs showing the athletes 'at work' portrayed all the men in active poses but several static shots of women. Thus, as was noted above, media sports texts can be seen to be 'bearers' of social ideologies (in this case of gender) that project meanings that simultaneously draw on already dominant ways of seeing the world (such as men 'do' and women 'are') and contribute substantially to the maintenance of those perspectives (it always was and has to be that way), which, in turn, powerfully condition the ways in which the social world operates (men lead and women follow).

This broad, schematic theory of social and cultural reproduction is, however, open to various criticisms on grounds of functionalism, its somewhat mechanical view of how ideologies work within texts, its neglect of the power of the reader, and its inability to deal with contestation, multiple meanings and ambiguities. Were this ideological system to work cleanly and comprehensively, no new ideas and practices could emerge, and the social world would be a much less kaleidoscopic and complex place. The role of media analysts, in particular, would be reduced to reading texts and connecting them to prevailing social perspectives and practices. This is an important task which has continued to provide much of the impetus for a critical approach to the study of society and culture, but it is only part of a much wider 'project' of understanding how culture in multifarious forms is produced under rather different circumstances with a diverse range of outcomes that include both reproduction and transformation. It is important, then, to be aware that all texts have many potential and conflicting meanings according to context and readership, and 'decoding' them may offer up subversive or surprising significatory possibilities. But it would be naive indeed to argue that 'meaning making' is a vast, open game in which every sign has the same chance as every other sign to be taken up and used as definitive of 'how it is'. Sports photographs are no different from any other kind of text in that they are neither the innocent nor the 'natural' products of value-free sport and sports culture. As Duncan argues in her analysis, using Foucault's (1979) concept of the 'panopticon' (self-monitoring and self-discipline imposed by feeling constantly under surveillance), of women's body images in the body and fitness magazine *Shape*:

> Most poststructuralist media theorists . . . contend that texts carry multiple meanings and that those meanings are constructed by both the texts and the readers or viewers themselves. Although there are 'preferred' meanings

invited by texts, all texts contain the possibility of their own subversion, and some readers may find pleasure in resisting those preferred readings. Thus there may be some *Shape* readers who resist the panoptic gaze, or who focus on the strength and power of the body ideal presented therein rather than on the beauty/slenderness motive. My goal, then, is not to argue that every reader uncritically accepts the body beautiful ideology, nor is it to argue that every *Shape* article is potentially disempowering, but I do wish to demonstrate that there are compelling discursive mechanisms that encourage the panoptic gaze and yet conceal its source and motives from 'view'.

(Duncan 1994: 52–3)

Duncan is arguing that it is possible to see the media texts that forge a linkage between women's health, beauty and slenderness and emphasize personal responsibility for achieving it (and culpability for not) as empowering, and it is also possible to reject these demands for women constantly to assess their self-worth in this way. But the merest acquaintance with how many women are on diets, have had eating disorders and carry around a negative body image (Heaven and Rowe 1990; Markula 2001) reveals just how compelling such gender discourses can be and, even for the most critically self-reflexive woman, to escape. Critcher (1993: 234), in arguing that 'textual analysis alone can never deliver anything adequate about audience response', has highlighted the dangers of establishing a theoretical agenda concerning the gendered sports image and then reading all media texts off it as inevitably consistent and straightforwardly understood by all readers irrespective of their social identity. Yet there is equivalent peril in celebrating a 'semiotic democracy' in which cultural power is equally distributed among everyone, so that the political catchcry of 'one person, one vote' is translated into 'one person, as many meanings as they like'. The mutual constraints of the power of the text, the autonomy of the reader and the influence of the social have to be carefully weighed, often with disappointingly inconclusive findings if the aim is to explain all meaning generation according to a single axial principle. These issues have been much debated in media reception and audience analysis, with a resultant greater attention given to the ways in which audiences are mobilized by the media rather than simply found, the empirical substantiation of assumed audience responses, and the socio-cultural influences on how texts are read, interpreted and used (Philo 1999; Ruddock 2001; Balnaves *et al.* 2002).

Before this discussion becomes overly abstract, we should return to the image of the sexualized male sports body and of the male body in general. As Jennifer Smith Maguire (2002: 449) has noted in an analysis of 'fitness publishing', the shaping of the fit body now involves both 'middle and new middle class men and women' as 'fitness conumers'. We have noted that many feminists have complained about an undue emphasis in the sports media on the sexual and physical appearance of sportswomen. What, then, are the implications of looking at sportsmen in this way? Is this a move towards a kind of equality – every athlete, male or female, gets ogled because for professional sportsworkers this experience just 'goes with the territory'? Is it likely to unite female and male athletes in resistance to being treated like strippers and 'page 3 girls', so that now men know what it is like to be regarded as a sex object, something will be done? Or does the more general power differential between men and women mean that sportsmen find being sexually objectified less oppressive, and that once they have posed for the calendars and pin-up shots men can still be taken seriously and not identified exclusively with the way they look, but women remain – as Duncan (1994) pointed out above – subject to the 'panoptic' gaze? These issues are complicated further when we take into account the rather heterosexist assumptions of most critical analysts. To what degree do these equations change when we are addressing the homosexual or bisexual gaze? What if the viewer feels homosexual desire (gay or lesbian) for the photographic sports object or, more disruptively, if that object of desire has 'gone public' about their own homosexuality? Thus it can be seen that changes in the way that athletes are portrayed in sports photography and in the relationships between viewer and photographic object/subject (a distinction made on the basis of how much room the person being photographed has to project something of themselves rather than be the 'plaything' of the viewer) have relevance for the whole field of gender relations, sexuality and, as will be discussed later, racial and ethnic identities.

Imaging sporting masculinity

Looking at and imaging the male body is an integral aspect of the culture surrounding post-war popular music. Every year, new pop icons (usually white), from the Bay City Rollers to Hanson, Bros to Take That, New Kids on the Block to the Backstreet Boys and 'N Sync, emerge to take the mantle (usually worn for only a short time) of *the* pop sensation at the centre of current adolescent female desire. More 'mature' audiences are also catered for in various genres through (again, usually white) male figures like Jon Bon Jovi, Chris Isaak and Mick Jagger, although black musicians like the late Marvin Gaye and Lionel Ritchie also have their followings. 'Queer' figures such as Michael Jackson and Prince stand out as anomalies – as, presumably, queer figures should (Seidman 1996). So, while we are used to gazing at images of male and female pop stars (such as Madonna and Jennifer Lopez) in an overtly sexualized manner, this explicit function of the image of the sportsman has been slow to emerge (Rowe 1995). The reasons for this tardiness in exploiting an obvious commercial opportunity have (as noted earlier) often been stated: sport is a traditional domain where men can look at and even touch or embrace other men without homophobic stigmatization. Furthermore, the archetypal 'expert', straight male sports fan 'officially' views the male sports body in technical rather than aesthetic or erotic terms; the body is an instrument of supreme

Sportsmen licensed to cuddle other men – and to advertise television
Picture by Darren Pateman, courtesy of the *Newcastle Herald*

sporting performance rather than an invitation to libidinal pleasure. As we have seen, to ward off the vulnerable passivity of the female sex object uncomplainingly and undemandingly receiving the gaze ('take me, I'm yours'), the male image is (hyper)active. He is moving not still, standing not reclining, confronting rather than seducing the camera's eye. In potentially opening themselves up to the 'feminization' of their body image by being portrayed in a sexualized manner, sportsmen seek to counter such a process by doing something – anything – rather than just receive the gaze.

But what happens if, like Andrew Ettingshausen, the male sports photographic subject is caught unawares? Miller (1998a) examines in some detail the notorious defamation case in which Ettingshausen successfully sued *HQ* magazine in 1993 for publishing without permission a picture of him naked in the shower. While he had allowed himself to be featured in other photospreads for women's magazines which clearly capitalized on his sex appeal (readers of the Australian edition of *Cleo* magazine had once voted him the 'Sexiest Man Alive'), Ettingshausen (whose popular nickname is ET) argued that the implication that he had connived in the photographic display of his penis to a wide audience showed him in a questionable light and threatened to undermine his reputation as a clean-living family man and his employment as a school development officer for the sport of rugby league. This case highlights three of the key areas of sensitivity that we have seen apply in the area of photographing the male sports body: preventing a view of the penis (an image much less policed in the case of women's genitalia), avoiding any suggestion of passivity or helplessness (as was felt to be precipitated by the 'unguarded' shot) and concentrating on its heterosexual rather than homosexual appeal. Despite the relative novelty of male sports stars adopting an explicit mode of sexual address, however, the case of ET was confined to the 'specular' availability of a heterosexual man to similarly inclined women.

Yet, the very need to carry out such 'hard ideological work' to exclude 'unacceptable' images and meanings of the male sports body confirms its semiotic vulnerability. As Miller (1998a: 107) argues, 'The male pinup draws out insecurity, instability, and contradictions in masculinity. Which kind of gaze is expected to consume it? Contrary to conventional masculine icons, the pinup pacifies the body'. Whereas once the imaging (in television as well as in still photography) of the male sports body was assumed to be only of technical interest to other, assumed heterosexual men, the appeal has been widened to incorporate 'single women and gays, because they have high discretionary income' (Miller 1998a: 107), not to mention the married women who control most household expenditure and constitute a large and, until the mid-1980s, largely neglected audience sector for media sport. For example, in the lead up to the Sydney 2000 Olympic Games, the Australian version of the women's magazine *Cosmopolitan* declared at the top of its front cover the exciting promise of 'SPORTING BODIES: 23 MALE ATHLETES – NAKED!'. In fact, many of the athletes were semi-clothed and, as the text described what they considered to be their greatest sporting moment, there was much hyperactivity as well as artful concealment of genitalia. No pretence was made that this was anything other than a 'scopophilic' exercise (that is, indulging in the pleasure of looking), with the photospread opening with the following text:

> Sport? Boring? Not any more. Forget Leo and Brad. When the Olympics roll around next year, we know which guys we'll be watching as closely as possible. On the track, on the field, in the pool and on the podium, these are the hottest bodies you're ever likely to see.
>
> (*Cosmopolitan* 1999: 195)

On the page opposite this text is an advertisement for Desire, an anti-perspirant endorsed with an image of athlete Heather Turland as a long-distance 'Mum on the run'! (p. 194). Thus, while the photospread may involve an unusually direct sexualization of the male athletic body, there are still strong traces of the conventional order in the article's lack of interest in their paternal status (and its contiguous advertisement's mention of a female athlete's maternal role).

The nature of this gaze on the male sports body can be further complicated by the 'seeping' of information into the frame from outside the world of sport. Take, for example, the cover of Guttmann's (1996) *The Erotic in Sports*, which is a reproduction of a striking *Sports Illustrated* photograph of the finely tuned body of US Olympic diver Greg Louganis entering the water in a perfect, aesthetically appealing and, for many, no doubt erotically pleasing dive. The viewer's reading of the photograph is, however, almost certainly changed by being in possession of the information that after retirement Louganis declared his homosexuality and HIV-positive status (a condition which he admitted to having when he bled from a head wound into the Olympic pool). In other words, the still sports photographic image is never entirely 'still'; it is always subject to revision and reformulation according to prevailing social ideologies and the circulation of cultural 'data'.

Similarly disruptive to the 'orderly' containment of images of traditional sports masculinity in the media are cases like that of another rugby league player, Ian Roberts, where the pictured Adonis came out as gay during his playing career after appearing nude in a gay magazine. The appearance of Ian Roberts in the inaugural issue of *Blue Magazine* in 1994 indicates the extent to which, once 'let off the leash', the photographic representation of prominent sportsmen can travel to some previously unexplored spaces. Roberts, a player famed for his formidable physique and toughness, had allowed his body to be used as a 'sexual ornament' before, most notably in the heterosexually targeted

'Men of League Calendar' that was part of the modernization and repositioning of the 'working man's sport' in the early 1990s. This marketing campaign
included a video of African American soul singer Tina Turner performing
'Simply the Best' and casting admiring glances at the footballers in a manner
calculated to induce other heterosexual women to see them in a new, sexualized
light (Lynch 1993). Roberts also figured prominently in swimwear in the 'Total
Fitness Body' Campaign, his attractiveness to women signalled by his poolside
female 'companion' – except that she was his sister, not his implied lover.
Roberts, who was in his thirtieth year before he 'came out', had previously
hidden his homosexuality from view by pretending to the press that he had a
'girl'.

Considerable consternation was caused for conventional masculine sports
culture by a self-declaration of homosexuality from a rugby league footballer
who had played for Australia in the most physically demanding position in the
game (prop) and whose muscular body had been much photographed, discussed and admired. His biography, *Ian Roberts: Finding Out* (Freeman 1997),
authored by the photographer who had persuaded him to pose for *Blue* magazine, contains a foreword that reproduces congratulatory and denunciatory
letters for 'coming out' and copious text on the tribulations of his life. It also
contains many photographs of Roberts as child and adolescent, in conventional
(and often spectacular) sports action and standard team photos, in an injured
state (including being carried off on a stretcher and another shot with blood
streaming down his face), doing charity work with children who are ill,
attending dance parties and other social gatherings in Sydney's 'gay precinct',
engaging in the usual 'horseplay' with teammates, and in various publicity,
calendar and magazine shots. It is difficult, therefore, to 'pin down' the images
of the sportsman to Connell's (1987) 'hegemonically masculine' identity of
heterosexuality and aggression (Miller 1998c). It is not difficult to imagine
many readers scrutinizing images of Roberts, looking for the 'tell tale signs' of
the hidden 'truth' of his sexual identity (Davis 1995).

Roberts' lack of 'camp' challenges stereotypes of the sporting male differently to the presentation of self by African American basketballer turned
wrestler Dennis Rodman, whose self-consciously outrageous, 'gender bending'
behaviour, which includes 'getting married' in a bridal gown, wearing leather
skirts, garish makeup and multi-coloured hair, and the prominent display of
body piercing. Like Roberts, Rodman is renowned for his toughness (in the
demanding role of 'rebounder'), but his flamboyance and black identity provide
new dimensions to his image of a 'different' kind of sportsman. Rodman's
image is also a sexualized one, but it is self-consciously 'queer' – that is, it
refuses an easy, fixed categorization as 'straight' or 'gay' (Seidman 1996). Both
of his books in the late 1990s, the 'New York Times Number One Bestseller'

Bad As I Wanna Be (Rodman with Keown 1996) – parodied, it should be noted, in the naked appearance of his ex-wife Anicka Rodman (with Scott 1997) on the cover of her own 'right of reply' book, *Worse Than He Says He Is: White Girls Don't Bounce* – and the rather less successful *Walk on the Wild Side* (Rodman with Silver 1997), have bizarre covers of a naked Rodman. They contain conventional action photographs of him on the basketball court alongside (especially in the latter book) many outlandish shots of him off it. The images of Rodman that circulate readily in newspapers, magazines and books, including academic works like Baker and Boyd's (1997) *Out of Bounds: Sports, Media and the Politics of Identity*, which has an apparently now *de rigueur* cover of Rodman in vinyl displaying his biceps and biting a metal chain, are clearly a major departure from the orthodox, traditional images of sportsmen that still form the vast bulk of sport photography. Indeed, they raise a question that I shall take up below of what constitutes a sports photograph in the first place.

It is still necessary to ask how such images can be read as an index of the state of sporting masculinity. One obvious response is to adjudge them to be mere effects of the American sports hype media machine, a 'freak show' designed to give celebrity status to a publicity-craving exhibitionist. There is no doubt some validity to such an assessment, but there is also something more culturally disruptive in the figure of a black elite basketballer known for his aggressive approach to the game (and hence gaining approval within traditional masculine sports culture) whose stock-in-trade is projecting an extraordinary visual image of himself while making pronouncements like 'I've fantasized about being with a man many times', 'the sports world is the ultimate prison of macho bullshit' (Rodman with Silver 1997: 179, 188) and 'people have assumed I'm bisexual. I don't do much to discourage that, since it fits into my idea of keeping people guessing' (Rodman with Keown 1996: 211). At the same time, Rodman's 'penis narratives' (Lafrance and Rail, 2001) – the self-enunciated homages to his own virility – speak of a much more traditional and constraining form of black masculine identity (Rowe *et al.* 2000)

'Keeping people guessing' is not the usual function of sports photography, which I have argued has been a rather conservative force that has tended to confirm rather than challenge dominant (especially patriarchal) roles, identities and structures of power. But, as it develops through the proliferation of genres and subjects – moving away from a reliance on action shots of men and 'honey' shots of women to a greater coverage of the aesthetic, 'ambient' and 'flexibly' sexual aspects of sport – it can be expected that the sports still image bank will play a more prominent role in recording cultural change and challenging prevailing social ideologies. I have concentrated in this section on the increasingly sexualized masculine sports image whereby 'thanks to the commodification of the male subject, men are brought out into the bright light of narcissism and purchase' (Miller 2001: 56), but there are other unorthodox sports images and their attendant gazes which form part of the changing discourses of identity that are a major feature of contemporary life (Giddens 1991). In sports photography, these involve negotiating the values that surround the body and trying to work through socialized, visceral responses to our own bodies and those of others (Shilling 1993; Falk 1994). Here the optic nerve meets athletic muscle to often discomfiting effect.

Variable subject, different gaze

The transformations of modernity and postmodernity have resonated through the 'body cultures' of different societies and epochs (Eichberg 1998). One relatively recent expression of such shifts in the culture of bodies is that we are not as limited as before to the body handed out at birth. Through appropriately scientific techniques and technologies, and less constrained by prescribed models of the body, it is believed possible to engage in 'building a better body' (Stratton 1999). Bodybuilding demands more than desultory exercise in pursuit of lower body weight and admiring comments from others about being 'in shape'. It requires working on each component of the body before a real or imaginary mirror (or lens) to produce the desired visible effect. The result may appear excessive and even repugnant to those outside the culture of the gymnasium. Muscularity in men is historically desirable in most body cultures as long as they do not become 'musclebound', but in women it is rather more culturally problematic. Heightened levels of muscularity among women is frequently represented as freakish and 'butch', and homophobically derided as a sign of lesbianism (Wright and Clarke 1999; Miller 2001). In the face of such media-exacerbated hostility, there are often attempts to recuperate the imaged muscular female body for a conventional binary model of masculine men and feminine women. For example, Angela Ndalianis has written of the representational tensions within bodybuilding 'muscle' magazines like *Flex*:

> But, as the old saying goes, 'a picture tells a thousand words', and in bodybuilding magazines it tells a story that attempts to bring back into play a gendered power structure. While, in one way, the written word serves to break down years of a subculture that was dominated by rigid boundaries that served to contain and construct gender according to a system of power negotiated around sexual difference, the image often contradicts the word, aiming covertly to re-establish the status quo and set up clear gender demarcations.
>
> (Ndalianis 1995: 19)

In this case, 'serious' debates in the magazine over the issue of 'femininity vs muscle' were undercut by the use of 'images of these [female] bodybuilders posing seductively in conventional "feminine" poses – and most of them either wear thong backs or high heels' (Ndalianis 1995: 20). Thus the traditional sexualization and patrolling of the 'socially approved' appearance of sports-women is still occurring in sports photography at the same time as some of the presentational rules are being at least partially rewritten for men. Such issues are made more complex when other social variables are introduced that demand greater analytical scope to go beyond the prime concerns of white, heterosexual men and women. Given that few professional sportspeople have ever 'come out', especially when at the peak of their careers (Rowe and Miller 1999), and that sports photography adheres mainly to an heterosexual/sexist ethic, gay men and lesbian women have largely been 'out of the frame' as photographic subjects and unacknowledged as textual readers. This state of affairs has begun to be challenged by new readings of both conventional and unconventional sports images. For example, the postmodern pseudo-sports television show *Gladiators* (a moving image show, of course, but one that, as with most popular television and film, has produced many still print and Internet images) is opened up to the kind of reading advanced by Kathryn Goldie:

> Lesbianism and male homosexuality flutter over and around *Gladiators*, but are manifested in different ways. Each requires a different containment strategy as required by a patriarchal and heterosexual social order. How-ever, the juxtaposition of sport, bodybuilding, wrestling and cartoon superhero genres creates enough tensions and ambiguities to defy a single reading of the muscular body, either on display or in action. Despite *Gladiators*' best efforts to construct non-threatening heterosexual hege-monic power relations, homoeroticism and the possibility of oppositional reading strategies remain.
>
> (Goldie 2002: 79)

Interrogating the power of sports representation and the politics of reading media sports texts creates many opportunities to analyse the relationship between social inequality and cultural power. In these 'image stakes', Linda D. Williams (1994) notes the double disadvantage of black sportswomen. On the assumption that 'no feature is so important to a magazine as its cover' (Williams 1994: 51), she conducted a study of the covers of *Sports Illustrated* between 1954 and 1989, finding that, while only 114 (6 per cent) of the 1835 covers in the period involved women, only 5 of these featured black sports-women (4 per cent of magazine covers with women appearing and 0.3 per cent of total covers), with 4 appearing in the short period between 1987 and 1989

(Williams and Lumpkin 1990). When we consider this 'quantitative' neglect alongside the 'qualitative' question of the manner in which black women have been typically represented, then the intersection of gender and racial ideologies in sports photographs is revealed to be an area worthy of more detailed analysis and critique. In broad terms, according to Kent Ono (1997: 86) 'Throughout U.S. history, African American women are constructed as inherently sexual and excessively available'. With specific regard to the swimsuit issue of *Sports Illustrated*, Davis (1997: 90–1) argues that the neglect and then highly selective inclusion of women of colour has meant that the 'models with African ancestry . . . typically possessed very light-color skin and facial features that conform to the Anglo-American beauty ideal', and suggests that there is 'indisputable textual evidence that racially-biased standards of beauty', not to mention gender-based standards of sexism, 'influence the swimsuit issue'. But it is not only black women's representation in sports photography that demands attention. The racialized dimension of photography is especially important in the use of the black male sports body in the advertising of products, where the sexualized component (which is also a key element of the cultural construction of black men; Mercer 1992) is 'bundled' with a more extensive admixture of contemporary style and cool (Carrington 2001). This prime role of the black male sports image in the selling of products is one of part male pin-up, part style guru. It is reliant on an 'in your face' sexual address that (Dennis Rodman included) rejects feminized complaisance as resolutely as any traditional sports photograph of the tough, unyielding sportsman. Before moving to a brief discussion of this genre, we might ask, finally, how a sports photograph becomes sexual or erotic. 'Sexiness' may be consciously cultivated in stronger or weaker forms by deploying a titillating mode of address associated with 'cheesecake' photography and pornography. As a corporeal discipline, sexiness can be a bi-product of the inherently sensual expression of the sporting body in some sports. Guttmann (1991, 1996), as noted above, argues that many (especially feminist poststructuralist) critiques of sport have not been sufficiently well informed about the historical linkage of sport and the erotic, and have been blind or resistant to the erotic quality of toned bodies and athletic movement. In making a plea for 'mutually admiring male and female gazes (and for gay and lesbian ones as well)' (Guttmann 1996: 163), he contrasts the 'travesties' of trying to make (in this case sportswomen) sexy to the 'marvel' of the eroticizing effect of 'athletic performances' (Guttmann 1991: 261). Perhaps, then, the most sexually appealing photographic images of sportspeople are not those in which they are playing at being sexy, but where they become unconsciously so by playing their sport well (although, obviously, some sports lend themselves better to 'balletic' moments of beauty than others). But returning sports photography to the field of action leaves vast quantities of imagery sprinkled throughout newspapers and magazines. These are the aforementioned 'secondary media sports texts' (including some of the images discussed above), which have a less direct relationship with the practice of sport, but nonetheless draw on sports news, celebrities and mythologies. It might be objected that, in the strict sense, they use sport rather than constitute sports photography *per se*, so calling into question the precise characteristics of the still sports image.

The uses of sport in photography

In this chapter, I have concentrated on two types of sports photograph. The first and most unequivocally sporting is the action photograph, but we have seen, second, that pictures of sportsmen and women take many forms, such as pin-up and aesthetic images. These photographs rely on representing recognizable aspects of sport, like the body of a famous athlete or 'signs' of sport such as uniform or equipment. There are other types of sports photograph to be examined that do not concentrate on the bodies of athletes in motion or in repose, but which take in the wider context of the event by putting to the fore the crowd or the venue. These 'atmosphere' or 'ambient' shots are most commonly found in the sports sections of broadsheet newspapers and in specialist magazines that have the space to present sumptuous photo-essays of major sporting occasions and the many photographic subjects that surround them. Sports images, then, appear both in the parts of the media clearly designated for them and also spread far beyond the sports pages into the realm of general news and human interest stories. The 'sports action' emphasis is reduced to such an extent in such cases that the photograph becomes a hybrid of sports photo, 'society' image, 'mood' shot, and so on.

Let us take, for example, the British tabloid *The Sun* newspaper's 'exclusive' front page story 'Our Love', in which pop singer Spice Girl Victoria Adams (professionally known as Posh Spice) and Manchester United and England soccer player David Beckham display their engagement rings and discuss their 'Romance of the Decade' (Coulson 1998). All of pages 2 and 3, traditionally areas of 'quality' newspapers that carry 'serious' news, are taken up with interviews with the happy couple and several more photographs, while the centre pages are devoted to more photographs and pronouncements on the union by Debbie Frank, '*Sun Love Astrologer*'. Clearly, sport is an important element of this 'photostory' – the engagement of a leading footballer and a member of a world famous pop group is a publicist's wet dream – but its qualifications as a media sports text are attenuated by the lack of direct concentration on sport itself. Posh'n'Becks have before and since been a well on which the media can draw deeply for photographic material. Their 1999 wedding in an Irish castle, for example, drew huge media coverage, with the wedding pictures sold exclusively for £1 million to *OK!* magazine, whose wedding issue in turn sold between 350 and 400 times more than usual (Cashmore 2002: 32–3). Then there have been two children and numerous interviews and photo opportunities. Such texts, with a stronger or weaker connection to sport, are diffused across the media, with sport as the focus or as an ancillary aspect that helps to secure interest by association. It is this associative function that is crucial to the imagery of advertisements using sport as a key element in addressing potential consumers. Sports myths, especially those of heroism, patriotism and team-work, are readily available to corporate enterprises like banks, computer companies and motor vehicle manufacturers. They have the capacity to stir the blood of consumers and induce them to feel well disposed towards the product or service because they already feel positive about a national team or champion athlete. Often, the alluring image is of a black sportsperson (usually male) who comes from a social group more commonly associated by the news media with criminal activities, social dysfunctionality and economic dependence than with spectacular feats in sport or in any other field of action.

The use in advertising and promotion of still images of black male athletes was mentioned above as one of the most prevalent practices in contemporary consumer persuasion. Flicking through newspapers and magazines, multiply retired basketballer Michael Jordan (and, in another Nike advertisement, unnamed Kenyan runners) can be seen endorsing 'air' athletic footwear; his former colleague Scottie Pippen is selling 'Ginsana Capsules and Tonic'; multi-medal-winning athlete Carl Lewis is modelling the Nike 'Apparel' range; while Tiger Woods appears to cover entire blocks of Madison Avenue shopfronts. To vary the picture a little, Venus Williams can be seen bearing the Reebok logo. It could be argued that such positive images of a minority group subject to deeply entrenched racism and suspicion within dominant white culture are welcome signs of social progress. Yet, as McKay (1995: 192) observes, the attractive images of highly privileged black men pumping out slogans like 'Just do it' (Nike), 'There is no limit' (Puma) and 'Life is short. Play hard' (Reebok) help conceal the alienation and degradation of so many of their peers, and of the exploited 'people of colour' in the Third and Fourth Worlds who work for miserly wages (with no or highly circumscribed rights of labour organization) to produce expensive leisure goods for more affluent consumers in other countries (Miller *et al.* 2001). At the same time, important acts of black militancy are drained of their political punch, as occurred with the aforementioned victory dais black power protest by Tommie Smith and John Carlos at the 1968 Mexico Olympics, which was rendered a quarter of a century later as a full-page colour advertisement for Puma sports shoes in a magazine mainly 'aimed at affluent young blacks' (McKay 1995: 192). For Boyd (1997; and also Maharaj 1997), the outcome of selecting and decontextualizing aspects of black male culture, linking it to the appealing aspects of sport, and then fashioning the combination into consumer iconography (extending from the orthodox to the more threatening figure of the 'bad nigga') is not the liberation and enhancement of an oppressed minority, but the commodification and expropriation of their difference and resistance (Marquesee 1999). Perhaps there is a self-reinforcing element in such arguments – racial oppression is both cultural marginalization and 'mainstreaming' – but it is important to remember that there is more to racial equality than a billboard with a sassy image of an athletic, affluent black man selling overpriced leisurewear.

Conclusion: sports images on the move

In this chapter, I have not attempted an exhaustive review of every type and genre of sports photograph and ways of reading them, but rather to demonstrate how they have proliferated in the media and are linked to specific viewerships, ideologies, myths and other texts in a way that makes them important components of contemporary culture. The still sports image, perhaps sepia-toned for nostalgic effect, vibrantly coloured for dramatic impact or glowingly lit for full sensual appeal, is important for the tasks of creating sport's social memory ('Do you remember when?'), securing audience attention ('Did you see that?') and extending its appeal ('What a bod!'). The magazine *Sports Illustrated* has received a good deal of attention in this chapter, which is appropriate given its influential history as a popular site of sports photography since 1954, and the controversy surrounding the annual swimsuit issue that it has published since 1964. If *Sports Illustrated* has felt some concern about criticism of, especially, its gender politics (Davis 1997: 6–7), it has also provocatively drawn attention to this aspect of its activities. Its September 2002 issue contained a spoof article on Simonya Popova, an invented 17-year-old Uzbekistani tennis player who clearly parodied the much photographed, greatly enriched, but poorly performed Anna Kournikova. The virtual Simonya, fashionably and provocatively dressed in *Sports Illustrated*, led many would-be media interviewers to seek her out through the bemused and then highly unamused Women's Tennis Association. The Popova prank, in seeking to make fun of Anna Kournikova's apparently successful formula involving photogen(et)ics, marketing and indifferent tennis playing, only served to highlight the magazine's hypocrisy in view of its long record of sexualizing the bodies of sportswomen. *Sports Illustrated*'s critique was not, ultimately, of the state of women's tennis, but of itself and of its fellow commercial sports media who had created the image-based Kournikova phenomenon in the first place.

Despite such postmodern japes involving the manipulation of self-consciously sexy sports imagery, the predominant form of sports photograph remains, paradoxically, the body-focused action shot. Here the subject is in motion but the medium is capable only of stopping the action and freezing the instant. What happens, then, when the static sports image becomes animated? Our attention now turns to the moment when the wall poster comes to life and the still media sports text starts to move.

Further reading

Birrell, S. and McDonald, M.G. (eds) (2000) *Reading Sport: Critical Essays on Power and Representation*. Boston, MA: Northeastern University Press.

Guttmann, A. (1996) *The Erotic in Sports*. New York: Columbia University Press.

Hargreaves, Jennifer (1994) *Sporting Females: Critical Issues in the History and Sociology of Women's Sports*. London: Routledge.

Miller, T. (2001) *Sportsex*. Philadelphia, PA: Temple University Press.

SCREENING THE ACTION: THE MOVING SPORTS IMAGE

In an ideal world, a competitive television environment would strike the perfect balance: gradually introducing non-enthusiasts to the intricacies and pleasures of new and diverse sports, using all the sophisticated wizardry of new technology while remaining faithful to the innate spirit of the game. All the evidence suggests that, while a visual spectacle is enhanced by innovative camerawork, both commentary and contextual artifice is increasingly exploited to entice the uncommitted. In the end, the overwhelming considerations are those which transcend any concern for honest reproduction.

(Steven Barnett 1990: 170)

Introduction: action, drama and narrative

If the still sports photograph seems to lodge in the mind, its neatly defined and structured image easily conjured up in fine-grained detail, the moving sports image often seems to fill up any spare cerebral and perceptual space, crowding out other subject matter with its movement, colour, noise and melodrama. Much critical attention is given (for reasons outlined in Chapter 1) to television, but sport is also the subject of many films (Bergan 1982) and even some theatre (Fotheringham 1992). Programmers have devised myriad ways of presenting sports television – live and delayed broadcasts with multiple-camera locations and sophisticated studio technology, sports 'magazine' programmes, quiz shows, dramas, studio comedies and variety 'turns' that appear in different parts of TV schedules. Most sports TV formats are heavily dependent on the recorded live action which, once placed in the vaults of television companies, is permanently (when correctly stored and preserved) available for repackaging as highlights, memories, 'what happened next' questions and funny moments. The core audience for TV sport is traditionally regarded as the male 'sports nut'. Yet not only are substantial numbers of women enthusiastic sports participants and viewers, but television also makes available sports texts to men and women alike who do not count themselves among this established fraternity and growing sorority (as noted in Chapter 3, for example, men only shaded women by 51 to 49 per cent in the TV viewership of the 2002 Korea/Japan World Cup). Given that the logic of all television is to secure and expand an audience, it is necessary to analyse the textual strategies adopted by TV producers to win over uncommitted viewers to the joys of sport on television. While it should be recognized that the many decisions taken and tasks performed in producing live sport may not 'hang together' in terms of a single determining logic (Stoddart 1994b; Silk *et al.* 2000), strong attempts are made to give such broadcasts a coherent identity that can be easily interpreted. As was noted in Chapter 3, this might require them to be faked a little; that is, to be 'plausibly live' (Farred 2001; Rivenburgh 2003) in convenient time slots. As one leading commercial media sports executive has said of the Olympic Games on television, ' "The Americans want their stories 'chewed and digested' from 7 or 7.30 till midnight" ' (Alex Gilady quoted in Bernstein 2003: 125).

'Action-dependent' sports television does not simply rely on an appeal to the senses through the immediate stimulation of sight and sound. Viewers would quickly tire of a TV sport that consisted of much sound and fury which signified nothing (as has tended to be the fate of fabricated, pseudo-sports TV competitions like *Gladiators*) and so must be made to feel that what is happening on screen actually matters. By inducing (or reinforcing) the identification of viewers with sportspeople and teams – for example, as local or national representatives – sports TV producers tap into the affective power of territoriality as it applies to sectors of cities, whole urban areas, regions, nations, even entire continents and hemispheres (de Moragas Spà *et al.* 1995). In this way, the unfolding TV sports event – an important component of news, as we saw in Chapter 2 – is also a narrativized construction, with twists and turns in the plot, heroes and villains, and, in the traditions of Greek and Elizabethan drama, a serious purpose of confronting the great public and private moral dilemmas of the day. In its grandest manifestation as global mega-media event, sport, according to Dayan and Katz's (1992: 25) typology of the 'story forms, or "scripts" ' that create narrative opportunities, can be read principally as 'Contest', although there are also openings for 'Conquest' (such as breaking world records) or 'Coronation' (like epic opening ceremonies) encodings.

In the case of fictional film and drama, where the starting point is narrative, character and dramatic tension, sport is used as a means of attracting those already interested in sport and as a dramatic vehicle for those who are not. Fictionalized sports texts, therefore, tend to be highly charged moral tales or allegories in which the state of the nation or the gender and racial/ethnic orders can be glimpsed through sport. How successful such mythologized treatments of sport will be is heavily dependent on the historical, social and cultural position of particular sports and their persuasiveness in making substantial groups of people care about the outcome (in this case narrative resolution) and feel an affinity with the players (character identification). Before interrogating the sports drama text, we need first to 'cut to the chase' – for ratings on free-to-air or subscribers for pay TV. This task involves a close inspection of the premium TV sports text – live action coverage.

The front row seat in the living room versus 'being there'

If we consider the activity of going to a live sports event 'in the flesh' as a specific kind of embodied consumption of a text, then watching that same event 'remotely' on television was in the first instance a compensation for the absence of the sensory experience of moving with the crowd, soaking up the atmosphere and all the sights and smells of an event unique in space and time. If the sports fan at the stadium feels part of history and a strong sense of consuming the sports text under superior conditions (often saying something like, 'you just *had* to be there when we won the trophy for the first time in 50 years'), then at least those watching on television at home or in the pub get some exposure to the text (albeit two-dimensionally on a small screen from a vantage point determined by television producers and camera people) in the absence of such an intimate encounter with it. At the same time, some aspects of the sports television viewing experience may be advantageous – such as no (or minimal) entry cost (for free-to-air television), no traffic jams, wet clothes, restrictions on alcohol consumption or violent encounters with rival spectators (apart from family members and bar patrons). When the comforts of home or the pub are placed alongside technical improvements in television broadcasts such as bigger screens, high-definition images, stereo surround sound, multiple camera angles and slow-motion replays, then it might be concluded that this is more than mere compensation for not being there. It may, instead, be a more satisfying and pleasant way of experiencing sport and participating in 'the live broadcasting of history' (Dayan and Katz 1992). Indeed, a considerable number of people may, as noted in Chapter 1, choose to pay per view as if they were going to the match, especially where they are looking for comprehensive coverage of simultaneous events (or by compulsion if the option of seeing top live television sport for free has, as in the case of British Premier League soccer, been largely taken away from them). As Samuel Weber (1996: 113) reminds us, television literally means 'seeing at a distance', a technology that allows us to overcome some of the limitations of the body. But watching sport on television is not a disembodied act: it generally involves one body in a state of excitement watching others performing *in extremis*. The viewing body is, nonetheless, also disciplined. It has to consent to being exposed at a specified time to the images of the sporting event provided on screen. This freedom–constraint dialectic is now played out in more complex ways as the viewing contexts of sports television have diversified.

The conventional binary stadium–home classification of the sports spectating experience has become increasingly unsatisfactory as presentational techniques of sport have changed and more is known of the sociality of spectatorship. Watching on screen rather than at the stadium has tended to be regarded as an inferior, inauthentic experiential context for sport, but spectators conditioned to expect the full panoply of televisual devices (close-ups, multiple, multi-angle slow-motion replays, 'post-match' interviews, and the like) now demand the comforts of the domestic TV hearth alongside the special experience of 'being there' in real space and time (Eckersley and Benton 2002). This is an intriguing reversal, whereby the place-based events that were once broadcast to dispersed homes are now also serviced by the same media technologies to prevent paying spectators from wishing they were getting a better, cheaper view at home. Watching the crowd watching major sports events, there is constant recourse to large screens for replays and close-ups of the action, sometimes to the consternation of officials when the legitimacy of their rulings is called into question. The after-action interviews with sportspeople, designed initially for the TV audience, are now amplified for those in the stadium. For spectators in the cheapest seats with distant and/or obscured views of the field of play, there is considerable dependency on the television images provided. During the Sydney 2000 Olympics, for example, I attended what has become known as the 'The Cathy Freeman Final', when the Aboriginal runner, who had also lit the Olympic cauldron during the Opening Ceremony, won a much-anticipated 400 metres final. The event was given special significance following the intense discussion of the impact that a Freeman victory might have on the fraught issue of reconciliation between White Australia and its Indigenous people (Hanna 1999; Lenskyj 2000). From my seat high in a stand, Freeman was only a tiny, insectoid figure with the naked eye, requiring more time to be spent watching Freeman on than off screen. At the same time, it was possible to give attention to several simultaneous performances in sports like discus, pole vault and triple jump, whereas for living-room viewers producers tighten the frame and concentrate the action. Nonetheless, being able to access directly the unique, scarce resource of stadium attendance, and its intense, vibrant atmosphere, created a collective history-laden atmosphere impossible to replicate in the domestic environment (Rowe 2000a). The cultural capital generated by 'being there' is still, then, considerable in sport, despite the hybrid, mediatized character of the in-stadium experience. This is especially the case when that event, the Olympics, constantly proposes a deeply mythologized link to the Games of antiquity (Toohey and Veal 2000).

Emphasizing the (albeit diminished) distinctiveness of physically attending sports contests should not, however, obscure the many different ways in which spectator and screen can interact. The home can be rather more than an isolated, privatized space for watching television sport. Viewing television is typically a highly sociable activity (Morley 1992), and live television sport is especially well suited to the construction of collective social encounters. Again, research during the Sydney 2000 Olympics (Rowe 2000b) revealed that TV sport can encourage all manner of carnivalesque behaviour. Within households there was much intra-familial, inter-generational and peer interaction, with the opportunity to invite neighbours and friends into homes to watch the Games, eat, drink and converse. According to Dayan and Katz (1992: 205), media events 'transform the home into a "public space"', but they disapprove of those sporting occasions when these small-scale social interactions spill over into carnivalesque expressions of fandom:

> The high holidays of football, soccer, and baseball – the Super Bowl, the World Cup, the World Series, and so forth – are among the mainstays of media use. Living-room celebrations of these games, and of the Olympics, involve rituals of conviviality, knowledgeable exchange, and a level of attention and sociability far exceeding that of everyday television. This sociability can reach disastrous heights, as in the parody of communitas which has marred recent European soccer matches and in the explosions of enthusiasm which may now be seen in the streets of cities whose teams have just won a televised game; television spectators pour out of their homes and jam the streets in frenzied cavorting and motor carnivals.
>
> (Dayan and Katz 1992: 207)

Setting aside Dayan and Katz's rather moralistic, fun-defying tone, the social phenomena that they describe – the flag-waving sports fans congregating on the streets and the loud sounds of car horns – indicate that the domestic environment, however handsomely served by widescreen televisions and surround sound, cannot always satisfy the urge to take part in a grander spectacle. During the 2002 World Cup, 'Big-screen viewing became a major feature – for example, an incredible 4.2 million Koreans took to the streets to watch their national team's victory over Italy' (FIFA 2002). As sports spectators abandon the home for the street, they also become part of the sports spectacle that, ironically, is relayed by television back to domestic screens as additional, visible evidence of the spectacular nature of the sports event itself. Such spontaneous expressions of the desire of television viewers to demonstrate their sporting passions in public or quasi-public spaces can be governed and rationalized in various ways. These include watching major sports events on large television screens in clubs, pubs and bars (sometimes, as noted in Chapter 3, of necessity because of the exclusive capture of major sports contests by pay TV) and in designated 'live sites' created by the authorities in city squares and parks. During the Sydney 2000 Olympics, for example, TV viewing sites were strategically located near the main stadium and in various places in the central business district (Rowe 2000b). Sports television out of the home, therefore, creates new viewing experiences and new ancillary media sports texts, as spectacular displays of fandom beyond the stadium attract media coverage, and some sports fans seek to match the paying spectators present by dressing and performing for the cameras. This distinction of the cash nexus may, it has already been noted, be eliminated where a paying crowd assembles before a large screen. As Boyle and Haynes (2003: 109), for example, have noted, the leading Scottish football club Glasgow Celtic 'beamed back' six away matches to the stadium in the earlier part of the 1999–2000 season to an average paying audience of over 9000 per game. This viewership is larger than the crowds physically attending many sporting events.

The 'spectacularization' of sport through television and the apparently increasing desire of sports spectators to become integral components of the sporting text itself intertwine the practice, mediation and experience of sport. As Robert Rinehart argues:

> . . . the games and sports themselves have become inseparable from their atmosphere: the sport experience is not one that easily lends itself to separating out 'the sport' from the totality of the 'sporting experience' . . . Furthermore, these sporting experiences . . . have themselves commingled, so that each borrows from and is informed by the other.
>
> (Rinehart 1998: 7)

In this blurring of sport and its experience, there is a corresponding breaching of the boundary between performer and spectator. Marvin Carlson, after noting the complexity and contestability of the concept of performance, records the ethnolinguist Richard Bauman's view that:

> all performance involves a consciousness of doubleness, through which the actual execution of an action is placed in mental comparison with a potential, an ideal, or a remembered original model of that action. Normally this comparison is made by an observer of the action – the theatre public, the school's teacher, the scientist – but the double consciousness, not the external observation, is what is most central. An athlete, for example, may be aware of his [or her] own performance,

placing it against a mental standard. Performance is always performance *for* someone, some audience that recognizes and validates it as performance even when, as is occasionally the case, the audience is the self.

(Carlson 1996: 5–6)

In the realm of sport, this double consciousness of the performer is reproduced across a very wide field through the agency of the media. The multiple opportunities for watching the self, watching the self being watched, watching what's being practised against some normative standard – the kind of surveillance and disciplining of the human subject analysed by Foucault (1979, 1980) – are available not just to the professional athlete, but to a battery of contributors, from coaches and marketeers to television commentators and directors to sponsors and fans. As Yi-Fu Tan (1990: 243) argues, in a football stadium, despite clear spatial and role 'demarcation . . . In a physical-emotional way, spectators participate as much as they can'. When we stretch the concept of the stadium, via the media, to the home, school, workplace and street, then perhaps we are, as Rinehart (1998) puts it, 'Players All', and often with aspirations to become an integral part of the media sports text. Thus, spectacular fan displays in and outside the stadium, like the loud chants of English cricket's 'Barmy Army', the visual displays of Barcelona football club fans, and the bright hair of Swedish tennis supporters, become critical 'reading material' in sport. There are, as a consequence, attempts by commercial corporations (like Nike and Vodafone) to harness 'spontaneous' fan behaviour for advertising and promotion, and by national sports associations to make their fans brighter and noisier (as in the case of the Australian rugby union). The media sports text, like its audience, is becoming more difficult to govern and interpret.

Peak sports organizations have also begun to recognize this diversifying range of sports viewing possibilities. FIFA (2002), for example, while measuring a 'cumulative in-home audience of 28.8 billion viewers' for Korea/Japan 2002, also for the first time assessed 'out-of-home viewing – a key factor in understanding today's audiences – [which] has added 2.5 billion to the total'. FIFA also noted that 'Futuristic options were on trial, with 16×5 wide screen viewing and delivery to mobile phones', signalling improvements in the quality of some sports TV images at the same time as others could be delivered in miniature but with greater spatial flexibility. Thus, the sports audience is already more complex than the in-stadium/at-home binary model allows and, as will be discussed in the Afterword, promises to diversify further with the availability of new technologies.

Irrespective of the rich range of sports viewing forms and contexts, human subjects must first be induced to sit or stand before the screen, to pay directly per view, or to be willing to pay for the option of doing so, even if that option is not always exercised (that is, induced to subscribe to a service). Like any other small screen genre, sports television typically presents itself as compulsive viewing. In the case of live television, part of this pitch connects to news discourse – real events are unfolding before the viewers' eyes and history is being made, and so on. Such promotions can work only if sports events are imbued with the necessary sense of significance, without which all sport looks like a series of bizarre manoeuvres observing arcane rules for no apparent reason. Sport as news is dependent on conventional news values (Hartley 1982; Critcher 1987), and the consequent placing of happenings in hierarchies and categories. Just as news is sorted by criteria of importance (the assassination of a monarch or president taking precedence over a politician's photo opportunity), then organized and presented to heighten its dramatic appeal, so sport is awarded significance in the media (as well as receiving it from outside). Different media spaces can be utilized to give live sports events prominence and appropriate *gravitas*. Newspapers can endlessly preview the 'big game', radio bulletins update listeners on the lead-up to it, and television news sets the stage for the major sports event to be televised live. Once shown, the action sports television text can then be replayed in numerous ways, and act as the subject of a post-mortem which can plug the gap until the next big sports event.

By tracing the features of the communicative apparatus that surrounds the live sports text in the electronic media, it is readily apparent that even the most important sports moments are not permitted to speak for themselves. We have already discussed in Chapter 4 the aural commentary that accompanies and helps direct responses to the visual text alongside the recorded sounds (increasingly within the range of more sophisticated microphones) of the crowd, sports competitors and officials, and ball against bat, body against body, and so on. Beyond the more efficient capture of the sounds and sights (from helicopter shots to extreme close-ups to slow-motion replays) of sport is the organization of the action into an intelligible narrative that vastly extends its range of meaning and cultural resonance. In bringing us this action, the electronic media also help to produce it as something greater, so that what appears on screen connects with other cultural and social phenomena in a variety of ways. Andrew Tudor (1992), for example, advances this argument in examining British television coverage of the 1990 soccer World Cup. After noting the well-known sports TV audience research studies (such as by Comisky *et al.* 1977) which demonstrate how 'it is commentary above all that provides the television audience with a framework through which events can be viewed, interpreted and emotionally glossed' (p. 391), he assesses the coverage of a match between England and Cameroon in terms of the national and racial stereotypes produced by 'British television's commitment to sustaining a partisan and nationalistic England narrative' (p. 407). While Tudor observes that the discursive positioning of English and African people was not always consistent, there was a strong tendency to represent Cameroon as ' "happy-go-lucky" amateurs' lacking England's 'old bulldog spirit', and an unfolding process of 'discursive upgrading' which 'involves narrators in constructing a coherent narrative by progressively spelling out the system of oppositions on which the account of national (football) character depends, and by reinterpreting these oppositions as necessary' (p. 410). Yet, Tudor goes on to argue that distinguishing 'us' as superior to 'them' also lays bare the anxieties that 'we' might feel about the state of the nation and our personal wellbeing (O'Donnell 1994). It is for this reason, perhaps, that there is so much emphasis in television sport and its commentary on the final score in sports contests as an absolute and unquestioned measure of success and failure, so that 'Televised sports allows viewers to take comfort in the possibility of unequivocal decisions, of being able to distinguish winners and losers, as well as in the possibility of "records" that are quantifiable and measurable' (Weber 1996: 127). Of course, if the hoped-for victory does not occur, it is also necessary, short of mass suicide, to come to terms with failure (a painfully acquired skill at which English sports supporters excel). This loss rationalization process opens up other narrative possibilities present in the age-old popular cries of 'we wuz robbed', 'string up the Board', 'the ref was bent', and so on. Alternatively, ridicule and abuse constitute common responses. When, for example, the England association football team lost to lowly rated Australia in February 2003, the online version of *The Sun* newspaper digitally grafted the head of England coach Sven Goran Eriksson (enhanced with outsized marsupial ears) onto a kangaroo's body, alongside the headline '**Get tough or HOP OFF** *Your message to Sven after Aussie disaster*'. Television, however, because of its 'liveness', tends to handle such moments with greater restraint, even poignancy. Thus, the BBC brought down the curtain on England's 2002 World Cup campaign, after its defeat by Brazil in June 2002, with a succession of touching, slow-motion images to the mournful strains of 'Stop Crying Your Heart Out' by the pop group Oasis.

The analytical possibilities afforded by the moving sports image go well beyond showing the sensitive side of contemporary sporting masculinity. The television sport package, complete with its own visual grammar and semiotically anchored by commentary, is readily available for the exploration of socio-cultural power in, outside and through sport. Considerable space now exists in cultural, media and sport studies, and in sociology, that opens such texts for close inspection in seeking to understand their ways of working with the ideologies and mythologies at hand. Simply consulting recent issues of one academic resource, *Journal of Sport & Social Issues*, provides a plethora of analyses of TV sport and its relationship to various dimensions of the socio-cultural order. Ketra Armstrong (1999), for example, analyses how the Nike leisurewear company tries to communicate with Black audiences through television (and also print) advertisements; Grant Farred (2000) appraises a new form of 'cool sports talk' on an ESPN programme that combines postmodernism with a productive engagement with questions of race; Eileen Kennedy (2001) examines the BBC's coverage of women's tennis at Wimbledon and finds it largely infantilizing; while Daniel Mason (2002) has tracked Canadian responses to transnational broadcasting innovations in its national game of hockey. The best of such work connects the institutional pressures on, and workings of, television and other media with the transformations of sport, relationships with fans and audiences, and broader socio-cultural processes like globalization as they relate to classed, racialized, ethnicized, 'nationalized', gendered and other significant forms of power (Bernstein and Blain 2003).

Television sport, the prime audiovisual domestic genre and medium, is especially well equipped to focus closely on what Turner (1992: 12) regards as the prime object of contemporary anxiety in the 'somatic society' – the body. Therefore, as Samuel Weber (1996: 127) proposes, 'televised sports reconfirms the individual body as focal point of a reality that television itself calls into question. The body that appears in the televised sporting event is one that accepts its limitations only in order to surpass them, in an infinite progress of record-breaking and record-making'. Here again the anxious viewing subject is seen as scrutinizing screen sports images – especially the extraordinary performances of athletic bodies – for signs of social and personal 'truth' (Davis 1995). In televised sport such linkages are made not only with non-sporting matters (from the state of national morale to the health of the economy to the quality of the national gene pool), but also between the media sports text and other familiar types of text. As the action unfolds on screen, it becomes recognizable as drama both on and off it.

It is useful, then, to appraise the media techniques and textual uses that turn televised live sports action into television drama. Rose and Friedman (1997: 3), using Siegfried Kracauer's theory of distraction developed in the 1920s, have proposed a particularly strong relationship between television sport and 'a uniquely masculine experience of spectatorship' that questions the gendered segregation of television viewing patterns. They argue that in television viewing hierarchies, soap opera (especially of the daytime variety) tends to be denigrated as 'light' entertainment for bored housewives, so that:

> in their very structure, soaps habituate women to the 'interruption, distraction, and spasmodic toil' [Modleski 1983: 71] which is characteristic of housework. At the same time, by focusing the female spectator's gaze on others, encouraging her to read their needs, desires, and intentions

from facial expressions and body language, the soap opera reflects
and reinforces the cultural imperative which requires women to do the
emotional work in their relationships.

(Rose and Friedman 1997: 4)

In contrast to the traditional positioning of women as concerned above all
else with emotions and relationships (as is exemplified by the current revival of
the 1960s term 'chick flick' to describe films that deal deeply with human,
especially romantic, relationships in contrast to the spectacular 'shoot 'em up'
and car-chase action of the typical 'guy's movie'), Rose and Friedman (1997: 4)
describe the traditional 'masculine mode of spectatorship' as one expected
'to avoid the emotional register, emphasizing instead the classical masculine
pleasures in voyeurism and objectification, and constructing a more linear,
goal-oriented structure of looking'. So, if men are culturally trained not to get
too emotional and involved in their viewing activities, we would expect television sport – until quite recently a predominantly male viewing choice and
still one dominated by men in terms of which sports get watched on TV and
when (Sargent *et al.* 1998) – to be sober and cool, appreciating the technical
excellence of the athleticism on show, and balanced in its appreciation of the
merits of all competitors and teams. Such a television sports spectator would
scrupulously honour the Olympic ideals of fair play and respect for taking part
rather than for winning. The familiar picture of the unhinged and hysterical
male viewer supporting an individual or team as they engage in live sports
competition is hardly in accord with this view. As Rose and Friedman go on
to say:

> The sports gaze depends not on distance, fragmentation, or objectifica-
> tion, but on identification, nearness, and participation. The male viewer's
> relationship to the image is in fact quite similar to that of the female
> soap viewer: he is alternately absorbed in multiple identifications and
> distracted. Rather than emphasizing a voyeuristic and objectifying gaze,
> television sports seems to invite the viewer to engage in a distracted,
> identificatory, and dialogic spectatorship which may be understood as a
> masculine counterpart to soap opera's 'maternal gaze'.
>
> (Rose and Friedman 1997: 4)

In suggesting that male (and, presumably, female) television sports spectators
have a similar relationship with the moving sports text as do *aficionados* of
screen melodrama (McKay and Rowe 1997), Rose and Friedman could be proposing either that sports fans want their television sport that way or that the
practical logic of securing and holding mass audiences in television inevitably
impels the text towards a deeply emotional engagement between text, subject

and viewer. In fact, both possibilities exist – the affective power of sport is such that few committed spectators who identify closely with the people performing on screen (which include athletes, coaches and other fans) can watch in a cool, detached way. The terms 'committed' and 'identify' are of paramount importance because, as we saw in discussing sports photography in Chapter 5, it is perfectly possible for male spectators to objectify sportswomen in a sexually voyeuristic fashion when they have no respect for their activities as athletes. But once sporting qualities come to the fore – as in the case, say, of female Olympic swimmers involved in close races against rival nations – then it is likely that the emphasis on 'just looking' in a voyeuristic way will recede (at least temporarily) in favour of an active absorption in the sport itself.

Second, the logic of (especially commercial) television is deeply reliant on fostering a sense of audience involvement. If men and women care about their sport, then that level of emotional commitment will have at least to be matched, if not stimulated and exceeded, by sports television. The huge general popularity of sport does not of itself deliver audiences in specific instances. There is constant competition between individual sports (like basketball and football) and between sport and other forms of popular entertainment (such as music or film) for audiences. Television sports audiences have to be 'primed', therefore, and can always be profitably expanded. But first the missing millions must be found.

Audience hunting

As I discussed earlier, it makes little sense for a mass medium to exclude or alienate men who do not regard themselves as 'sports nuts', or gay men and women who like sport, or women who could be encouraged to develop an interest in it by various means. Miller (1998a: 107), for example, notes that half of the British television audience of 24 million for a match during the 1990 soccer World Cup were women, which led one newspaper to speculate that 'TV production houses and female viewers were both engaged by the "bum not the ball" '. Playing up the human interest or broader entertainment side of sport (normally associated with 'soft' news and 'low' drama) to appeal to larger television audiences can, of course, annoy the purist sports spectator. While the application of new camera and sound technologies (such as miniaturized lenses and microphones on the field of play) are likely to be much welcomed by regular viewers who are looking for an ever closer simulation of the actual event, the explanation of rules or moves or various comic innovations are anathema to the 'expert' viewer. As Barnett has noted:

When [Kerry] Packer's Channel Nine finally wrenched Test cricket away from the Australian Broadcasting Corporation, it invested considerable financial and technical resources into coverage. Some of the innovations – aerial shots of field placing, split-screen comparisons of respective bowling actions – were valuable contributions to a better view and a better understanding of the game. Others were little more than cheap production tricks which had little to do with explaining a complex game to the uninformed. At the most banal level came the introduction of a ridiculous cartoon duck, which tearfully accompanied a batsman dismissed for nought (in cricket terminology a 'duck') to the pavilion . . . Cartoon characters in live sports have only one objective – to keep those with minimum interest in the game (particularly children) tuned in. This is, no doubt, precisely why Sky imported the same triviality into their coverage of the 1990 West Indies–England Test series (along with the excitable commentary of Tony Greig).

(Barnett 1990: 169)

Barnett (1990: 169) also notes the use of 'honey shots' of 'scantily clad young women in the stands' to dissuade heterosexual men not 'riveted' by the sport from changing channels, the equivalent tactic to the sexualization of male sports performers for heterosexual women. But the dramatization, 'cartoonization' and sexualization of television sport do not exhaust the repertoire of techniques for keeping and holding large audiences. Sports authorities and television companies have also devised new 'telegenic' forms of sport that lend themselves well to fixed television schedules and reshape sports contests in a manner that accentuates even more the melodramatic character of live sport.

Looking further at the game of cricket, for example, we can see that the one-day form has been moulded well to the demands of television in terms of its structure and guaranteed result. Unlike viewers of Test cricket, impatient audiences with busy lives will not be required to watch at least thirty hours of live action over five days only for the event to end inconclusively as a draw. The one-day game, as distinguished from its traditional three-, four- and five-day counterparts, allots a fixed number of overs for each side to bowl. The side with the lower score after this allocation or which is dismissed before the other's score is reached loses. Draws are extremely rare, as they rely on the improbable outcome of 'tying' the scores rather than the passage of time, and, even then, a victor can if necessary be declared on a 'count back' (such as the number of wickets lost). The rules are also varied to encourage more spectacular action, such as hitting the ball adventurously in the air rather than more cautiously along the ground. This aim is achieved through the imposition of fielding restrictions, especially during the first fifteen overs (which in the traditional game usually involves a careful jockeying for initial advantage), which make it less likely that an ambitious, big-hitting batter will be caught in the 'deep'; operating a quota for the number of overs allowed to be bowled by any one bowler, in order to give batters the opportunity to face some less specialist bowlers and so score more runs; applying a much stronger test to the assessment of 'wides' and 'no balls', the illegal deliveries that must be repeated and are penalized by the awarding of extra runs. Such tailored changes to the game (no doubt unfathomable to those who do not have an intimate knowledge of the game of cricket, but the source of endless disputation for those who do) are designed to ensure that the televised one-day cricket match is fast and furious, encouraging high scores and high drama.

Harriss (1990) has observed how making cricket more television friendly through these changes aligns it with the dramatic form (even before the contribution of commentators and producers is factored in), so that in 'the age of late capitalism based on mass consumption, cricket becomes a postmodern, decentred spectacle that emphasizes a glossy surface without depth' (p. 118). The introduction of coloured uniforms in place of the traditional stately white, and of day–night matches under floodlights to accommodate the audience's work and TV viewing schedules, have helped turn a notoriously staid game into a fully integrated leisure package. The World Cup of cricket, held every four years and most recently in 2003 in South Africa and Zimbabwe (in the latter case somewhat controversially given the state of its domestic politics), creates a definable world one-day champion cricket nation as opposed to the winners and losers of sundry bi- and tri-nation series. Television is seen here to be both cause and effect of the transformation of cricket (and, no doubt, other sports like tennis and golf) from the controlled and stately progress towards victory based on a rationalized 'cost–benefit analysis' to a much flashier spectacle dedicated to instant gratification by seizing the ephemeral attention of a media-saturated and more diverse audience:

> The one-day spectacle is packaged in much the same way as a one-hour television melodrama. There is some variation in each individual episode, but the conclusion is inevitably a hectic chase sequence. The paradox of one-day cricket is that, like the television melodrama, while it emphasizes action it does so only within the framework of a formula. Also like the television melodrama, the plot of each game is circumscribed by the structure of the series as a whole. This eliminates complexity and allows the viewer to be immersed quickly and easily in the immediate plot.
>
> (Harriss 1990: 118)

It might be suggested that the kind of melodrama described by Harriss is much more action dependent (in the manner of TV shows in which social order is perpetually challenged, like *24*, *X Files*, *NYPD Blue*, *Law & Order*, *Boomtown*, *The Sopranos*, *Prime Suspect*, *Rebus* and *Cracker*) than that discussed by Rose and Friedman (which is closer to daytime and evening 'soaps' and dramas like *Days of Our Lives*, *The Young and the Restless*, *Passions*, *Neighbours*, *Home and Away*, *Melrose Place*, *Dawson's Creek*, *Chicago Hope* and *ER*). This specific point – which, while valid, requires a more detailed analysis of the concept of melodrama (see Brooks 1976) than is possible here – does not rebut the more general proposition that live television sport moves well beyond the territory of describing action on the field and into the space of narrativizing and mythologizing its subject. In fact, it plainly draws on both the action and 'feeling' oriented sub-genres of melodrama to construct a media text that we could typify as combining the spectacular physical, often violent elements of action drama with the detailed characterization, emotional concentration and relational emphasis of 'human' drama. The outcome can properly be described as inter-textual and multi-genre in nature, not always satisfying individual viewers but ceaselessly working to link what is on the screen in a meaningful and attractive way to other media texts and life experiences.

Because television sport is a moving spectacle of varying pace (golf, for example, is positively pedestrian when compared with ice or field hockey), it relies on capitalizing on the visual drama of movement when it is readily access-ible and producing a sense of rapid momentum when it is not. Even sports that already seem frenetic are sped up by television in pursuit of the uncommitted viewing eye, yet this constant acceleration of the rhythm of the sports TV text is to some degree in tension with the impulse to slow it all down and see it more clearly from numerous angles and in minute detail. By making the spectacle of sports television louder and more frenetic in a drive to interpellate, in Althusser's terms, potential viewers ('Oy! Look!'), and then distract (in Kracauer's sense), even transfix them ('Don't Look Away For A Moment!'), programmers are attempting to occupy the exterior and interior spaces of homes and minds. This urgent mode of address is also associated with a traditional split between British and American styles of sports broadcasting.

It is useful to trace some of the major changes in the way that images of sport are presented on the small screen. To do so, we need to know something of the history of the principles governing the capturing of 'reality' for television and, in particular, of recording and transmitting sports events. As Whannel points out, in the earlier part of the twentieth century, when protocols for the reflection of the world by television were being developed:

> television merely took over a lot of standard realist conventions from film-making – the 180-degree rule, the principle of complementary angles, and so on . . . These conventions aimed at transparency, strengthening

the claim to television to reflect events and minimising its own active construction of representations.

(Whannel 1992: 32)

Thus the television camera was thought of as an unseen eye, its 'sweeping' of what was before it from a single, static position simulating the experience of the spectator watching from a particular vantage point. The key to this form of television, as in all forms of realism, was to make the infrastructure of communication invisible, turning two-dimensional (and initially monochrome) perception into three-dimensional (colourful) experience. When single cameras were supplemented by others, the consequent shifting of perspectives made it harder to hide the production decisions being made on behalf of the viewer, sacrificing a degree of 'reality effect' for a technologically enhanced view of the action. A tension quickly emerged between a rather 'Olympian' view of the sports action (watching from a suitable distance in a detached, objective manner) and a more 'dramaturgical' approach reliant on close-up shots that engaged the viewer much more closely with the personalities of the participants. To some degree, this was also a struggle between those who took a high-minded, serious approach to the visual reportage of sports events and those who saw it merely as one form of popular entertainment, which, like others, should be presented using all the available, audience-pleasing techniques (Whannel 1992: 33). The development of such techniques included rapid-fire editing, which could give to even the most ponderous sports contest the appearance of a series of lightning strikes.

One way to establish the existence of such shifts from slower to faster styles of sports television presentation is to quantify for comparative purposes the length and duration of shots in individual live sports programmes. The variables measured include any changes that might occur over time and differences between countries influenced by one or other of the major sports broadcasting traditions. Fiske's (1983) case study of televised cricket in Australia revealed that average shot-length was 6 seconds out of a total average of 46–9 shots per over. When Whannel (1992: 99) replicated the study in England in 1991, he found considerable differences – an average shot length of 8 seconds (one-third longer) with an average of only 32 shots per over (29–30 per cent fewer). This variation can be explained, as suggested earlier in the mention of the Packer Cricket 'Revolution', by a change of broadcast philosophy (mirroring a wider historical shift as the first colonial power, Britain, was superseded by the second dominant force of media and cultural imperialism – the USA) that saw some commercial television stations in Australia depart from the patented BBC model of broadcasting restraint and embrace the more upbeat American style (Barnett 1990). In 1998, my own update of these studies revealed some similarities and variations. An October one-day match between the unobtrusively named Queensland Bulls and the Tasmanian Tigers revealed an average shot length of less than 6 seconds (5.7), but an average number of shots per over of only 29. The explanation of this uneven finding is that the average over length was only 166 seconds, barely half that of those sampled by Fiske (although some allowance should be made for variation in types of bowling). The Australian cricketing audience's assumed attention span, it seems, shrunk markedly in those fifteen years. A brief comparative study I conducted in the September of that year of a UK one-day game between Essex and Nottingham revealed an average shot length of a little under 8 seconds (7.95) and an average number of shots per over of only 24 (23.66). The English, it seems, have maintained their reputation for a more sedate brand of TV cricket. But, with an average over length of only 188 seconds, the screen action is positively frenetic by earlier standards.

Goldlust (1987) also carried out a limited empirical study of the different forms of sports television by performing comparative visual component and shot analyses of tennis, baseball and football in the USA and cricket in Australia. Goldlust, like the aforementioned writers, operated with the:

> somewhat artificial, but still meaningful, distinction between an emphasis on commercial *entertainment* values best represented by the American networks and *journalistic* values emphasizing accuracy and 'objective' reporting of events that has become the established ethos within the BBC and a significant element of its institutional self-image.
>
> (Goldlust 1987: 98)

While Goldlust did not perform any quantitative analysis of British sports television, recording only 'his impression that the distinction would still hold' (p. 100) on the basis of viewing British TV soccer for three weeks on both the public BBC and the commercial channels (and finding that the average shot length in West German TV coverage of the 1974 soccer World Cup was almost double that of the BBC), he found general evidence of a move towards 'a "high tech" form of "snap, snap" television typified by contemporary American network coverage of sports' (p. 100).

Of course, variations in the structure and form of very different sports like tennis and American football impose constraints on how television will cover them (for example, the average length of a segment from the Masters tennis match sampled was over twice that of the Super Bowl), and there are cultural variations of various kinds – the amount of commentary 'hype' tolerated, the quantity of background information provided, and so on. Gordon and Sibson (1998) have also shown in their comparative analysis of US and Australian television coverage of the 1996 Atlanta Olympics that there are perceptible differences in how broadcasters from different countries handle the same live sports 'feed' (that is, in how they process the same raw textual material). But the most significant finding is that the now entrenched methods of television, much imitated or directly imported from the USA in countries like Australia, have the impact of eroding the differences between sports with wildly varying histories, tempos and spectatorships. Above all, this is an impulse constantly to shift the viewer's perspective and to provide a barrage of sights and sounds to prevent their attention from wandering and their hand straying to the remote control button, so that:

> illustrative of the overall tendency towards fragmentation of viewpoint is that the longest shot of any kind over all four telecasts lasted 51.2 seconds and this was a close-up of a baseball pitcher warming up before an innings, while graphics listing the team line-up were superimposed over the picture. Overall, rarely did any shot exceed twenty-five seconds in length – in the [one-day] cricket the longest was only nineteen seconds.
>
> The multiplicity of viewing perspectives provided by the television coverage is further increased in that the slow-motion replays are often from one or more camera positions different from that shown in the live segments.
>
> The analysis above sensitizes us to the extent to which the sporting event is transformed through the dictates of what is considered to be 'good television' into a form of rapidly alternating images and visual perspectives that has much in common with the editing style of many other contemporary commercial television programmes.
>
> (Goldlust 1987: 105–6)

Furthermore, in noting Fiske's (1983) calculation of the rough approximation of average shot length in sports, adventure and news programmes, it can be suggested that the logic of television is towards a homogeneous rendering of its subject – any subject, from sport to strikes to soap opera. When it is considered that since Goldlust and Fiske did these appraisals there has been an enormous development of television sport's scope and technique (Wenner 1998; Boyle and Haynes 2000; Brookes 2002), it is clear that television is having a profound impact on ways of seeing sport that, for younger and rising generations, seem timeless and matural. The more traditionalist lovers of sport worry about the power of television to make sport in its own image – that is, for sporting traditions to be discarded in favour of the *Sturm und Drang* (the flashing, thunderous spectacle signifying not too much when the billows of dry ice have cleared) that viewers have become conditioned to expect and demand. In the world of free-to-air, network television at least, where there is little toleration of specialist, minority interest, the moving media sports text also seems to be a

convergent and more uniform one. In theoretical terms, this trend exposes one
of the paradoxes of postmodernization (Crook *et al.* 1992) – as differentiation
(say, of news and entertainment media functions) gives way to hyper-
differentiation ('hard' versus 'soft' news within the genre of journalism), the
result is often de-differentiation (the collapse of boundaries between functions
and genres). So, as Real points out in his analysis of the televising of the
Olympics:

> The fast-paced Olympic television presentation of multiple events with
> on-screen graphics and announcer commentary is the opposite of the
> classical coherent, single-authored, focused artistic experience. Underlying
> this postmodern presentation is the commercial incentive to maximize
> viewing audience by promotion and titillation, by superlatives and
> historical allusions, by giving the audience what it expects but in an even
> fancier form than it had hoped.
>
> (Real 1996: 242)

In likening the experience of watching the TV Olympics to that of taking in
pop video channels like MTV and the strange film and television of directors
like David Lynch and Quentin Tarantino, Real is proposing that sport has
joined many other mediated cultural forms in being overwhelmed by a (post)-
culture of fragmentation, pastiche and promiscuous borrowing from any style
or genre at hand. Following Jameson's (1984) characterization of postmodernism as the 'logic of late capitalism' (noted above), such arguments taken
to their fullest extent foresee the complete collapse of all divisions between
texts. This is an improbable development given that the media sports text is still
recognizable as such. Few in full possession of their faculties would mistake
a sports broadcast for a children's programme or a soap opera, yet this does
not mean that elements from them (the infantilization of the audience or the
dramatization of the action) have not infiltrated the sports text (and, presumably, vice versa). Watching such disparate television shows as the card-game
based *Late Night Poker*, quiz shows *Who Wants to be a Millionaire?* and *The
Weakest Link*, and 'reality' programmes like *Big Brother, Survivor, Temptation
Island, The Bachelor* and *Joe Millionaire*, the interpenetration of sport and
other TV genres is apparent. Each of these shows contains a strong element of
competition, and borrows freely from sports television and other genres (such
as romance and current affairs). In more muted form than the global media
event, this could be regarded as the triumph of the 'Contest' script (Dayan and
Katz 1992: 25). So, just as the conventions of sports television have bled into the
weft and weave of the entire, ever-shifting fabric of TV, live (including delayed
or replayed) television sport has soaked into the embroidered threads of other
genres in its eternal quest for audiences. The series of disconnected cohorts that

form and re-form across the media sports cultural complex that we call 'the audience' (Ruddock 2001; Balnaves *et al.* 2002) has to be held together for long enough to register with advertisers, sponsors, sports organizations and governments. Given the stringent demands of these 'stakeholders', nothing can be left to chance and no screen sport can just rely on its assumed intrinsic appeal.

What we have seen is something not altogether surprising given the nature of sports mythologies and the reliance of the popular media on narrative – the deployment of different styles and genres to transform what could be the 'spartan' act of sports viewing into a luxurious wallowing in spectacle. In the process, the 'real' events on screen are coupled with the 'fictional' elements of story telling and myth making. As Cunningham and Miller (1994) point out, a key element of this narrativizing impulse is, as in other entertainment forms, the creation and promotion of sportspeople as celebrities. Hence, it can be said that 'TV sport is an individualizing genre, announcing, auditing and ending the careers of stars' (Cunningham and Miller 1994: 77). That television is a visual medium gives it a huge advantage over its rival, more flexible electronic medium – radio – in that the viewer to an extent mimicks the everyday encounters of individuals, searching their gestures for meaningful signs of character and personal history. In accentuating the specific character traits of athletes, though, the collective aspects of sport (especially uncomfortable questions of society and politics) are often strategically played down (Hilliard 1994; Benedict 1997). Thus, while national or city teams routinely have group traits ascribed to them by television commentators (tough, flamboyant, sneaky, and so on), the simplest and most direct way of developing drama through character is to focus closely on single sportspeople. It is not a very long step from creating sports stars through television to their appearance (as either themselves or another character) on film and then to film stars playing them on the big screen. Feature films that are not documentaries or biographies are moving media sports texts that obey a different logic to live action in starting with the 'fictional' (or fictive) and working backwards to the 'real' practice of sport.

Screen of dreams

We have noted above how actual sports action, when caught on screen, is invested with the quality of dramatic fiction. What happens, then, when sport appears on screen as fiction? If 'unscripted' screen sport already has recognizable actors, plots, sets, and so on, then its fictional counterpart might be expected to develop these into an even more structured and mythologized cultural entity that operates in the space between the 'real' and the 'imaginary'. Fictional moving media sports texts are subject to different imperatives than

those which operate in the non-fictional. Miller (1996) suggests that more attention should be given to documentary and instructional films (for an example,
see Robbins's (1997) discussion of the basketball documentary *Hoop Dreams*.
These texts, however, are not discussed in any detail here because I am interested primarily in representations that take the audience further from sport
as a formal institution in order to see it anew. For media texts regarded as
'actuality', the drive is to get up as close to the sporting subject as possible,
to reveal its 'reality' in ever more finely grained and multi-perspectival detail.
Once the veracity of the action appearing on screen is established, it is possible
to build up the fictional and mythological qualities that turn sport from a series
of physical manoeuvres into a meaning-laden cultural practice. In the case of
fictional works, it is necessary to move in the opposite direction – from the
invention of a fictional world to the 'truth' of sport and human existence. As in
the case of photographic images and literary texts, the treatment can vary
widely from a focus on sport above all else to deploying sport as a means
of reaching a large audience in the service of theme, narrative, character and
mise-en-scène. I am more concerned here with films such as *The Loneliness
of the Long Distance Runner* (1962), *This Sporting Life* (1963), *Rocky* (1976),
Raging Bull (1980), *Chariots of Fire* (1981), *Field of Dreams* (1989), *White Men
Can't Jump* (1992), *Jerry Maguire* (1996) and *Fever Pitch* (1997) in which sport
is integral, rather than those in which it is incidental. An example of such an
incidental use of sport on film is the scene in *Men in Black* (1997) where the
baseball crowd in Queens, New York, is seemingly so caught up in the sports
action that the only person to see a spaceship flying overhead is a transfixed
outfield catcher searching the night sky for a descending ball. Many films use
sports stadia as locations because of the narrative possibilities of large crowds
(usually a desperate search for a 'needle in a haystack' and/or a threat of
carnage). Others feature prominent sports stars like O.J. Simpson in the *Naked
Gun* (1988) series, Kareem Abdul-Jabbar in *Flying High* (1980) and Michael
Jordan in *Space Jam* (1997). But bona fide fictional sports films put sport and
the social relations and mythological constructions that surround it at the heart
of the film (Bergan 1982; Rowe 1998).

When we set about reading a sports film, the same questions apply as to
the analysis of any text: what is its message at manifest and latent levels, to
whom does it hope to appeal, why has this subject and this approach to it been
selected? Some of these questions may seem deceptively simple to answer. For
example, it is obvious that sport will be chosen as a subject for film because
sports fans constitute a ready-made and willing audience for such films. Yet
if sports fans are so eager to conduct a pursuit of the 'real' in and through
media sport, how tolerant will they be of a Hollywood studio or any other
production house using sport to 'tell stories'? Sarris (1980: 50) is unequivocal on

this matter: he likes sport and film but not together, because 'Sports are now. Movies are then. Sports are news. Movies are fables'. It might also be the case that a prominent place for sport in fiction film will deter non-sports fans at the box office. Thus, sport on film, unless it is to be very carefully targeted to relatively small, specialized audiences, needs to be tailored to the needs of sports and non-sports fans alike by doing justice to the sporting elements of the film for the former and expanding its concerns to the satisfaction of the latter. To be a broad audience pleaser (and not 'box office poison'), the issues confronted in the fictional sports film must simultaneously illuminate the sporting world, the other worlds with which it comes into contact, and the relations (actual and metaphorical) between them. For this reason, fictional sports films tend to be allegorical (Rowe 1998), framed as grand moral tales in which sport is represented as a metaphor for life and, not uncommonly, life is represented as a metaphor for sport. To demonstrate this point, it is instructive to examine some well-known sports films and to tease out the themes that link sports mythologies to the concerns of everyday life.

One of the definitive sports films of the early 1980s (not least because of its sweeping, stirring electronic soundtrack by Vangelis) was the British film *Chariots of Fire*. Released in the early years of the Thatcher government, it was a popular choice for exhibition at fund-raising events for the Conservative Party, who had their own 'prototype' champion elite athlete seemingly drawn from the frames of the film – Sebastian Coe (later to become a Conservative Member of Parliament). *Chariots of Fire* is a quintessential sports film (in this case based on real historical events and characters) in that it deals squarely with the mythological possibilities of transcendence of class, ethnic prejudice and human selfishness through sport. The main featured runner, Harold Abrahams (played by Ben Cross), has to overcome the snobbishness and anti-Semitism of the masters of his Cambridge college; deal with the problem of being at the same time teammate and competitor with other athletes, including one drawn from the same aristocratic class that has ridiculed him; compensate for his own lack of material resources, and so on. In the most famous scene from the film, he is shown on a training run on the beach, the rhythmic pulse of the soundtrack (overlaid with a grandiose melody) matching the pace of the runner striving against the odds for sporting victory. This scene contrasts with another of a training run in the private grounds of a stately home involving an aristocratic athlete jumping hurdles on which are placed glasses of champagne. The 'feel good' quality of his final success, the patriotic fervour induced by international sporting competition, and the nostalgic atmosphere of a film (including an evocation of the Olympianism of antiquity, as the title indicates) set in a time before big business had penetrated to the core of high-performance sport, made the Oscar-winning *Chariots of Fire* appeal to sports fans and to others. Sport has (as we have seen) extraordinary affective and connotative power, making many people feel deeply moved, and encouraging them to translate sporting values and measures of success and failure to other spheres. Hence, not only are sport and sports metaphors deployed in advertising, but they can also be used readily as the vehicle for the fictional handling of many pivotal social issues.

If we take a very different film to *Chariots of Fire* like *Jerry Maguire*, the 'cut throat' world of US sports agents provides a very effective setting for an exploration of the ethics of capitalism, the need for balance between working and personal lives, and the nature of alliances (economic and friendly) between Black and White. In the film, Jerry Maguire (played by Tom Cruise), a successful and ruthless sports agent, momentarily penetrates the amorality of his occupation and embarks on a brief crusade to restore more altruistic values to the duties of representing athletes in contract negotiations. Instead of chasing more money and clients, he decides to safeguard their interests by limiting the number but improving the quality of his business relationships, even making room to consider the broader health of sport itself. By the time he 'comes to his senses', realizing that his newfound and publicly expressed ethical commitment was no more than a passing fancy, he is sacked from his firm and abandoned by most of his clients (including those who had professed their unshakeable loyalty to him). Cut adrift by his usual class allies, Jerry Maguire is supported only by Dorothy Boyd, a single mother from a working-class background (played by Renee Zellweger) with whom he becomes romantically involved, and Rod Tidwell (Cuba Gooding Jr), an African American footballer with a rather uncertain career trajectory who keeps demanding 'Show me the money!' Ultimately, Maguire becomes successful through the ascendancy of his once doubtful but loyal client and saves the marriage that he has placed in jeopardy, which, as Miller (1997) points out, is somewhat unusually represented as more fragile than his client's own conjugal relationship – the Black family generally shown to be in crisis because of the lack of commitment of the Black male.

A pivotal scene in *Jerry Maguire* is when his client appears to have broken his neck during an important football match, only to become a sports celebrity through the degree of showmanship he displays as he rises from his prone position to 'milk' the applause of the crowd. Sport is shown, finally, to be about 'caring', commitment, forging alliances between unlikely people of different race and class in the pursuit of dual successes in sport and commerce. Hence, the tension between capitalism and sport is resolved by reassuring the audience that ethical and humane business practice in sport brings more rather than less financial success, while also guaranteeing that sport is never reduced to mere capital accumulation. The relationship between new capitalist and old sporting values in the USA is a constantly recurring theme in films about the quintessential American sport – baseball. *Field of Dreams*, with *Bull Durham* (1988) a key text in the sub-genre of the baseball film in what Sobchack (1997) calls 'Post-American Cinema' (by which she means a nation that has fragmented and lost any sense of common cultural identity), is preoccupied with the problems of (in this case rural) capitalism and the erosion of authentic feeling and cohesive, self-sustaining community. In the film, a struggling mid-West farmer, Ray Kinsella (played by Kevin Costner, who also appears in *Bull Durham*, presumably on account of his all-American boy image), hears a mysterious heavenly voice whispering 'If you build it, he will come'. The 'it' is a new baseball field on his farmland and the 'he' is a long dead and much-wronged player 'Shoeless' Joe Jackson. *Field of Dreams* invests sport with the magical power not only of bringing back the dead, but also of reviving collective memory and the values of a society which had sold its precious cultural assets – like sport – to the highest bidder. Kinsella, reluctantly at first, takes up the challenge, and sustains his faith despite objections from his bank and family, recruiting an unlikely ally in Terence Mann (James Earl Jones), a reclusive elderly black writer and former activist who shares his belief in the redemptive power of baseball. Finally, the field is built, the ghostly players return to earth, the family farm is saved by charging tourists and baseball nostalgia 'buffs' to visit this ethereal sports theme park, the wrongs done to 'Shoeless' Jackson are righted, Kinsella's family stays together, an old man is made happy, the racial divide is bridged – and the golden age of America restored in Iowa. The allegorical role of sports film – so strong in the baseball sub-genre given its reputation as the USA's national pastime (McGimpsey 2000) – is clearly demonstrated in *Field of Dreams*, with the condition of sport being presented as both symptom and solution to the dilemmas of social and personal life.

If this is an overtly mystical vision lacking in irony and scepticism, then *Fever Pitch* (1997), a film of a bestselling autobiographical book by the British writer Nick Hornby (1992), provides a much more down-to-earth and self-critical take on sports culture that is no less aware of the power of its romance. In the book and film (for which Hornby wrote the screenplay), a middle-aged man Paul (Colin Firth) recalls how soccer helped salvage an unhappy childhood by giving him something to do with his father during 'weekend visits', initiating him into masculine culture, and providing him with something to be truly committed to – Arsenal Football Club. This was no childhood fad, however, as support for Arsenal became an all-encompassing, adult obsession. The film sets up an antagonism between the immature world of football supporting and another, more 'grown-up' world symbolized by his girlfriend, Sarah (Ruth Gemmell). In a watershed moment in *Fever Pitch*, the male protagonist breaks

Living room legend: fantasy football for the confused adult male
Still from *Fever Pitch*, a Wildgaze Films Production for Channel Four Films

up with his (unknown to him, now pregnant) girlfriend after taking her onto the rowdy, male-dominated terraces of Arsenal's Highbury Stadium. On the same day in 1989, in Sheffield's Hillsborough Stadium, ninety-five football fans were crushed to death (when police allowed too many people into too small an area from which no escape was possible because of security fencing). Paul's response to these horrific events is matter of fact: football fans all over Britain will go back to unsafe grounds because they are compelled by their passion to do so, a fatalistic attitude that his girlfriend finds unfathomable, especially when it applies to a pursuit as 'trivial' as watching a football team. In reflecting on his life through the bottom of a vodka glass, Paul weighs the competing claims of the sports world in a lengthy soliloquy, confused about 'whether life's shit because Arsenal are shit, or the other way round'; considering the time and money spent and the relationships neglected in his pursuit of sports fandom; relishing moments of fans' absorption when 'everything else [has] gone out of their heads' and they feel at 'the centre of the whole world'; savouring the predictable structure of a life organized around the yearly soccer season; and then finally acknowledging that 'some stuff', like having a partner and becoming a father, is more important than supporting Arsenal and going to football matches.

Here the familiar filmic preoccupation with the relationship between the sports and wider worlds is evident, albeit in a much more knowing and self-critical manner than an heroic, nostalgic baseball film like *Field of Dreams* (no doubt also reflecting a cultural difference between a modest British film with no superstars and a shambling schoolteacher 'hero' who wears Arsenal boxer shorts, and a Hollywood 'blockbuster' with a mega-star male lead who has injected a stylish, late-1980s element into the rural struggle memorably depicted in John Steinbeck's *The Grapes of Wrath*). *Fever Pitch* is, ultimately, a rite of passage film, with the male protagonist negotiating the transition from a life dominated by football fandom to a richer, more varied and responsible existence. The cathartic moment of a dramatic and unexpected Arsenal victory that provides the film's climax is also the instant of liberation from obsessive football fandom, when sport's place in the world comes into perspective. The allegorical quality of *Fever Pitch* is apparent, even if its tone is reflective and quizzical. Sport's screen of dreams perennially returns to the place where the magical world of sport is compared with the prosaic existence beyond – with the latter usually found wanting. This time, it is sport – and Arsenal Football Club – that loses out.

Sport continues to be a major subject for film and an opportunity for filmmakers to explore both the sports world and the sport–society relationship. Oliver Stone's American football fable, *Any Given Sunday* (1999), uses a troubled franchise as a site for an exploration of the ways in which the nobler aspects of sport (from the film's perspective the warrior-like nature of contact sport) are being undermined by corporate commercial interests. In this regard, as in *Field of Dreams*, this loss of higher moral ground and the threat of cynical manipulation symbolizes a wider trend in the USA. *Any Given Sunday* covers a familiar range of issues in sports film. One of these is inter-generational succession between players, in this case Dennis Quaid's Jack 'Cap' Rooney, the Sharks' champion but declining quarterback and the up-and-coming Willie Beamen (Jamie Foxx). It is also between owners and coaches in the form of Al Pacino's ageing coach Tony D'Amato facing the new order imposed by owner Christina Pagniacci (Cameron Diaz), the daughter of the late team owner who was also a long-time friend and supporter of D'Amato. That Beamen is black and Pagniacci a young woman complicates the equations of power. It makes possible the airing of racial issues (like the question of 'stacking', or the highly ideological allocation of sports roles according to assumed racial characteristics; see, for example, Anderson 1993) and also those concerning gender and class, with the Ivy League-educated Pagniacci bringing a ruthless, market-oriented approach to sport that the older, less formally credentialled D'Amato opposes. Her presence among naked athletes in the locker room echoes the 'Lisa Olson' case discussed in Chapter 2, a double intrusion of sex and capitalist management into homosocial sporting space. Beamen, like Rod Tidwell in *Jerry Maguire*, has the concern with gaining material security from a short-lived and dangerous sporting career that is characteristic of the class location of the majority of African Americans. The film covers the politics of franchise location (Nunn and Rosentraub 1997; Whitson 1998), with the owner threatening to move the team from its base in Florida unless it receives a substantial civic subsidy to renovate the stadium. It addresses the decadence of professional sports culture and the mistreatment of women (Benedict 1997) as well as the calculated damage to the bodies of the mostly black athletes in a reproductive cycle of exploitation and abuse.

In getting up close to sport, *Any Given Sunday* foregrounds corporeality – both the brutality and, on occasions, beauty of the game (all to the rhythmic strains of music by the likes of Fat Boy Slim and Gary Glitter), but also the 'back stage' management of the body that makes the visible sports performance possible. The film shows the cold calculations of catastrophic injury, career and players contracts, and the tolerance of needle-deadened pain, that keep the sporting show on the road for the amusement of the paying spectators of gladiatorial combat (as discussed below). That staple of team sports films, the locker room motivational talk by the coach, is aired on several occasions as an opportunity to connect homespun philosophies of sport and life. The climactic moment, as in virtually every sports film that relies on substantial on-field action, is an improbable, heart-stopping victory that saves the team and reconciles its principal antagonists. *Any Given Sunday* is, above all, acutely aware of the crucial importance of the media to sport, scanning the communicative infrastructure (including a cameo by the director as a drunken sports commentator!) almost as closely as it covers the sporting action on the field and the power plays off it. At various points in the film, there are arguments about the on-field tactics and personnel likely to be most favoured by the audience, especially the vast TV spectatorship. The team's economic dependency on television is recognized, with its poor performance threatening its viability because, as is pointed out, 'Without the playoffs there's no more TV money'. *Any Given Sunday* is, then, a quintessentially American sports film in the tradition of *Field of Dreams* and *Jerry Maguire*, both attracted to, and horrified by, the culture that it has produced and reveals.

Sports films, it has been shown, tend to be characterized by a strongly articulated national cultural identity. *Bend It Like Beckham* (2002) is, then, as English (more specifically than British, although there is no English nation as such) a film as *Any Given Sunday* is American. Gurinder Chadha's film is principally from the perspective of British citizens whose origins and continuing cultural reference points are in the Indian sub-continent, a form of contemporary Englishness that has caused some discomfort to those adhering to a traditional, white model of identity, even 'a sense of crisis and dislocation' (Maguire 1999: 203). *Bend It Like Beckham* is concerned with the aforementioned popularity of the England and then Manchester United (now Real Maddrid) footballer and with a desire to emulate him, but with the twist that the person who wishes to be and 'bend it' like Beckham (a reference to his famed ability to swerve the football around the obstacle of the human walls that are built in soccer matches to protect the goal from free kicks) is a young girl of East African origin (presumably one whose family was expelled by the late Uganda dictator Idi Amin) living in west London, Jesminder 'Jess' Bhamra (played by Paminder Nagra). The film examines the clash of various cultures, especially as they relate to ethnicity and gender, with Jess trying to pursue her sporting ambitions in the face of opposition from her traditional Sikh family. In the process she establishes a friendship with the girl who recruited her to the Hounslow Harriers, Jules (Keira Knightley), whose 'tomboy' appearance and lack of interest in teenage boys, and some misinterpreted encounters with Jess, leads her mother to believe, erroneously, that she is a lesbian. Problems of cultural exchange, co-existence and integration are compounded on a personal level by romantic rivalry between Jess and Jules for the affections of their coach, Joe (Jonathan Rhys Meyers). Predictably, Jess scores a dramatic winning goal in a final by bending a free kick around a wall, which, in her mind, consists of the women in her family who had tried to prevent her being there (her father assents to her, at the last moment, leaving her sister's wedding celebrations to play in the second half). Ultimately, there are multiple reconciliations, and both Jess and Jules leave for the USA on soccer scholarships, with Jess on the point of departure spotting Posh'n'Becks being hustled through Heathrow airport in celebrity fashion. Jess also asserts her independence from Joe, refusing to allow her feelings for him to prevent her from taking up the opportunity, and so striking a blow for autonomous, youthful feminism.

The film has various sub-themes, including the problematization of sexuality in women's sport (as Jules says, 'Mother, just because I wear trackies and play sport does not make me a lesbian') and *in loco parentis* responsibility of coaches (although sidestepping the controversial area of sexual harassment of female athletes by male coaches; see, for example, Brackenridge 1997). Jess and Joe's afflictions are compared and contrasted: her leg disfigured by burns and his career-ending knee injury; her problems with her parents and his unresolved anger towards his father; she suffering racial abuse on the field by being called a 'Paki', his experience, as an Irishman, of English hostility. Class differences are also glimpsed within the Punjabi community and in the consumerist tastelessness of Jules's hyper-feminine, lingerie-selling mother (played by Juliet Stevenson). But the grandest theme of the film is sport's (especially football's) capacity to reach across and challenge divisions of culture, ethnicity, gender and generation. In this regard, once more, the sports media are crucial, with the the film opening with a fantasy sequence of Jess, in her bedroom beneath a huge poster of Beckham, scoring a goal for Manchester United in a televised match from a cross by Beckham. She receives high praise from real-life BBC commentators Garry Lineker, John Barnes and Alan Hansen, until her mother is interviewed by them and claims that 'She's bringing shame on the family'. In Jess's daydream it is television that is shown to confirm her cultural status, the link between cultures that is also the benchmark of success. In the film's closing credits, it is noted that it was made 'With the participation of BSkyB and British Screen', a case of sports television allowing film to enhance its global profile. Michael Giardina (2003) is critical of the cultural politics of *Bend It Like Beckham*, arguing that it 'Effaces the everyday hardships and struggles of daily life in favour of a reformulated, faux progressive New Labour vision of race, gender, and class relations' (p. 78). It is certainly a 'feel good' film, in common with most of those already discussed. Sports films often show much human conflict and suffering, but they are usually resolved and assuaged in the denouément. *Bend It Like Beckham*'s genial, woman-centred multiculturalism may be oceans apart from the macho sensory assault of *Any Given Sunday*, but both films end in hugs and smiles and are testimonies to sport's symbolic healing power.

The association football boom in Britain has spawned new sports films like the rise–fall–rise narrative *Mean Machine* (2001), in which jailed former

England captain Danny Meehan, played by Vinnie Jones, redeems himself after 'throwing' a match and thus having, as one inmate complains, 'sold out his country'. The spoof documentary *Mike Bassett: England Manager* (2001) is the story of an incompetent lower league manager (played by Ricky Tomlinson) who gets the job only because better qualified candidates have been deterred from taking it by the ferocity of the English tabloid press. Soon, the tabloids call him 'The Most Hated Man in Britain', but after the mandatory unlikely win under pressure (which also occurs in *Mean Machine*) another declares 'Bassett's face found on a Shroud'. Cameos by Martin Bashir (noted most recently for his documentary on Michael Jackson) and legendary players Pele and Ronaldo enhance its comic realism. In the USA, sport and proto-sport are still popular subjects for film, including violent, futuristic treatments of gladiatorial com-petition in *Futuresport* (1998) and the remake of *Rollerball* (2001), in which the 'world's most dangerous game' is played out in post-Cold War 'Central Asia' (and in which *Any Given Sunday*'s LL Cool J also appears). Sports drama (often made for television) is a stock screen genre, with remakes like *Brian's Song* (2001), 'real life' fictional treatments like *Rudy* (1993) and 'gritty' narratives like *Varsity Blues* (1999) regularly telling the story of sportsmen triumphing against the odds (with the occasional sportswoman in such films as *A League of Their Own* (1992)). The sports film has a tendency to traverse the boundaries of the real and the mythic. During the presidency of Ronald Reagan, for example, he sometimes reprised his role as the heroic but tragic footballer George Gipp in *Knute Rockne, All American* (1940), calling on the citizenry to 'Win one for the Gipper'. Whether in fantasy or naturalistic form, the fictional sports film still finds a prominent place in the media sports cultural complex, linking live TV texts, journalism, biography and literature, and making it harder still to find cultural space free of sport.

Conclusion: 'there's always the sport'

The above discussion of sport in fictional film demonstrates its richness as a source of mythologies, allegories and narratives. The rise and fall of the 'standard' sports career lends itself particularly well to narrative film. In a short time-span there are exultant and despairing moments, with the inevitability of athletic decline and the likelihood of personal trauma offering many emotional possibilities to be exploited. The seeds of the filmic treatment of sport, however, are already present in sports television, which as argued earlier has an affinity with melodrama both in its presentation and reception. In sports films melodrama tends to be formative, while in live sports TV the action is taken as the material out of which melodrama can be made. This does not mean, however, that sports TV and film do not display some similarities and cannot produce hybridic texts. As shown earlier, *Any Given Sunday* follows the established tendency in sports TV to get ever closer to the action and uses the technology and technique of film to make the viewer feel, rather disconcertingly, that they are receiving the physical punishment meted out in gridiron games. Before it, Martin Scorcese's *Raging Bull* (1980) positioned the film spectator as the recipient of punches in the boxing ring, the sound of the crowd fading as if they had received the crushing blows to the head experienced by the real historical character Jake La Motta (played by Robert De Niro). In the epic film *Gladiator* (2000), director Ridley Scott uses contemporary protocols of sports television to represent the ancient 'sport' of gladiatorial combat. The modern sportsman–ancient gladiator parallel is also a common theme in sports film – the coach Tony D'Amato in *Any Given Sunday* is shown to be a devotee of the 'sword and sandal' epic film *Ben-Hur*, repeatedly watching Charlton Heston circle the Colosseum in a chariot. John Nelson, *Gladiator*'s senior visual effects advisor, reveals in a newspaper interview that:

> The gladiator sequences, which are at the heart of Scott's film, were shot to mimic the way modern-day sporting events are shown on television, Nelson said, to subliminally make them more real to today's audiences. There is, for example, the 'blimp shot', a favourite at the Super Bowl, in which the camera seems to float over the top of the massive Colosseum.
>
> There is even what the film-makers called their 'Wembley shot'. In every soccer event broadcast from Wembley Stadium in London, Nelson said, there has always been a shot from the uppermost rows looking down toward the stadium floor over a sea of raised arms, so *Gladiator* has this perspective, too.
>
> (Lyman 2000: 15)

Here film has borrowed some of the tricks of the sports television trade, but the latter has also deployed film technology, such as when CBS covered the 2001 Super Bowl using the EyeVision technology developed for the film *Matrix*, allowing '270-degree views of players, with stop-action shots from simultaneous angles' (Meacham 2001: 2). Despite such fusions of sports television and film, it is the cultural power of the former that has preoccupied cultural critics and business analysts alike. The academic canon on sports television that has been built up since the mid-1980s (including Rader 1984; Chandler 1988; Klatell and Marcus 1988; Barnett 1990; Wenner 1989, 1998; Whannel 1992) has reflected changes in society and culture that have been filtered through sports TV, as well as marking those trends in visual broadcast sport that have echoed across society and culture in a continuous feedback loop.

When we take into account all the other print and broadcast media sports texts, from documentaries to full-length feature films to radio commentaries and newspaper sports columns, sport's amoeba-like cultural capacity to divide and re-form is formidable. This dynamic, ever-changing quality of media sport has to be monitored constantly, and in the next, closing chapter we shall take a detour into a future showing urgent signs of waiting to be born. In 1970, Raymond Williams (1989: 95) opened a television column with the statement 'There's always the sport. Or so people say, more and more often, as they become sadder about what is happening to the rest of television'. Three decades later, it is necessary to ask whether sport on television is perhaps in decline and a source of angst rather than eternally buoyant and a relief from sadness.

Further reading

Barnett, S. (1990) *Games and Sets: The Changing Face of Sport on Television*. London: British Film Institute.

Bergan, R. (1982) *Sports in the Movies*. London: Proteus.

Bernstein, A. and Blain, N. (eds) (2003) *Sport, Media, Culture: Global and Local Dimensions*. London: Frank Cass.

de Moragas Spà, M., Rivenburgh, N.K. and Larson, J.F. (1995) *Television in the Olympics*. London: John Libbey.

Real, M. (1996) *Exploring Media Culture: A Guide*. Thousand Oaks, CA: Sage.

Whannel, G. (1992) *Fields in Vision: Television Sport and Cultural Transformation*. London: Routledge.

AFTERWORD: SPORT INTO THE ETHER(NET) – NEW TECHNOLOGIES, NEW CONSUMERS

Another subscriber model, equally well thought out in my view, is the ESPN site. Rather than simply repurposing its television content, ESPN enhanced and broadened the content offering. For the score-obsessed sports junkie, stats and scores are available on demand. No more having to tune in to all-news radio at fifteen minutes after the hour; no more phone calls to a 900 number droning on through an endless list of scores that the consumer might have no interest in at all. ESPN.com, by virtue of its interactivity, allows the consumer to get the information desired in the shortest possible time. On-line discussion areas on this same site further foster the building of a community around the ESPN brand.

(Michael J. Wolf 1999: 211)

Introduction: the coming of cybersport

One fear of every academic author is the instant obsolescence of their work occasioned by a sudden cultural or technological shift. In a dynamic area like media sport this is a reasonable concern, although we can have absolute confidence that, even with its recent decline in profitability, there will be more rather than less of it in the future. What we need to consider is not whether media sports texts will disappear or decline, but how their form, content and uses will change. The media will have to deal with transformations in sport (the rise of new sports and the decline of old ones) and sport must handle new media technologies that will provide, through digital compression and the like, not only many more sports TV channels, but also the opportunities for viewers to use interactive technologies and to design their own sports programming. The institutions of sport and media will also have to come to terms with changes in each other's administrative structures and patterns of ownership, and with new (perhaps supra) state policies on sport and media.

It is easy, in an orgy of technophilia, to imagine that new machines and capabilities will sweep away the old, but historical knowledge teaches that technological changes have been a constant feature of the media sports cultural complex, and that these are always moulded by social, cultural, economic and political factors. We have also learnt not to underestimate the importance of the sports media as a force within culture, or the wide-ranging repercussions of the cultural items that pass within and through the force field of sports texts and their associated meanings. The sports media are both an index of wider changes and an influence on them, part of the eternal dialectic of social production, reproduction and transformation. A brief update on the 'future present' of sports media will aid, finally, in an understanding of the direction, pace and nature of change in the media sports cultural complex.

From consumer to *auteur*

In most of the foregoing discussion it has been recognized that, whatever the uses, meanings and gratifications of media sports texts, the process has generally revolved around the acceptance or rejection of already created material for persons constructed as audiences by professional media organizations. I have already discussed (in Chapter 4) the use of existing print technologies to produce the amateur or semi-professional print sports texts called fanzines. Analogous activities can involve the video recording of sports contests for training and/or entertainment purposes, taking photographs for sale to team members and their families, phoning in sports reports and results of events not covered by the professional media to radio stations, as well as the perennial sports club newsletter (and not, of course, forgetting the formidable powers of the Zybrainic Sportswriter). New media technologies, however, aided by the intermeshing of telecommunications, computers and broadcasting (Wejbora 2003) and the 'key processes of digitization, convergence and interactivity' (Boyle and Haynes 2003: 96), expand the possibilities of cultural production into areas normally associated with consumption, enabling fans to produce their own custom-made texts out of the raw material supplied. The passive sports media consumer may become both all-powerful media *auteur* and athlete 'replicant'. As one men's magazine contributor (with a rather depressingly predictable focus) puts it:

> Imagine you're watching one of your favourite sports, like female mud wrestling. With the Internet, you'll be able to zoom in on a contestant,

bring up her statistics (including bust size), and even monitor her pulse and body temperature (so you know just how hot she is) . . . But the biggest advantage the Internet will offer is viewer shot selection. While we already have things such as race cam, you're at the mercy of the program director as to when it's shown.

With Internet broadcasting, however, you'll be able to choose which camera you want to look through at any one time, meaning that when a car crashes and burns during the Grand Prix, you will be able to look through the race cam to watch the medics arrive.

If that doesn't tickle your fancy, then there's set to be another development within the not too distant future – athlete cam. Thanks to miniature cams strapped to the athlete's body, you'll finally get close enough to the action to almost smell the sweat.

And when virtual reality arrives, you'll also be able to feel the blows of a hard tackle in a rugby match, provided both you and the footballer wear virtual reality bodysuits.

(Kaufman 1998: 139)

Using digital technology to be 'able to see the replay from any angle you so choose, or [you might want] to flip between two simultaneous matches' (Shipp, quoted in Austin 1998: 5) and to create the home virtual stadium, 'when anyone will be able to buy a headset and decoder and actually feel like they are part of the game' (Cockerill 1997: 52), combine the partial appropriation of the media technology once the preserve of media professionals with the simulation of the experience not only of attending sports events 'in the flesh' as spectators, but also of participating as 'cyber' athletes. Hence, we are taken well beyond the 'seeing at a distance' that (as noted in Chapter 6), Weber (1996) views as the characteristic feature of television. Paradoxically, the new media technology is artificially trying to produce the 'feel' of 'having been there' as participant or spectator long after television first lured sports players and fans away from stadia towards the armchair. Of course, only a tiny proportion of potential athletes and fans can ever be 'actors' in the unique space and time of actual sports events. Digital media technology, therefore, delivers 'actuality' in place of the impossible.

Less ambitiously, those same technologies feed the other huge appetites of followers of sport – for information and dialogue. Web sites like Soccernet receive approaching 100,000 'hits' a day (up to 800,000 during peak events), providing 'news and analysis of games in the English and Scottish leagues as well as World Cup pages, a soccer store, newsletter, spot the ball and indexes in Argentina, Chile, Colombia, The Netherlands, Spain and Uruguay' (Austin and Harper 1998: 4), and planning to 'introduce animated action replays – running a television image through software that converts it into a graphic representation of the game. It's the next best thing to television, and allows fans to replay match action again and again' (Hadfield, quoted in Austin and Harper 1998: 4). A cursory check in July 1998 through the Yahoo! search engine's UK and Ireland sites found 4271 categories and 14,591 sites devoted to sport. By April 2003, there were 126 densely organized 'Directory Category Matches' and almost 40 million 'Web Matches'. All major and many minor sports now have web sites dedicated to merchandising and marketing (among other functions), just as all major media organizations have online information services. As Tom Loosemore, a senior producer of BBC Online states:

> On the Web, the live is much less important than the nearly live – the real value is the Monday morning syndrome, when you come into work and catch up with the goals you missed at the weekend. The secret, in my opinion, is a comprehensive and up-to-the-minute news sports offering that gives you all the background that TV and radio can't give you, when *you* want it.
>
> (quoted in Austin and Harper 1998: 4)

This conception of the (mostly male) white-collar worker logging on in search of the latest sports news points to a future of ever more abundant and readily available media sports texts. Rather than, as is often the case, this being seen as a 'zero sum' game within and between media, as new forms inevitably supplant others, it is instead the co-existence and constant supplementation of the existing sports media. Assuming that saturation point is not reached – and on current indicators it seems far distant as sports fans absorb more media content and the media recruit more sports fans – the only likely outcome is maximal media sport, more minutely targeted. Women, for example, as was noted in Chapter 6, were once neglected by sports press and television. They are now watching some sports (like association football) and some events (like the Olympics) in very significant numbers, but there is certainly room to develop female audiences across the spectrum of sports. As discussed in Chapter 2, newspaper sports editors are also looking to expand their still modest female readerships. The latest media male and female audience frontier for sport is cyberspace. For the diminishing ranks of the sports-resistant global population, the only alternative, as implied in the Introduction, may be solitary confinement.

The Internet has enabled an extension not only of the ways by which the professional media can contact sports fans, but also of those same fans' opportunities to communicate with each other. Newsgroups like 'rec.sport.soccer' allow sports fans to debate issues like ground safety and the merits of different teams and players, while netzines operate as both sports forum and shrine.

Fans' web sites are particularly useful for non-elite sports clubs neglected by the mainstream media. For example, a devotee of Plymouth Argyle Football Club living in an alien location (London, perhaps, or Australia) may take comfort (if that is the word) every Monday morning during the soccer season in accessing 'www.argyle.org.uk'. Members of P@SOTI (Plymouth Argyle Supporters on the Internet) can also use its messageboard for information on how to get to matches, to comment on team performances, or for rudimentary political debates (such as occurred when one posted a link to a racist web site). The site can also be used to exchange information about media sport, such as when, in early 2003, a US-based supporter informed fellow fans in that country that they could watch the team live in an FA Cup match on Fox Sports World (the subsequent national humiliation described in Chapter 3 was, therefore, also international). It is such syntheses of the speed-fixated global and the stubbornly local that characterize the condition of postmodernity. Larger if less 'organic' sports teams like Manchester United, with its 'estimated global fan base of 20 million' (*Sydney Morning Herald* 2000: 39), are able to use their listed Internet arm manutd.com to communicate with merchandise purchasers in countries like India and Indonesia. The Internet can also be used to develop additional revenue streams through 'webcasting' of delayed and archived footage, although any impact on Manchester United's own pay TV service would have to be managed with care. With large media companies taking stakes (from strategic to controlling) in sports teams (such as Granada Media in Liverpool and Arsenal football clubs), and some clubs wanting to produce, sell and distribute even their primary media content (in the form of live television, media and sport convergence), it is advancing on several, simultaneous fronts. The profundity, pace and profitability of change may not have matched the optimistic predictions of the late 1990s, but there is no doubt that the sport and cyberworlds are more than passing acquaintances, and are in the process of becoming firm friends.

Many new developments in cybersport were caught up in the dot.com disaster that was, ironically, ushered in by the new millennium. The case of Quokkasports is instructive in coming to an appreciation of the distinction between the possible and the sustainable. In early 2000, the San Francisco-based, Nasdaq-listed company formed in 1996 was in the ascendant. As a pioneer of interactive spectator sports, it had 'blue chip' strategic investors (several of whom subsequently had their own severe problems) like Intel, TCI/Liberty, MediaOne, British Telecom and Hearst Communications. It managed the web site for the 2000 America's Cup yachting race (which registered over 800 million 'hits'); established partnerships with Major League Baseball, and the IOC and NBC on the 2000 Sydney Olympics, with contracts for successive Summer and Winter Games; had the interactive rights for various motor cycle, car and yacht races, and even for a Japanese climbing expedition on Mount Everest (Kennedy 2000: 33, 36). Quokkasports' commitment to sporting interactivity involved wiring competitors for words and pictures and, in the case of a round-the-world yacht race, allowed visitors to chart the progress of the craft and even to compete against them in a virtual race. The mountaineers' physiological data like heart rates were relayed alongside meteorological conditions in pursuit of what co-founder John Bertrand called ' "Immersive coverage. Many other sites do what we call horizontal coverage but we go for total immersion so you get the inner story" ' (Kennedy 2000: 33, 36). The inner story of sport, however, was subsumed by the outer story of media economics, and by the northern spring of 2001 Quokkasports had laid off most of its staff and filed for Chapter 11 bankruptcy protection, a victim of 'an online advertising drought and investor apathy' (Mariano and Olsen 2001). In this fate Quokkasports was not alone, with the sports sites Broadband Sports and Rivals.com closing, and CBS Sportsline at that time sacking sixty staff (Mariano and Olsen 2001). The naive belief that the cybereconomy is 'weightless' proved to be wishful thinking, as operations like Quokkasports, despite their innovative, interactive melding of television and the Internet in unlikely media sports like ocean-going yacht racing, went down with all hands, as did many other Internet sports companies like Sportal, which was bought in 2001 by UKBetting for just £2 (Gibson 2002c). Sports.com, the sports site supplying many other general sites with information and images, went into administration at just the moment that it was expected to flourish – the first day of the 2002 Korea/Japan World Cup. In analysing new media sport technologies, therefore, it is important not to become immersed in the conceptual environment that it creates, the intellectual equivalent of virtual reality where there are no reference points beyond the world created by helmet and gloves. The achievements and possibilities of media sport beyond broadcasting and print require sceptical appraisal. The continuing health of mega-media sports events like the World Cup and the Olympics has been clearly demonstrated in this book. If the post-broadcast era is yet to arrive, there are signs that new producer–text–consumer relations are emerging and so re-drawing various features of the media sport landscape.

Change to the organization and experience of media sport takes a variety of forms. It may involve new television devices or gadgets designed to enhance viewer information and pleasure, such as the adaptations of computer-game technology that create virtual representations of the trajectories of penalty kicks in rugby union ('AXA Angle') and the movement of the ball in cricket, tennis and baseball ('Hawk-Eye'). 'Tagging', the attachment of transmitters to athletes and even animals like horses and dogs, can produce 360-degree, three-dimensional models of sports contests (Timms 2002). There is a danger, though, that such hi-tech gadgetry will not please sports fans, some of whom 'believe we are fast approaching saturation point, where new toys distract from, rather than enhance, the viewer's experience' (Meacham 2001: 2). Sometimes this new technology may also fail to live up to its promise, as when EyeVision, developed by Carnegie Mellon Robotics for the film *Matrix* and then used for multi-camera, 270-degree TV coverage of the Super Bowl (see Chapter 6), 'was found wanting during the most critical period of the 2001 Superbowl, when a single camera angle was required' (p. 2).

Enhancing orthodox sports TV broadcasts, even where it allows viewer choice of camera and the capacity to call up data, is, however, less disruptive to the prevailing broadcast sport order than the use of the Internet as a broadcaster. For this reason, the IOC banned webcasting at the 2000 Sydney Olympics (and beyond; Boyle and Haynes 2003) out of fear of jeopardizing its expensively sold TV broadcast rights. However, it sold to WebMedia.com the much less in-demand worldwide Internet broadcasting rights and US TV rights to the Sydney 2000 Paralympics (Higgins 2000). Here an event that would not normally receive the close attention of broadcasters (four hours of the 1996 Atlanta Paralympics were broadcast in the USA, only 2 per cent of the coverage devoted to the Atlanta Olympics) can be disseminated to dispersed audiences via television and the Internet. As larger contracts come up for renewal, however, and organizational realignments take place involving television companies and Internet service providers, moving sports images will be received by additional means. In late 2002, AOL Time Warner and BT vied to pick up the lapsed rights to delayed coverage of the English Premier League before more comprehensive negotiations over the next round of Premier League rights (Gibson 2002b). The launch of new broadband sports networks can be seen to be putting considerable pressure on the traditional dominance of television in sport. For example, *Wisden*, the highly traditional cricket magazine (owned by the Getty family), went online in 2001, streaming the first live cricket match on a pay-per-view basis, while in early 2002 the media company Granada was the first to screen an English Premier League match on the Internet (again, as pay-per-view). Internet betting agencies are also substantial beneficiaries of the convergence of broadcasting and computing, and live webcasts of horse races from around the world are now common (Dodson 2002). As Boyle and Haynes (2003: 109–10) note, in 1999 Glasgow Celtic became the first British football club to provide live video coverage of a home match on its web site. With the BBC web site showing live coverage of a snooker tournament in early 2003, it can safely be expected that the Internet will produce more live, 'as live' and edited sport events.

The Internet is also unquestionably now a significant source of sports information. Aided by highly unfriendly time-zone deadlines for newspapers, the BBC web site had record traffic during the month of the 2002 World Cup, while:

> guardian.co.uk/football quadrupled its best-ever traffic. On one day it overtook the news front as the most popular site and provided us with a new one-day traffic record of more than 4m impressions. To put this in context, September 11 and 12 showed 2.4m and 2.7m page impressions respectively. In June we had 10 days with 2.8m or more page impressions.
>
> (Bell 2002)

Without having even to search the web, sports information services like Infostradasports send out regular emails to subscribers full of sports statistics and event previews. Other non-broadcast developments involve the cultivation of online sports 'communities' where web sites can provide information on events, players and products, but can also enable, for example, amateur golfers to take part in an online golf competition by filing their weekly scores to a web site (Johnston 2000). The short message service (SMS) technology that took off so spectacularly in the early twenty-first century in the wake of the mobile phone boom has been quickly harnessed to sports results, competitions, merchandising and advertising. Association football clubs like Arsenal and Manchester United have been quick to exploit the flexibility of mobile phones through, respectively, O2 and Vodafone (Carter 2002). As noted in Chapter 3, the more sophisticated mobile phones are now able to handle moving sports images, although television companies are highly resistant to live sports viewing of this kind (Wray 2003). Thus media sport can be seen to be much more than watching television, catching radio broadcasts and reading print texts. Virtually every new communication technology and service seeks a sporting application, because sport is universally seen as a key driver for their uptake. This means that media sport is hunting down customers at every breathing moment and in every conceivable space. The primary justifications for these developments in media sport are flexibility, interactivity, agency and empowerment. No sports fan need be out of range or constrained by faceless cultural producers making choices on their behalf on a 'one size fits all' basis. The customization of media sport and the enlistment of consumers as co-producers, therefore, can be interpreted within a post-Fordist framework of flexible and reflexive accumulation, production and consumption of cultural goods (Hall 1989; Lash and Urry 1994). It is also, paradoxically, both a sign of gathering globalization (each site is connected to every other) and something of a repudiation of it (the splintering of cultural practice). The key analytical response to these shifts, however, is that they do not necessarily represent a transformation of prevailing socio-cultural relations and their formations of power (Wejbora 2003); indeed, they may reinforce existing inequalities and promote new ones.

The driving force for most of the changes described above, no less than for the earlier structures and processes described in Chapter 3, has been the development of commercial markets rather than of cultural citizenship. This is an unsurprising conclusion in the context of advanced capitalism. But as was also argued in Chapter 3, marketized media that involve direct exchange create inequalities of access and use that limit the 'empowerment' of media consumers to those of sufficient means to purchase them. It is important, therefore, to go beyond the attractive 'pitch' for new media sport and to ask who will benefit from these innovations, and whether and how they might be made generally available (Rowe 2003). The much-cited precedent for new forms of media delivery – BSkyB's 'life' saving (for itself) capture of the English Premier League over a decade ago – is hardly an auspicious one in social justice terms. The politics of media content are also not rendered redundant by new, shiny devices and handy services. For example, Sagas *et al.* (2000) found in their US study of the Internet coverage of sport on selected web sites that they reproduced, rather than transcended, the entrenched gender inequality that characterizes more traditional media sport. Again, this is not surprising given that much of the flexibility of form and use described above involves the repackaging of sports content that originates in traditional media. Because a sports match is being watched on a mobile phone or a story read on a web site does not automatically block racist or ethnocentric stereotypes in commentary or overcome the neglect of the sports and sportspeople normally invisible in much traditional media sport. No corner of the media sports cultural complex, therefore, however freshly painted and enthusiastically touted, can be allowed to escape the critical eye of the cultural analyst.

Conclusion: look and learn

The excitable hype-speech that pours out of the purveyors of new media sports technologies (and not a few cultural analysts who trade in theories of 'the people's' effortless ideological autonomy, resistiveness and capacity for progressive textual decodings and uses) is perhaps counterbalanced by the rather pessimistic academic assessments of the influence of the media on sport. Stoddart (1994c: 280), for example, in reviewing the tendency of 'Many critics [to] regard television as the greatest of all change agents in twentieth century', judges (in the Australian context) that:

The overwhelming thrust of academic analysis of all this has been gloomy, to wit, that television has ruined sport. These findings represent a

misshapen view of what sport was like BT (before television), and an
assumption that Australian society (and its foreign counterparts) had produced a sports form in syncromesh with its broad social patterns. Those
assumptions are flawed seriously and will be redressed only by a full-scale
analysis of Australian sport's [and that of other countries'] historical
interaction with the media.

(Stoddart 1994c: 281)

It is, I think, reasonable to be critical of the *a priori* assumption of the malign
influence of the media on sport, and of the sports media on the wider culture
and society. What is incontestable is that media coverage – its presence or
absence – has had an incalculably large impact on sport, and that the sports
media are a key component of the fabric of contemporary culture. The current
recession in TV sport and the spectacular crash of technology companies in
March 2000 has demonstrated a hitherto largely unacknowledged vulnerability
of the media. As was discussed in Chapter 3, the impact on sport has been
shrinking broadcast revenues and somewhat retarded online development.
Historians like Stoddart are right to caution against grand generalizations
about how sport has been devoured by the media. Each sport has its own
distinctive history, its own way of negotiating how it is represented in the print
and broadcast media, just as individuals and social groups interpret and use the
sports media according to their own reading positions and relations within and
across texts and social institutions (over which they can, as socially produced
subjects, exert only limited control). But where sociologists (even those con-
vinced, like myself, of the importance of properly grounded historical analysis)
tend to part company with some historians is over the necessity of theorizing
social change and unravelling the connections between apparently disparate
social phenomena (Rowe and Lawrence 1998).

The contention of this book has been that media sports form is, indeed, to
a substantial (though by no means absolute) extent in 'syncromesh with its
broad social patterns'. Those broad social patterns are the major social structures (class, gender, racial/ethnic) and processes (capital and other forms of
accumulation, postmodernization, 'mediatization', globalization) that, once
apprehended, make it possible to distinguish between common or unique,
connected or distinct phenomena in sport, media and culture. As the book's
title suggests, the relationships between these two large institutions, the textual
outcomes of their union, and the vast universe of culture which makes them
and which they help make, do not obey 'iron' laws of cause and effect, supply
and demand. The unruly trinity of sport, culture and the media is not, like its
spiritual counterpart, three facets of the same, stable entity. Instead, it is a more
dynamic metaphor of contested power and protean forms.

There are undoubted dangers in 'mediacentricity', in exaggerating the power of the media over sport and over everything else that they touch (Blain 2003), as well as of the centrality of sport itself. The author might be said to have a certain vested interest in presenting an all-consuming picture of the wall-to-wall world of sport. But everyone is connected in some way to the media sports cultural complex – all those words and images spewing forth, all that money, technology and personnel set to work to give us more. The conclusion to the first edition of this book was written during the 1998 soccer World Cup Finals in France alongside a cumulative audience of 'an estimated 37 billion people worldwide' (Austin 1998: 4) and, like most of them, a long way from the action on the pitch. This conclusion is being written five years later, sandwiched between the 2002 Korea/Japan World Cup, the most watched event in the history of television (as noted in Chapter 3), and the 2004 Athens Olympics in the home of the Modern Games that will certainly seek to break that global TV viewing record. The cultural power of media sport is undiminished and, moreover, enhanced. In 1998, I pondered the sudden demonization of the sent-off David Beckham (now 'Posh Spite!' according to the tabloids), whereas now he is the much-worshipped subject of film, television and the press, he 'reigns in Spain', and academics are trying to explain the once resistible rise of Posh'n-'Becks. This is but one example of the speed and extent of change in the media sports cultural complex. But five years ago there were rumours of a new European soccer Super League that would further blur the boundaries of national cultures, and drugs scandals in athletics, swimming, rugby league, basketball and cycling (the 'Tour de Drugs!'). Here continuity rather than change can be stressed. There are still attempts to establish a European Super League, although a world club championship staged in Brazil in 2000 gave a glimpse of a deracinated future, with England's Manchester United withdrawing in that season from its domestic FA Cup, the oldest continuous football competition in the world. The spur, it seems, was one of sport's enduring features – institutional politics – in this case England's failed attempt to host the 2006 World Cup (Sugden and Tomlinson 1999: 180–1). There have been many sports drug scandals since, including one involving the leading Australian cricketer Shane Warne, who had to leave his teammates behind in South Africa and Zimbabwe during the 2003 World Cup of Cricket. Sometimes, then, the sheer, relentless presence and force of media sport feels like the cultural counterpart of a tsunami, and at others more closely resembles the predictable, warm flow of the jacuzzi. The corruption scandal that gripped the International Olympic Committee in 1999 may have saddened some of the more terminally naive sports romantics, but it provided fantastic quantities of front-page copy and 'shock horror' lead stories. There have been more outrages to consume the media's interest since, including the judging of some events during the 2002 Salt Lake

City Winter Olympics, and more scandals can be as safely anticipated as the next Enron-style corporate collapse. From all these cultural data there is no exit and the door is alarmed. By learning a little more about how media sport is set before us and what the media sports text can be made to mean, perhaps we can take back a little of the cultural power that we have ceded to it.

GLOSSARY OF KEY TERMS

Capitalism: the form of social and economic organization most consistently associated with the pursuit of private wealth; the defence of private property; the creation and exchange of commodities for profit; and the direct 'sale' by workers (the working class) of their 'labour power' to employers (the ruling class). Over the past two or three centuries of its existence, capitalism has gone through various stages. The current 'late' or 'advanced' phase of capitalism is characterized by marked shifts in class relations and identities linked to changes in the organization both of paid work in the 'public' world (such as the shift from manual to non-manual labour) and of unpaid work in the 'private' world (like the large-scale movement of women into the workplace and pressures for gender equality at home and at work).

Code: see **text**.

Commodification: the process by which people and things acquire value which enables them to be exchanged for profit. In sport, for example, amateur play and players have been turned into exchangeable services and products.

Communication: see **media**.

Culturalization: the process by which *culture* – the *signs*, symbols, meanings and values circulating within and between societies – has become increasingly central to the operation of all social institutions, including the political apparatus and economic structures (see *mediatization*).

Cultural economy: a term used to describe both the cultural industries (such as publishers, music companies and art galleries) and the manner in which forms of culture (like films, books, music, and even ideas and values) take on the appearance of ordinary commodities, with their value rising and falling according to critical reception, status, scarcity, public demand, and so on.

Discourse: the social and cultural framework of institutions and (often unacknowledged) assumptions that organize everyday language, thought and behaviour.
Because multiple discourses exist and are connected to structures of power, social
life is characterized by competition between discourses for legitimacy (for example,
monarchism versus republicanism) and, consequently, 'sovereignty' over groups in
society.

Fordism: the highly organized method of mass production typified by the assembly line
and reliant on a corresponding level of mass consumption of vast numbers of the
same product. Limited and more flexible production and greater product choice
that does not disturb this overall 'regime' is known as *neo-Fordism*. A substantial
change in the direction of small-batch production, rapid response to shifts in consumption patterns, and more discerning, demanding consumers is often described
as *post-Fordist*.

Genre: the recognizable and predictable qualities of *texts* (see below) which allow us to
classify them into types (for example, horror films, rap records and detective
novels), and so represent an implicit 'contract' between text producer and consumer. Smaller categories (such as different types of 'techno music') are known as
sub-genres.

Globalization: the much debated process through which constraints of time and space
are weakened by accelerated forms of economic, social, cultural, political and technological exchange. There is considerable disputation over the history, extent and
desirability of the globalization process and its relationship to other processes
such as *Americanization* and *localization*.

Ideology: the element of discourse that applies most directly to a group's interests. For
example, competing ideologies like 'the free market must decide' versus 'the market
must be controlled in the interests of everyone' are likely to reflect the degree of
benefit that individuals and groups can derive from the different arrangements for
distributing wealth that they promote.

Inter-textual: see **text**.

Media: all the organizations, large and small, through which pass various types of
message in the process of *communication* (by which meaning is exchanged).
The term is increasingly restricted to specialist organizations with the substantial
technology, knowledge, information and capital at their disposable to enable
large-scale or 'mass' communication.

Media sports cultural complex: a concept that embraces all the *media* and sports
organizations, processes, personnel, services, products and *texts* that combine to
create the broad, dynamic field of contemporary sports culture.

Mediatization: the extension of the influence of media into all spheres of social life in a
manner linked to the larger process of *culturalization* (see above).

Modernist: see **postmodernity**.

Myth: wide-ranging cultural beliefs and meanings that are usually so familiar that they appear to be natural, universal and eternal elements of society. Sport, which generates strong emotions, antagonisms, hierarchies and romantic ideals, is particularly prone to be *mythologized*.

Narrative: the outcome of the organization (or *narrativization*) of events which might be turned into a 'story', involving a plot, scenes, characters, narrators, and so on.

Neo-Fordism: see **Fordism**.

Political economy: an analytical approach that links socio-economic power (for example, ownership of a major newspaper chain) with politico-cultural power (such as the promotion of conservative values through the owner's newspapers or the shaping of newspaper stories by commercial rather than cultural or ethical considerations). The master concepts in *political economy* are *class* and *class conflict*, although there is often substantial departure from elements of *Marxism* that have often underpinned it (such as the inevitability of a proletarian revolution).

Post-Fordism: see **Fordism**.

Postmodernity: logically, the 'condition' that has superseded *modernity*, the rather imprecise term for societies that have undergone the process of *modernization* (which includes the development of industries and markets; political institutions that represent the citizenry; tolerance of dissenting opinion and different values, and so on), usually on the basis of a general belief in 'progress'. *Postmodernity* arrives after *modernity* has become 'exhausted' or begins to disintegrate under the weight of its own contradictions, which include the accelerating pace of global economic change, the fragmentation of social experience and identity, and a loss of faith in 'grand narratives' (like socialism, free enterprise and technological liberation). The more restricted terms *modernist* and *postmodernist* are applied to the cultural trends and *texts* (see below) of their respective epochs, although there is disagreement over the extent to which they might co-exist, and also over how they may reflect or affect the entire condition of society.

Sign: see **text**.

Sport: recreational and professional competitive, rule-governed physical activity. While physical play and game contests have clearly existed in many societies and epochs, sport of a regular and organized kind is the product of a *modernist* (see above) social institution with its origins in Victorian England.

Sub-genre: see **genre**.

Text: the outcome of a specific combination of elements (*signs*) which takes on or produces meanings (through the process of *signification*) governed by systematic rules (*codes*). The concept of *text* was once dominated by the written form, but it is now common to describe and analyse a wide variety of visual, musical and other textual forms. References to other texts or relations between *texts* are known as *inter-textual*.

REFERENCES

Althusser, L. (1971) *Lenin and Philosophy and Other Essays*. London: Monthly Review Press.

Amis, M. (1989) *London Fields*. London: Jonathan Cape.

Anderson, D. (1993) Cultural diversity on campus: a look at collegiate football coaches, *Journal of Sport and Social Issues*, 17(1): 61–6.

Andrews, D.L. (1996) Deconstructing Michael Jordan: reconstructing postindustrial America, *Sociology of Sport Journal*, 13(4): 315–18.

Andrews, D.L. (2004) Speaking the 'universal language of entertainment': News Corporation, culture and the global sport media economy, in D. Rowe (ed.) *Critical Readings: Sport, Culture and the Media*. Maidenhead: Open University Press.

Andrews, D.L. and Jackson, S.J. (eds) (2001) *Sport Stars: The Cultural Politics of Sporting Celebrity*. London: Routledge.

Ang, I. (1991) *Desperately Seeking the Audience*. London: Routledge.

Anon. (1992) Obituary: death of the Right Honourable Game Football, in I. Hamilton (ed.) *The Faber Book of Soccer*. London: Faber & Faber.

Appleton, G. (1995) The politics of sport and pay TV, *Australian Quarterly*, 67(1): 31–7.

Arlott, J. (1968) Untitled article, 11 September, in M. Engel (ed.) (1986) *The Guardian Book of Cricket*. Harmondsworth: Penguin.

Armstrong, K.L. (1999) Nike's communication with black audiences: a sociological analysis of advertising effectiveness via symbolic interactionism, *Journal of Sport & Social Issues*, 23(3): 266–86.

Attwood, A. (1998) Football crazy, *Sydney Morning Herald*, 17 January.

Austin, K. (1998) The main game, *Sydney Morning Herald – The Guide*, 8–14 June.

Austin, K. and Harper, C. (1998) Have a ball, *Sydney Morning Herald Icon*, 6 June.

Aymar, B. (ed.) (1994) *Men in Sports: Great Sport Stories of All Time, From the Greek Olympic Games to the American World Series*. New York: Crown Trade.

Baird, K. (1994) Attitudes of Australian women sports journalists, *Australian Studies in Journalism*, 3: 231–53.

Bairner, A. (2001) *Sport, Nationalism, and Globalization: European and North American Perspectives*. Albany, NY: State University of New York Press.

Baker, A. and Boyd, T. (eds) (1997) *Out of Bounds: Sports, Media, and the Politics of Identity*. Bloomington, IN: Indiana University Press.

Bakhtin, M. (1968) *Rabelais and His World*. Cambridge, MA: MIT Press.

Balnaves, M., O'Regan, T. and Sternberg, J. (eds) (2002) *Mobilising the Audience*. St Lucia, QLD: University of Queensland Press.

Barnes, S. (1989) *A Sportswriter's Year*. London: Heinemann.

Barnes, S. (2000) Seven days that sent tremors through SW19, *The Times*, 1 July.

Barnett, S. (1990) *Games and Sets: The Changing Face of Sport on Television*. London: British Film Institute.

Barry, D. (1992) Why the NBA isn't as offensive as you think, in T. McGuane (ed.) *The Best American Sports Writing 1992*. Boston, MA: Houghton Mifflin.

Barthes, R. (1973 [1957]) *Mythologies*. London: Paladin.

Barthes, R. (1977) The rhetoric of the image, in *Image-Music-Text*. London: Fontana.

Barthes, R. (1978) *A Lover's Discourse*. New York: Hill & Wang.

Baudrillard, J. (1981) *For a Critique of the Political Economy of the Sign*. St Louis, MO: Telos.

Baudrillard, J. (1983) *Simulations*. New York: Semiotext(e).

BBC (2001) *Annual Report and Accounts 2000/2001* (www.bbc.org.uk).

Becker, K. (1992) Photojournalism and the tabloid press, in P. Dahlgren and C. Sparks (eds) *Journalism and Popular Culture*. London: Sage.

Bell, E. (2002) It's a funny old game, *MediaGuardian*, 1 July.

Bell, J.B. (1987) *To Play the Game: An Analysis of Sports*. New Brunswick, NJ: Transaction.

Benedict, J. (1997) *Public Heroes, Private Felons: Athletes and Crimes Against Women*. Boston, MA: Northeastern University Press.

Bennett, T. (1998) *Culture: A Reformer's Science*. Sydney, NSW: Allen & Unwin.

Bennett, T. *et al.* (1977) *Mass Communication as a Social Force in History* (DE353 – Unit 2). Milton Keynes: Open University Press.

Bergan, R. (1982) *Sports in the Movies*. London: Proteus.

Bernstein, A. (2000) 'Things you can see from there you can't see from here': globalization, media, and the Olympics, *Journal of Sport & Social Issues*, 24(4): 351–69.

Bernstein, A. (2003) Meeting the industry: an interview with Alex Gilady, in A. Bernstein and N. Blain (eds) *Sport, Media, Culture: Global and Local Dimensions*. London: Frank Cass.

Bernstein, A. and Blain, N. (eds) (2003) *Sport, Media, Culture: Global and Local Dimensions*. London: Frank Cass.

Birrell, S. and McDonald, M.G. (eds) (2000) *Reading Sport: Critical Essays on Power and Representation*. Boston, MA: Northeastern University Press.

Bittner, J.R. (1983) *Mass Communication: An Introduction*, 3rd edn. Englewood Cliffs, NJ: Prentice-Hall.

Blain, N. (2003) Beyond 'media culture': sport as dispersed symbolic activity, in A. Bernstein and N. Blain (eds) *Sport, Media, Culture: Global and Local Dimensions*. London: Frank Cass.

Blain, N. and Boyle, R. (1998) Sport as real life: media sport and culture, in A. Briggs and P. Cobley (eds) *The Media: An Introduction*. Harlow: Longman.

Bloom, J. (2000) *To Show What an Indian Can Do: Sports at Native American Boarding Schools*. Minneapolis, MN: University of Minnesota Press.

Blue, A. (1987) *Grace Under Pressure: The Emergence of Women in Sport*. London: Sidgwick & Jackson.

Boreham, T. and Pegler, T. (1998) Idlers deny industry a sporting chance, *The Australian*, 4 March.

Bourdieu, P. (1978) Sport and social class, *Social Science Information*, 17(6): 819–40.

Boutilier, M.A. and SanGiovanni, L. (1983) *The Sporting Woman*. Champaign, IL: Human Kinetics.

Boyd, T. (1997) The day the niggaz took over: basketball, commodity culture, and black masculinity, in A. Baker and T. Boyd (eds) *Sports, Media, and the Politics of Identity*. Bloomington, IN: Indiana University Press.

Boyle, R. and Haynes, R. (2000) *Power Play: Sport, the Media & Popular Culture*. Harlow: Pearson Education.

Boyle, R. and Haynes, R. (2003) New media sport, in A. Bernstein and N. Blain (eds) *Sport, Media, Culture: Global and Local Dimensions*. London: Frank Cass.

Bracewell, M. (1997) *England is Mine: Pop Life in Albion from Wilde to Goldie*. London: HarperCollins.

Brackenridge, C. (1997) 'He owned me basically': women's experience of sexual abuse in sport, *International Review for the Sociology of Sport*, 32(2): 115–30.

Brierley, S. (1998) Advertising and the new media environment, in A. Briggs and P. Cobley (eds) *The Media: An Introduction*. Harlow: Longman.

Brohm, J.M. (1978 [1976]) *Sport: A Prison of Measured Time*. London: Pluto.

Brookes, R. (2002) *Representing Sport*. London: Arnold.

Brooks, P. (1976) *The Melodramatic Imagination: Balzac, Henry James, Melodrama, and the Mode of Excess*. New Haven, CT: Yale University Press.

Brown, A. and Walsh, A. (1999) *Not for Sale: Manchester United, Murdoch and the Defeat of BSkyB*. London: Mainstream.

Brown, P. (1996) Gender, sport and the media: an investigation into coverage of women's sport in the *Newcastle Herald* and the *Sydney Morning Herald*. Unpublished doctoral dissertation, University of Newcastle, Newcastle, NSW.

Brown, P. and Rowe, D. (1998) The coming of the leisure society? Leisure time use in contemporary Australia, in D. Rowe and G. Lawrence (eds) *Tourism, Leisure, Sport: Critical Perspectives*. Melbourne, VIC: Cambridge University Press.

Bunn, R. (1999) 'The inflationary spiral in the cost of TV transmission rights', Interview in *Diffusion EBU*, Winter, pp. 4–7.

Capling, A. (2001) *Australia and the Global Trade System*. Melbourne, VIC: Melbourne University Press.

Cardus, N. (1926) Kent v. Lancashire, 1, 2 and 3 July, in M. Engel (ed.) (1986) *The Guardian Book of Cricket*. Harmondsworth: Penguin.

Carlson, M. (1996) *Performance: A Critical Introduction*. London: Routledge.

Carlton and United Breweries Best Australian Sports Writing and Photography 1996 (1996) Melbourne, VIC: Heinemann.

Carrington, B. (2001) Postmodern blackness and the celebrity sports star: Ian Wright, 'race' and English identity, in D.L. Andrews and S.J. Jackson (eds) *Sport Stars: The Cultural Politics of Sporting Celebrity*. London: Routledge.

Carrington, B. and McDonald, I. (eds) (2001) *'Race', Sport and British Society*. London: Routledge.

Carter, M. (2002) Match of the day, *MediaGuardian*, 12 August.

Cashman, R. (1994) Cricket, in W. Vamplew and B. Stoddart (eds) *Sport in Australia: A Social History*. Melbourne, VIC: Cambridge University Press.

Cashman, R. and Hughes, A. (1998) Sydney 2000: cargo cult of Australian sport?, in D. Rowe and G. Lawrence (eds) *Tourism, Leisure, Sport: Critical Perspectives*. Melbourne, VIC: Cambridge University Press.

Cashmore, E. (2000) *Making Sense of Sport*, 3rd edn. London: Routledge.

Cashmore, E. (2002) *Beckham*. Cambridge: Polity.

Chandler, J.M. (1988) *Television and National Sport: The United States and Britain*. Urbana, IL: University of Illinois Press.

Chenoweth, N. and O'Riordan, B. (2002) The sick business of sport, *Australian Financial Review*, 4 June.

Chibnall, S. (1977) *Law and Order News*. London: Tavistock.

Chippindale, P. and Horrie, C. (1990) *Stick It Up Your Punter! The Rise and Fall of the Sun*. London: Heinemann.

Chomsky, N. (1989) *Necessary Illusions*. Boston, MA: South End Press.

Clarke, J. and Critcher, C. (1985) *The Devil Makes Work: Leisure in Capitalist Britain*. London: Macmillan.

Cockerill, M. (1997) The great sport hijack, *Sydney Morning Herald Sport*, 15 February.

Cohen, S. (1980 [1972]) *Folk Devils and Moral Panics: The Making of Mods and Rockers*. Oxford: Martin Robertson.

Cohen, S. and Taylor, L. (1976) *Escape Attempts: The Theory and Practice of Everyday Life*. London: Allen Lane.

Cohen, S. and Young, J. (1973) *The Manufacture of News: Deviance, Social Problems and the Mass Media*. London: Constable.

Coleman, N. and Hornby, N. (eds) (1996) *The Picador Book of Sportswriting*. London: Picador.

Collodi, C. (1911) *Pinocchio: The Story of a Puppet*. London: J.M. Dent.

Combe, C. (1997) Structural change in the UK broadcasting industry during the 1990's. Unpublished paper, University of Westminster, London.

Comisky, P., Bryant, J. and Zillman, D. (1977) Commentary as a substitute for action, *Journal of Communication*, 27: 150–3.

Connell, R.W. (1987) *Gender and Power*. Sydney, NSW: Allen & Unwin.

Correy, S. (1995) Who plays on pay?, *Media Information Australia*, 75: 80–2.

Cosmopolitan (1999) Sporting bodies 2000, December.

Coulson, A. (1998) Our love, *The Sun*, 26 January.

Cramer, J.A. (1994) Conversations with women sports journalists, in P.J. Creedon (ed.) *Women, Media and Sport: Challenging Gender Values*. Thousand Oaks, CA: Sage.

Creedon, P.J. (1994a) Women in toyland: a look at women in American newspaper sports journalism, in P.J. Creedon (ed.) *Women, Media and Sport: Challenging Gender Values*. Thousand Oaks, CA: Sage.

Creedon, P.J. (1994b) From whalebone to spandex: women and sports journalism in American magazines, photography and broadcasting, in P.J. Creedon (ed.) *Women, Media and Sport: Challenging Gender Values*. Thousand Oaks, CA: Sage.

Critcher, C. (1987) Media spectacles: sport and mass communication, in A. Cashdan and M. Jordin (eds) *Studies in Communication*. Oxford: Basil Blackwell.

Critcher, C. (1993) In praise of self abuse, in C. Brackenridge (ed.) *Body Matters: Leisure Images and Lifestyles*. Eastbourne: Leisure Studies Association.

Crook, S., Pakulski, J. and Waters, M. (1992) *Postmodernization: Change in Advanced Society*. London: Sage.

Crosswhite, J. (1996) Pay TV and its impact on women's sport, in R. Lynch, I. McDonnell, S. Thompson and K. Toohey (eds) *Sport and Pay TV: Strategies for Success*. Sydney, NSW: School of Leisure and Tourism Studies, University of Technology, Sydney.

Cunningham, S. (1992) *Framing Culture: Criticism and Policy in Australia*. Sydney, NSW: Allen & Unwin.

Cunningham, S. and Jacka, E. (1996) *Australian Television and International Mediascapes*. Cambridge: Cambridge University Press.

Cunningham, S. and Miller, T. (with Rowe, D.) (1994) *Contemporary Australian Television*. Sydney, NSW: University of New South Wales Press.

Curran, J. (1981a) The struggle for a free press, in J. Curran and J. Seaton (eds) *Power Without Responsibility: The Press and Broadcasting in Britain*, 4th edn. London: Fontana.

Curran, J. (1981b) The industrialisation of the press, in J. Curran and J. Seaton (eds) *Power Without Responsibility: The Press and Broadcasting in Britain*, 4th edn. London: Fontana.

Curran, J. (1998) Newspapers: beyond political economy, in A. Briggs and P. Cobley (eds) *The Media: An Introduction*. Harlow: Longman.

Curry, J. (1998) Posada wants career to enter present tense, *New York Times Sports Wednesday*, 28 January.

Dandaneau, S.P. (2001) *Taking It Big: Developing Sociological Consciousness in Postmodern Times*. Thousand Oaks, CA: Pine Forge.

Davis, L.A. (1997) *The Swimsuit Issue and Sport: Hegemonic Masculinity in Sports Illustrated*. Albany, NY: State University of New York Press.

Davis, T. (1995) The practice of gossip, in P. van Toorn and D. English (eds) *Speaking Positions: Aboriginality, Gender and Ethnicity in Australian Cultural Studies*. Melbourne, VIC: Victoria University of Technology.

Dayan, D. and Katz, E. (1992) *Media Events: The Live Broadcasting of History*. Cambridge, MA: Harvard University Press.

DeLillo, D. (1997) *Underworld*. New York: Scribner.

de Moragas Spà, M., Rivenburgh, N.K. and Larson, J.F. (1995) *Television in the Olympics*. London: John Libbey.

Denison, J. and Markula, P. (eds) (2003) '*Moving Writing': Crafting Movement in Sport Research*. New York: Peter Lang.

Diamond, J. (1994) Match of the day, every day, *The Guardian*, 11 April.

Dodson, S. (2002) The net's £300m bet, *MediaGuardian*, 4 February.

Duncan, M.C. (1990) Sports photographs and sexual difference: images of women and men in the 1984 and 1988 Olympic Games, *Sociology of Sport Journal*, 7(1): 22–43.

Duncan, M.C. (1994) The politics of women's body images and practices: Foucault, the panopticon, and *Shape* magazine, *Journal of Sport & Social Issues*, 18(1): 48–65.

Duncan, M.C., Messner, M. and Williams, L. (1991) *Coverage of Women's Sport in Four Daily Newspapers*. Los Angeles, CA: Amateur Athletic Foundation of Los Angeles.

Dunn, R.G. (1998) *Identity Crises: A Social Critique of Postmodernity*. Minneapolis, MN: University of Minnesota Press.

Dunning, E. (1999) *Sport Matters: Sociological Studies of Sport, Violence and Civilization*. London: Routledge.

Durkheim, E. (1960 [1893]) *The Division of Labour in Society*. Glencoe, IL: Free Press.

Dutton, K.R. (1995) *The Perfectible Body: The Western Ideal of Physical Development*. Sydney, NSW: Allen & Unwin.

Dworkin, S.L. and Wachs, F.L. (2000) 'Disciplining the body': HIV-positive male athletes, media surveillance, and the policing of sexuality, in S. Birrell and M.G. McDonald (eds) *Reading Sport: Critical Essays on Power and Representation*. Boston, MA: Northeastern University Press.

Dyer, G. (1982) *Advertising as Communication*. London: Methuen.

Eagleton, T. (1989) *The Ideology of the Aesthetic*. Oxford: Basil Blackwell.

Eckersley, O. and Benton, N. (2002) The venue versus the lounge room, *Australasian Leisure Management*, 35: 20–3.

Eco, U. (1986) Sports chatter, in *Travels in Hyperreality*. New York: Harcourt Brace Jovanovich.

Eichberg, H. (1998) *Body Cultures: Essays on Sport, Space and Identity* (J. Bale and C. Philo, eds). London: Routledge.

Elias, N. (1986a) The genesis of sport as a sociological problem, in N. Elias and E. Dunning, *Quest for Excitement: Sport and Leisure in the Civilising Process*. Oxford: Basil Blackwell.

Elias, N. (1986b) An essay on sport and violence, in N. Elias and E. Dunning, *Quest for Excitement: Sport and Leisure in the Civilising Process*. Oxford: Basil Blackwell.

Elias, N. (1986c) Introduction, in N. Elias and E. Dunning, *Quest for Excitement: Sport and Leisure in the Civilising Process*. Oxford: Basil Blackwell.

Elias, N. and Dunning, E. (1986a) *Quest for Excitement: Sport and Leisure in the Civilising Process*. Oxford: Basil Blackwell.

Elias, N. and Dunning, E. (1986b) Folk football in medieval and early modern Britain, in *Quest for Excitement: Sport and Leisure in the Civilising Process*. Oxford: Basil Blackwell.

Ellis, R. (1997) Albion want Royle, *Daily Star*, 18 December.

Engel, M. (1986) Introduction, in M. Engel (ed.) *The Guardian Book of Cricket*. Harmondsworth: Penguin.

Enzensberger, H.M. (1976) *Raids and Reconstructions*. London: Pluto.

Enzensberger, H.M. (1994) *Civil Wars: From L.A. to Bosnia*. New York: The New Press.

Errington, C. (2002) 'Go out and spend it . . .', *Evening Herald*, 7 January.

Errington, C. (2003) Argyle cut by daggers, *Evening Herald*, 15 January.

Evans, K. (2001) Commodified bodies: sport, image and gender. Unpublished Masters thesis, Monash University, Australia.

Falk, P. (1994) *The Consuming Body*. London: Sage.

Farred, G. (2000) Cool as the other side of the pillow: how ESPN's *Sportscenter* has changed television sports talk, *Journal of Sport & Social Issues*, 24(2): 96–117.

Farred, G. (2001) TV's time's up: the forgotten Games, *Journal of Sport & Social Issues*, 25(1): 3–5.

FIFA (2002) 41,100 hours of 2002 FIFA World Cup TV coverage in 213 countries, *Press Release*, 21 November.

Fiske, J. (1982) *Introduction to Communication Studies*. London: Methuen.

Fiske, J. (1983) Cricket/TV/culture, *Metro*, 62: 21–6.

Fiske, J. (1989a) *Understanding Popular Culture*. Boston, MA: Unwin Hyman.

Fiske, J. (1989b) *Reading the Popular*. Boston, MA: Unwin Hyman.

Foley, D. (1992) Making the familiar strange: writing critical sports narratives, *Sociology of Sport Journal*, 9(1): 36–47.

Fotheringham, R. (1992) *Sport in Australian Drama*. Melbourne, VIC: Cambridge University Press.

Foucault, M. (1979) *Discipline and Punish: The Birth of the Prison*. New York: Vintage.

Foucault, M. (1980) *Power/Knowledge: Selected Interviews and Other Writings, 1972–1977* (C. Gordon, ed.). New York: Pantheon.

Freeman, P. (1997) *Ian Roberts: Finding Out*. Sydney, NSW: Random House.

Fujiwara, Y. (2003) World Cup: the lessons, *European Broadcasting Union Diffusion Sport Dossier*, January, pp. 24–5.

Galtung, J. and Ruge, M.H. (1970) The structure of foreign news, in J. Tunstall (ed.) *Media Sociology: A Reader*. London: Constable.

Galtung, J. and Ruge, M.H. (1973) Structuring and selecting news, in S. Cohen and J. Young (eds) *The Manufacture of News*. London: Constable.

Gardner, S. (1998) Football shares hit fever pitch, *The Sunday Times Money*, 13 September.

Garrison, B. and Salwen, M. (1989) Newspaper sports journalists: a profile of the 'profession', *Journal of Sport & Social Issues*, 13(2): 57–68.

Garrison, B. and Salwen, M. (1994) Sports journalists assess their work: their place in the profession, *Newspaper Research Journal*, 15(2): 37–49.

Gellner, E. (1983) *Nations and Nationalism*. Oxford: Blackwell.

Giardina, M.D. (2003) 'Bending It Like Beckham' in the global popular: stylish hybridity, performativity, and the politics of representation, *Journal of Sport & Social Issues*, 27(1): 65–82.

Gibson, O. (2002a) Kirch stalls on BSkyB buy-back bid, *MediaGuardian*, 20 May.

Gibson, O. (2002b) Shoot-out over Premier League rights, *MediaGuardian*, 13 December.

Gibson, O. (2002c) BT to resurrect Sportal name, *MediaGuardian*, 22 November.

Giddens, A. (1991) *Modernity and Self Identity*. Cambridge: Polity.

Gildea, W. (1992) For Ali, greatness takes another form, in T. McGuane (ed.) *The Best American Sports Writing 1992*. Boston, MA: Houghton Mifflin.

Giulianotti, R. (1999) *Football: A Sociology of the Global Game*. Cambridge: Polity.

Given, J. (1995) Red, black, gold to Australia: Cathy Freeman and the flags, *Media Information Australia*, 75 (February): 46–56.

Goldie, K. (2002) Pectoral poseurs: gender and sexuality in *Gladiators*, in D. Hemphill and C. Symons (eds) *Gender, Sexuality and Sport: A Dangerous Mix*. Petersham, NSW: Walla Walla Press.

Golding, P. and Murdock, G. (1991, 2000) Culture, communications, and political economy, in J. Curran and M. Gurevitch (eds) *Mass Media and Society* (first and third editions). London: Edward Arnold.

Goldlust, J. (1987) *Playing for Keeps: Sport, the Media and Society*. Melbourne, VIC: Longman Cheshire.

Goodwin, P. (1998) *Television under the Tories: Broadcasting Policy 1979–1997*. London: British Film Institute.

Gordon, S. and Sibson, R. (1998) Global television: the Atlanta Olympics opening ceremony, in D. Rowe and G. Lawrence (eds) *Tourism, Leisure, Sport: Critical Perspectives*. Melbourne, VIC: Cambridge University Press.

Grainger, G. (1996) The Broadcasting Services Act 1992: present and future implications, in R. Lynch, I. McDonnell, S. Thompson and K. Toohey (eds) *Sport and Pay TV: Strategies for Success*. Sydney, NSW: School of Leisure and Tourism Studies, University of Technology, Sydney.

Gratton, R. (1999) The media, in R. Cashman and A. Hughes (eds) *Staging the Olympics: The Event and Its Impact*. Sydney, NSW: University of New South Wales Press.

Gruneau, R. and Whitson, D. (1993) *Hockey Night in Canada*. Toronto: Garamond.

Guttmann, A. (1978) *From Ritual to Record: The Nature of Modern Sports*. New York: Columbia University Press.

Guttmann, A. (1991) *Women's Sport: A History*. New York: Columbia University Press.

Guttmann, A. (1996) *The Erotic in Sports*. New York: Columbia University Press.

Guttmann, A. (2002) *The Olympics: A History of the Moden Games*, 2nd edn. Urbana, IL: University of Illinois Press.

Habermas, J. (1989) *The Structural Transformation of the Public Sphere*. Cambridge: Polity.

Hall, M.A. (1997) Feminist activism in sport: a comparative study of women's sport advocacy organizations, in A. Tomlinson (ed.) *Gender, Sport and Leisure: Continuities and Challenges*. Aachen: Meyer & Meyer Verlag.

Hall, S. (1989) The meaning of new times, in S. Hall and M. Jacques (eds) *New Times: The Changing Face of Politics in the 1990s*. London: Lawrence & Wishart.

Hamilton, I. (ed.) (1992) *The Faber Book of Soccer*. London: Faber & Faber.

Hanna, M. (1999) *Reconciliation in Olympism: Indigenous Culture in the Sydney Olympiad*. Petersham, NSW: Walla Walla Press.

Hargreaves, Jennifer (1993a) Gender on the sports agenda, in A. Ingham and J. Loy (eds) *Sport in Social Development: Traditions, Transitions and Transformations*. Champaign, IL: Human Kinetics.

Hargreaves, Jennifer (1993b) Bodies matter! Images of sport and female sexualisation, in C. Brackenridge (ed.) *Body Matters: Leisure Images and Lifestyles*. Eastbourne: Leisure Studies Association.

Hargreaves, Jennifer (1994) *Sporting Females: Critical Issues in the History and Sociology of Women's Sports*. London: Routledge.

Hargreaves, John (1982) Sport, culture and ideology, in Jennifer Hargreaves (ed.) *Sport, Culture and Ideology*. London: Routledge & Kegan Paul.

Hargreaves, John (1986) *Sport, Power and Culture*. Cambridge: Polity.

Harguem, A. (2003) The Arab example, *European Broadcasting Union Diffusion Sport Dossier*, January, pp. 20–3.

Harris, H. (1997) Tel 'broke rules': official, *Daily Mirror*, 27 March.

Harris, J. and Clayton, B. (2002) Femininity, masculinity, physicality and the English tabloid press: the case of Anna Kournikova, *International Review for the Sociology of Sport*, 37(3/4): 397–413.

Harris, K. (1988) What do we see when we watch the cricket?, *Social Alternatives*, 7(3): 65–70.

Harris, M. (1998) Sport in the newspapers before 1750: representations of cricket, class and commerce in the London press, *Media History*, 4(1): 19–28.

Harriss, I. (1990) Packer, cricket and postmodernism, in D. Rowe and G. Lawrence (eds) *Sport and Leisure: Trends in Australian Popular Culture*. Sydney, NSW: Harcourt Brace Jovanovich.

Hartley, J. (1982) *Understanding News*. London: Methuen.

Hartley, J. (1996) *Popular Reality: Journalism, Modernity, Popular Culture*. London: Arnold.

Harvey, D. (1989) *The Condition of Postmodernity: An Inquiry into the Conditions of Cultural Change*. Oxford: Basil Blackwell.

Haynes, R. (1995) *The Football Imagination: The Rise of Football Fanzine Culture*. Aldershot: Arena.

Heaven, P. and Rowe, D. (1990) Gender, sport and body image, in D. Rowe and G. Lawrence (eds) *Sport and Leisure: Trends in Australian Popular Culture*. Sydney, NSW: Harcourt Brace Jovanovich.

Hebdige, D. (1989) After the masses, in S. Hall and M. Jacques (eds) *New Times: The Changing Face of Politics in the 1990s*. London: Lawrence & Wishart.

Hemphill, D. and Symons, C. (eds) (2002) *Gender, Sexuality and Sport: A Dangerous Mix*. Petersham, NSW: Walla Walla Press.

Henningham, J. (1995) A profile of Australian sports journalists, *The ACHPER Healthy Lifestyles Journal*, 42(3): 13–17.

Herman, E.S. and Chomsky, N. (1988) *Manufacturing Consent: The Political Economy of the Mass Media*. New York: Pantheon.

Hesmondhalgh, D. (2002) *The Cultural Industries*. London: Sage.

Heywood, L. (2000) The girls of summer: social contexts for the 'Year of the Women' at the '96 Olympics, in K. Schaffer and S. Smith (eds) *The Olympics at the Millennium: Power, Politics, and the Games*. New Brunswick, NJ: Rutgers University Press.

Higgins, D. (2000) Web site ties up TV rights to Paralympics, *Sydney Morning Herald*, 7 August.

Higgs, C.T., Weiller, K.H. and Martin, S.B. (2003) Gender bias in the 1996 Olympics: a comparative analysis, *Journal of Sport & Social Issues*, 27(1): 52–64.

Hill, C. (1992) *Olympic Politics*. Manchester: Manchester University Press.

Hilliard, D.C. (1994) Televised sport and the (anti) sociological imagination, *Journal of Sport & Social Issues*, 18(1): 88–99.

Hirsch, P. (1971) Processing fads and fashions: an organization-set analysis of cultural industry systems, *American Journal of Sociology*, 17(4): 641–57.

Hirst, P. and Zeitlin, J. (eds) (1989) *Reversing Industrial Decline?* Oxford: Berg.

Holland, P. (1998) 'The direct appeal to the eye?' Photography and the twentieth-century press, in A. Briggs and P. Cobley (eds) *The Media: An Introduction*. Harlow: Longman.

Hornby, N. (1992) *Fever Pitch*. London: Victor Gollancz.

Huggins, T. (2003) Europe sees last of the big spenders, *Sydney Morning Herald*, 3 February.

Hughson, J. (1998) Is the carnival over? Soccer support and hooliganism in Australia, in D. Rowe and G. Lawrence (eds) *Tourism, Leisure, Sport: Critical Perspectives*. Melbourne, VIC: Cambridge University Press.

Ingham, A. and Loy, J. (1993) Introduction: sport studies through the lens of Raymond Williams, in A. Ingham and J. Loy (eds) *Sport in Social Development: Traditions, Transitions and Transformations*. Champaign, IL: Human Kinetics.

International Olympic Committee (2002) *Marketing Fact File* (www.multi-media.olympic.org/pdf/en_report.344.pdf).

International Review for the Sociology of Sport (1998) Review symposium, L.A. Davis, *The Swimsuit Issue and Sport*, 33(2): 189–203.

Jameson, F. (1984) Postmodernism: or the cultural logic of late capitalism, *New Left Review*, 146: 53–92.

Janowitz, M. (1968) The study of mass communication, in D. Sills (ed.) *International Encyclopaedia of the Social Sciences*, Vol. 2. London: Macmillan.

Jellie, D. (1998) Talking torque, *Sydney Morning Herald – The Guide*, 2–8 March.

Jennings, A. (1996) *The New Lords of the Rings: Olympic Corruption and How to Buy Gold Medals*. London: Simon & Schuster.

Jhally, S. (1989) Cultural studies and the sports/media complex, in L.A. Wenner (ed.) *Media, Sports and Society*. Newbury Park, CA: Sage.

Johnson, L. and Roediger, D. (2000) 'Hertz, don't it?' Becoming colorless and staying black in the crossover of O.J. Simpson, in S. Birrell and M.G. McDonald (eds) *Reading Sport: Critical Essay on Power and Representation*. Boston, MA: Northeastern University Press.

Johnston, L. (2000) Sport returns to the grass roots, *Sydney Morning Herald*, 13 March.

Kane, M. and Disch, L. (1993) Sexual violence and the male reproduction of power in the locker room: a case study of the Lisa Olson 'incident', *Sociology of Sport Journal*, 10(4): 331–52.

Kane, M. and Greendorfer, S. (1994) The media's role in accommodating and resisting stereotyped images of women in sport, in P.J. Creedon (ed.) *Women, Media and Sport: Challenging Gender Values*. Thousand Oaks, CA: Sage.

Kaufman, D. (1998) All angles covered, *Ralph*, June, p. 139.

Kellner, D. (1995) *Media Culture: Cultural Studies, Identity and Politics between the Modern and the Postmodern*. London: Routledge.

Kennedy, A. (2000) Cyber crewmen in America's Cup, *Sydney Morning Herald*, 7 February.

Kennedy, E. (2001) She wants to be a sledgehammer? Tennis femininities on British television, *Journal of Sport & Social Issues*, 25(1): 56–72.

Kerr, J. (1994) *Understanding Soccer Hooliganism*. Buckingham: Open University Press.

Kidd, B. (1982) Sport, dependency and the Canadian state, in H. Cantelon and R. Gruneau (eds) *Sport, Culture and the Modern State*. Toronto: University of Toronto Press.

Klatell, D. and Marcus, N. (1988) *Sports for Sale: Television, Money and the Fans*. New York: Oxford University Press.

Krane, V. and Waldron, J. (2000) The Gay Games: creating our own sports culture, in K. Schaffer and S. Smith (eds) *The Olympics at the Millennium: Power, Politics, and the Games*. New Brunswick, NJ: Rutgers University Press.

Kuper, S. (1994) *Football Against the Enemy*. London: Orion.

Lafrance, M. and Rail, G. (2001) Excursions into otherness: understanding Dennis Rodman and the limits of subversive agency, in D.L. Andrews and S.J. Jackson (eds) *Sport Stars: The Cultural Politics of Sporting Celebrity*. London: Routledge.

Larson, J.F. and Park, H.S. (1993) *Global Television and the Politics of the Seoul Olympics*. Boulder, CO: Westview Press.

Lash, S. and Urry, J. (1994) *Economies of Signs and Space*. London: Sage.

Law, A., Harvey, J. and Kemp, S. (2002) The global sport mass media oligopoly: the three usual suspects and more, *International Review for the Sociology of Sport*, 37(3/4): 279–302.

Leiss, W., Kline, S. and Jhally, S. (1990) *Social Communication in Advertising*, 2nd edn. London: Routledge.

Lenskyj, H.J. (2000) *Inside the Olympic Industry: Power, Politics, and Activism*. Albany, NY: State University of New York Press.

Lindsey, E. (2001) Notes from the sports desk: reflections on race, class and gender in British sports journalism, in B. Carrington and I. McDonald (eds) *'Race', Sport and British Society*. London: Routledge.

Lowes, M.D. (1997) Sports page: a case study in the manufacture of sports news for the daily press, *Sociology of Sport Journal*, 14(2): 143–59.

Lowes, M.D. (1999) *Inside the Sports Pages: Work Routines, Professional Ideologies and the Manufacture of Sports News*. Toronto: University of Toronto Press.

Lumpkin, A. and Williams, L.D. (1991) An analysis of *Sports Illustrated* feature articles, 1954–1987, *Sociology of Sport Journal*, 8: 1–15.

Lyman, R. (2000) Rome built the easy way, *Sydney Morning Herald*, 1 May.

Lynch, R. (1993) The cultural repositioning of rugby league football and its men, in A.J. Veal and B. Weiler (eds) *First Steps: Leisure and Tourism Research in Australia and New Zealand*. Leisure Research Series No. 1. Sydney, NSW: ANZALS.

Macdonald, K.M. (1995) *The Sociology of the Professions*. Thousand Oaks, CA: Sage.

MacNeill, M. (1998) Sports journalism, ethics and Olympic athletes' rights, in L.A. Wenner (ed.) *MediaSport*. London: Routledge.

Magee, J. (2002) Shifting balances of power in the new football economy, in J. Sugden and A. Tomlinson (eds) *Power Games: A Critical Sociology of Sport*. London: Routledge.

Magee, J. and Sugden, J. (2002) 'The world at their feet': professional football and international labour migration, *Journal of Sport & Social Issues*, 26(4): 421–37.

Maguire, J. (1990) More than a sporting touchdown: the making of American football in Britain 1982–1989, *Sociology of Sport Journal*, 7(3): 213–37.

Maguire, J. (1993) Globalization, sport development, and the media/sport production complex, *Sport Science Review*, 2(1): 29–47.

Maguire, J. (1999) *Global Sport: Identities, Societies, Civilizations*. Cambridge: Polity.

Maharaj, G. (1997) Talking trash: late capitalism, black (re)productivity, and professional basketball, *Social Text*, 50 (Spring): 97–110.

Maiden, M. (2002) Odds blow out on TV sports gamble, *Sydney Morning Herald*, 25 February.

Mariano, G. and Olsen, S. (2001) Quokka seeks refuge in bankruptcy court, *CNET News.com*, 27 April.

Markula, P. (2001) Beyond the perfect body: women's body image distortion in fitness magazine discourse, *Journal of Sport & Social Issues*, 25(2): 158–79.

Marquesee, M. (1999) *Redemption Song: Muhammad Ali and the Spirit of the Sixties*. London: Verso.

Martin, R. and Miller, T. (eds) (1999) *SportCult*. Minneapolis, MN: University of Minnesota Press.

Marx, K. (1967 [1867]) *Capital: A Critique of Political Economy, Vol. 1: A Critical Analysis of Capitalist Production*. New York: International Publishers.

Mason, D.S. (2002) 'Get the puck out of here!' Media transnationalism and Canadian identity, *Journal of Sport & Social Issues*, 26(2): 140–67.

May, N. (1984) *Gold! Gold! Gold! Norman May Looks at the Olympics*. Melbourne, VIC: Horwitz Grahame.

McCarthy, M. (2002) Bowl, Olympics compete for gold, *USA Today*, 31 January.

McCathie, A. (2002) Soccer stars see prices plummet, *Australian Financial Review*, 31 August.

McClure, G. (2003) The story that wasn't, *The Age Sporting Life*, 12 February.

McGimpsey, D. (2000) *Imagining Baseball: America's Pastime and Popular Culture*. Bloomington, IN: Indiana University Press.

McGovern, P. (2002) Globalization or internationalization? Foreign footballers in the English League, 1946–95, *Sociology*, 36(1): 23–42.

McGuane, T. (1992) Introduction, in T. McGuane (ed.) *The Best American Sports Writing 1992*. Boston, MA: Houghton Mifflin.

McGuire, M. (2003) Backflip puts pants back on Carey, *The Australian*, 11 February.

McHoul, A. (1997) On doing 'we's': where sport leaks into everyday life, *Journal of Sport & Social Issues*, 21(3): 315–20.

McKay, J. (1990) Sport, leisure and social inequality in Australia, in D. Rowe and G. Lawrence (eds) *Sport and Leisure: Trends in Australian Popular Culture*. Sydney, NSW: Harcourt Brace Jovanovich.

McKay, J. (1991) *No Pain, No Gain? Sport and Australian Culture*. Sydney, NSW: Prentice Hall.

McKay, J. (1992) Sport and the social construction of gender, in G. Lupton, T. Short and R. Whip (eds) *Society and Gender: An Introduction to Sociology*. Sydney, NSW: Macmillan.

McKay, J. (1995) 'Just do it': corporate sports slogans and the political economy of enlightened racism, *Discourse: Studies in the Cultural Politics of Education*, 16(2): 191–201.

McKay, J. (1997). *Managing Gender: Affirmative Action and Organizational Power in Australian, Canadian, and New Zealand Sport*. Albany, NY: State University of New York Press.

McKay, J. and Miller, T. (1991) From old boys to men and women of the corporation: the Americanization and commodification of Australian sport, *Sociology of Sport Journal*, 8(1): 86–94.

McKay, J. and Rowe, D. (1997) Field of soaps: Rupert v. Kerry as masculine melodrama, *Social Text*, 50(1): 69–86.

McKay, J. and Smith, P. (1995) Exonerating the hero: frames and narratives in media coverage of the O. J. Simpson story, *Media Information Australia*, 75: 57–66.

McQuail, D. (1987) *Mass Communication Theory: An Introduction*, 2nd edn. Newbury Park, CA: Sage.

Meacham, S. (2001) Too much of a good thing?, *Sydney Morning Herald – The Guide*, 25 June–1 July.

Meher-Homji, K. (2002) The drive to survive: veteran Waugh under siege but milestones await, *Sun Herald*, 22 December.

Mercer, K. (1992) Skin head sex thing: racial difference and the homoerotic imaginary, *New Formations*, 16 (Spring): 1–23.

Messner, M.A. (1992) *Power at Play: Sports and the Problem of Masculinity*. Boston, MA: Beacon Press.

Messner, M.A., Dunbar, M. and Hunt, D. (2000) The televised sports manhood formula, *Journal of Sport & Social Issues*, 24(4): 380–94.

Messner, M.A., Duncan, M.C. and Cooky, C. (2003) Silence, sports bras, and wrestling porn: women in televised sports news and highlights shows, *Journal of Sport & Social Issues*, 27(1): 38–51.

Millar, S. (1998) Courtship ends as soccer and TV are united, *The Guardian*, 7 September.

Miller, T. (1990) Sport, media and masculinity, in D. Rowe and G. Lawrence (eds) *Sport and Leisure: Trends in Australian Popular Culture*. Sydney, NSW: Harcourt Brace Jovanovich.

Miller, T. (1993) *The Well-Tempered Self: Citizenship, Culture, and the Postmodern Subject*. Baltimore, MD: Johns Hopkins University Press.

Miller, T. (1996) Film, in W. Vamplew, K. Moore, J. O'Hara, R. Cashman and I.F. Jobling (eds) *The Oxford Companion to Australian Sport*, 2nd edn. Melbourne, VIC: Oxford University Press.

Miller, T. (1997) '. . . the oblivion of the sociology of sport' (editorial), *Journal of Sport & Social Issues*, 21(2): 115–19.

Miller, T. (1998a) *Technologies of Truth: Cultural Citizenship and the Popular Media*. Minneapolis, MN: University of Minnesota Press.

Miller, T. (1998b) Hopeful signs? Arthur Ashe/working-class spectatorship (editorial), *Journal of Sport & Social Issues*, 22(1): 3–6.

Miller, T. (1998c) Scouting for boys: sport looks at men, in D. Rowe and G. Lawrence (eds) *Tourism, Leisure, Sport: Critical Perspectives*. Melbourne, VIC: Cambridge University Press.

Miller, T. (1999) Competing allegories, in R. Martin and T. Miller (eds) *SportCult*. Minneapolis, MN: University of Minnesota Press.

Miller, T. (2001) *Sportsex*. Philadelphia, PA: Temple University Press.

Miller, T., Lawrence, G., McKay, J. and Rowe, D. (2001) *Globalization and Sport: Playing the World*. London: Sage.

Miller, T., Rowe, D., Lawrence, G. and McKay, J. (2003) Globalization, the over-production of US sports, and the new international division of cultural labour, *International Review for the Sociology of Sport*, 38(4): 427–40.

Milmo, D. (2001) Kirch group scores with global World Cup TV rights, *MediaGuardian*, 16 July.

Milmo, D. (2002) Football cost too much, admits ITV, *MediaGuardian*, 27 November.

Modleski, T. (1983) The rhythms of reception, in E.A. Kaplan (ed.) *Regarding Television*. Los Angeles, CA: American Film Institute.

Moller, M. (2002) Reclaiming the game: rugby league, globalisation and masculinity. Unpublished doctoral dissertation, University of Sydney, Sydney, NSW.

Montgomery, M. (1986) *An Introduction to Language and Society*. London: Methuen.

Moore, D. (1996) Pay TV: the Confederation of Australian Sport perspective, in R. Lynch, I. McDonnell, S. Thompson and K. Toohey (eds) *Sport and Pay TV: Strategies for Success*. Sydney, NSW: School of Leisure and Tourism Studies, University of Technology, Sydney.

Moore, M. (1997) Seven's 2000 advantage, *Sydney Morning Herald – The Guide*, 9–15 June.

Morley, D. (1992) *Television, Audiences and Cultural Studies*. London: Routledge.

Mowbray, M. (1993) Sporting opportunity: equity in urban infrastructure and planning, in A.J. Veal and B. Weiler (eds) *First Steps: Leisure and Tourism Research in Australia and New Zealand*. Leisure Research Series No. 1. Sydney, NSW: ANZALS.

Murdock, G. (1992) Citizens, consumers, and public culture, in M. Skovmand and K.C. Schroder (eds) *Media Cultures: Reappraising Transnational Media*. London: Routledge.

Murdock, G. (1997) Base notes: the conditions of cultural practice', in M. Ferguson and P. Golding (eds) *Cultural Studies in Question*. London: Sage.

Murphy, D. (1976) *The Silent Watchdog: The Press in Local Politics*. London: Constable.

Nack, W. (1992) O unlucky man, in T. McGuane (ed.) *The Best American Sports Writing 1992*. Boston, MA: Houghton Mifflin.

Ndalianis, A. (1995) Muscle, excess and rupture: female bodybuilding and gender construction, *Media Information Australia*, 75 (February): 13–23.

Nisbet, R. (1967) *The Sociological Tradition*. London: Heinemann.

Norris, C. (1993) Old themes for new times: postmodernism, theory and cultural politics, in J. Squires (ed.) *Principled Positions: Postmodernism and the Rediscovery of Value*. London: Lawrence & Wishart.

Novak, M. (1976) *The Joy of Sport*. New York: Basic Books.

Nunn, S. and Rosentraub, M.S. (1997) Sports wars: suburbs and center cities in a zero-sum game, *Journal of Sport & Social Issues*, 21(1): 65–82.

O'Donnell, H. (1994) Mapping the mythical: a geopolitics of national sporting stereotypes, *Discourse and Society*, 4(3): 345–80.

Ono, K.A. (1997) 'America's' apple pie: baseball, Japan-bashing, and the sexual threat of economic miscegenation, in A. Baker and T. Boyd (eds) *Out of Bounds*. Bloomington, IN: Indiana University Press.

O'Regan, T. (1992) The international, the regional and the local: Hollywood's new and declining audiences, in E. Jacka (ed.) *Continental Shift: Globalisation and Culture*. Sydney, NSW: Local Consumption Publications.

Orwell, G. (1992 [1945]) The sporting spirit, in I. Hamilton (ed.) *The Faber Book of Soccer*. London: Faber & Faber.

Palmer, J. (1998) News values, in A. Briggs and P. Cobley (eds) *The Media: An Introduction*. Harlow: Longman.

Pedersen, P.M. (2002) Examining equity in newspaper photographs: a content analysis of the print media photographic coverage of interscholastic athletics, *International Review for the Sociology of Sport*, 37(3/4): 303–18.

Peterson, R. and Berger, D. (1975) Cycles in symbol production: the case of popular music, *American Sociological Review*, 40: 158–73.

Philo, G. (ed.) (1999) *Message Received: Glasgow Media Group Research 1993–1998*. Harlow: Addison Wesley Longman.

Pilger, J. (1998) *Hidden Agendas*. London: Vintage.

Pratchett, T. (1990) quoted in P. Cochrane, The end's nigh, but wait, *Sydney Morning Herald*, 17 August.

Preuss, H. (2000) *Economics of the Olympic Games: Hosting the Games 1972–2000*. Petersham, NSW: Walla Walla Press/Centre for Olympic Studies, University of New South Wales.

Pronger, B. (1990) *The Arena of Masculinity: Sport, Homosexuality, and the Meaning of Sex*. New York: St Martin's Press.

Rader, B. (1984) *In Its Own Image: How Television has Transformed Sports*. New York: Free Press.

Real, M. (1996) *Exploring Media Culture: A Guide*. Thousand Oaks, CA: Sage.

Real, M. (1998) MediaSport: technology and the commodification of postmodern sport, in L. Wenner (ed.) *MediaSport*. London: Routledge.

Redhead, S. (1991) *Football with Attitude*. Manchester: Wordsmith.

Reilly, R. and Stout, G. (eds) (2002) *The Best American Sports Writing 2002*. Boston, MA: Houghton Mifflin.

Richman, A. (1991) The death of sportswriting, *GQ*, September, pp. 254–61, 334–7.

Ridley, J. (2002) When Beckham scored with that penalty it was better than sex, *Daily Mirror*, 21 June.

Rinehart, R.E. (1998) *Players All: Performances in Contemporary Sport*. Bloomington, IN: Indiana University Press.

Rintala, J. and Birrell, S. (1984) Fair treatment for the active female: a content analysis of *Young Athlete* magazine, *Sociology of Sport Journal*, 1(3): 231–50.

Rivenburgh, N.K. (2003) The Olympic Games: twenty-first century challenges as a global media event, in A. Bernstein and N. Blain (eds) *Sport, Media Culture: Global and Local Dimensions*. London: Frank Cass.

Robbins, B. (1997) Head fake: mentorship and mobility in *Hoop Dreams*, *Social Text*, 50 (Spring): 111–20.

Robinson, S. (2002) Salacious allegations: culture, public relations and the sports scandal. Unpublished honours thesis, University of Newcastle, Newcastle, NSW.

Roche, M. (2000) *Mega-Events and Modernity: Olympics and Expos in the Growth of Global Culture*. London: Routledge.

Rodman, A. (with Scott, A.) (1997) *Worse than He Says He Is: White Girls Don't Bounce*. Los Angeles, CA: Dove.

Rodman, D. (with Keown, T.) (1996) *Bad As I Wanna Be*. New York: Bantam.

Rodman, D. (with Silver, M.) (1997) *Walk on the Wild Side*. New York: Bantam.

Rogers, E. (1993) Foreword, in J. Larson and H. Park, *Global Television and the Politics of the Seoul Olympics*. Boulder, CO: Westview Press.

Rojek, C. (1985) *Capitalism and Leisure Theory*. London: Tavistock.

Rose, A. and Friedman, J. (1997) Television sports as mas(s)culine cult of distraction, in A. Baker and T. Boyd (eds) *Out of Bounds*. Bloomington, IN: Indiana University Press.

Rowe, D. (1992) Modes of sports writing, in P. Dahlgren and C. Sparks (eds) *Journalism and Popular Culture*. London: Sage.

Rowe, D. (1995) *Popular Cultures: Rock Music, Sport and the Politics of Pleasure*. London: Sage.

Rowe, D. (1996) The global love-match: sport and television, *Media, Culture & Society*, 18(4): 565–82.

Rowe, D. (1997a) Apollo undone: the sports scandal, in J. Lull and S. Hinerman (eds) *Media Scandals: Morality and Desire in the Popular Culture Marketplace*. New York: Columbia University Press.

Rowe, D. (1997b) Rugby League in Australia: the Super League saga, *Journal of Sport & Social Issues*, 21(2): 221–6.

Rowe, D. (1997c) Big defence: sport and hegemonic masculinity, in A. Tomlinson (ed.) *Gender, Sport and Leisure: Continuities and Challenges*. Aachen: Meyer & Meyer Verlag.

Rowe, D. (1998) If you film it, will they come? Sports on film, *Journal of Sport & Social Issues*, 22(4): 350–9.

Rowe, D. (2000a) Cathy Freeman: live at Stadium Australia, 25 September 2000, *M/C Reviews Feature Issue on The Olympics*, 10(18): October (http://www.api-network.com/mc/).

Rowe, D. (2000b) Global media events and the positioning of presence, *Media International Australia incorporating Culture and Policy*, 97: 11–21.

Rowe, D. (2002) 'Public broadcasting: populist multiplex or edifying ghetto?', paper to *The Changing Meanings of Popular Culture for Public Broadcasting*, European Science Foundation Workshop, Amsterdam, June.

Rowe, D. (2003) Watching brief: cultural citizenship and viewing rights, *Culture, Sport, Society* (forthcoming).

Rowe, D. and Lawrence, G. (1998) Framing a critical sports sociology in the age of globalisation, in D. Rowe and G. Lawrence (eds) *Tourism, Leisure, Sport: Critical Perspectives*. Melbourne, VIC: Cambridge University Press.

Rowe, D. and McKay, J. (2003) Sport: still a man's game, in S. Tomsen and M. Donaldson (eds) *Male Trouble: Looking at Australian Masculinities*. Melbourne: Pluto.

Rowe, D. and Miller, T. (1999) Gays, in E. Cashmore (ed.) *Sports Culture: An A–Z*. London: Routledge.

Rowe, D. and Stevenson, D. (1995) Negotiations and mediations: journalism, professional status and the making of the sports text, *Media Information Australia*, 75: 67–79.

Rowe, D., Lawrence, G., Miller, T. and McKay, J. (1994) Global sport? Core concern and peripheral vision, *Media, Culture & Society*, 16(4): 661–75.

Rowe, D., McKay, J. and Miller, T. (1998) Come together: sport, nationalism and the media image, in L.A. Wenner (ed.) *MediaSport*. London: Routledge.

Rowe, D., McKay, J. and Miller, T. (2000) Panic sport and the racialized masculine body, in J. McKay, M. Messner and D. Sabo (eds) *Masculinities, Gender Relations, and Sport*. Thousand Oaks, CA: Sage.

Rubino, R. (2003) Funky football risks niche for TV exposure, *The Press Democrat*, 9 February.

Ruddock, A. (2001) *Understanding Audiences: Theory and Method*. London: Sage.

Sacks, H. (1992) in G. Jefferson (ed.) Vol. 1, *Lectures on Conversation* (2 vols). Oxford: Basil Blackwell.

Sagas, M., Cunningham, G.B., Wigley, B.J. and Ashley, F.B. (2000) Internet coverage of university softball and baseball web sites: the inequity continues, *Sociology of Sport Journal*, 17(2): 198–205.

Salwen, M. and Garrison, B. (1998) Finding their place in journalism: newspaper sports journalists' 'professional problems', *Journal of Sport & Social Issues*, 22(1): 88–102.

Sandomir, R. (2003) Good ratings for Arena League, *The New York Times*, 4 February.

Sargent, S.L., Zillmann, D. and Weaver III, J.B. (1998) The gender gap in the enjoyment of televised sports, *Journal of Sport & Social Issues*, 22(1): 46–64.

Sarris, A. (1980) Why sports movies don't work, *Film Comment*, 16(6): 49–53.

Schaffer, K. and Smith, S. (eds) (2000a) *The Olympics at the Millennium: Power, Politics, and the Games*. New Brunswick, NJ: Rutgers University Press.

Schaffer, K. and Smith, S. (2000b) The Olympics of the everyday, in K. Schaffer and S. Smith (eds) *The Olympics at the Millennium: Power, Politics, and the Games*. New Brunswick, NJ: Rutgers University Press.

Schlesinger, P. (1991) *Media, State and Nation: Political Violence and Collective Identities*. London: Sage.

Schudson, M. (1991) The sociology of news production revisited, in J. Curran and M. Gurevitch (eds) *Mass Media and Society*. London: Edward Arnold.

Schultz, J. (ed.) (1994) *Not Just Another Business: Journalists, Citizens and the Media*. Sydney, NSW: Pluto.

Seidman, S. (ed.) (1996) *Queer Theory/Sociology*. Oxford: Basil Blackwell.

Sekula, A. (1984) *Photography Against the Grain*. Halifax, NS: The Press of the Nova Scotia College of Art and Design.

Shaw, P. (ed.) (1989) *Whose Game is It Anyway? The Book of the Football Fanzines*. Hemel Hempstead: Argus.

Sheehan, P. (1998) Game, set and match: Murdoch, the champion of world sports, *Sydney Morning Herald – The Guide*, 23 February–1 March.

Shiller, R.J. (2000) *Irrational Exuberance*. Princeton, NJ: Princeton University Press.

Shilling, C. (1993) *The Body and Social Theory*. London: Sage.

Silk, M., Slack, T. and Amis, J. (2000) Bread, butter and gravy: an institutional approach to televised sport production, *Culture, Sport, Society*, 3(1): 1–21.

Silverman, D. (1993) *Interpreting Qualitative Data: Methods for Analysing Talk, Text and Interaction*. London: Sage.

Simson, V. and Jennings, A. (1992) *The Lords of the Rings: Power, Money and Drugs in the Modern Olympics*. London: Simon & Schuster.

Singer, T. (1998) Not so-remote-control, *Sport*, March, p. 36.

Sloop, J.M. (1997) Mike Tyson and the perils of discursive constraints: boxing, race, and the assumption of guilt, in A. Baker and T. Boyd (eds) *Out of Bounds*. Bloomington, IN: Indiana University Press.

Smith, A. (1997) Back-page bylines: an interview with Liz Kahn, Mary Jollimore, and Wanda Jamrozik, *Social Text*, 50(1): 87–95.

Smith, P. (1996) Pay TV: perspective from a popular sport, in R. Lynch, I. McDonnell, S. Thompson and K. Toohey (eds) *Sport and Pay TV: Strategies for Success*. Sydney, NSW: School of Leisure and Tourism Studies, University of Technology, Sydney.

Smith Maguire, J. (2002) Fitness publishing and the cultural production of the fitness consumer, *International Review for the Sociology of Sport*, 37(3/4): 449–64.

Smythe, D.W. (1977) Communications: blindspot of Western Marxism, *Canadian Journal of Political and Social Theory*, 1: 120–7.

Sobchack, V. (1997) Baseball in the post-American cinema, or life in the minor leagues, in A. Baker and T. Boyd (eds) *Out of Bounds*. Bloomington, IN: Indiana University Press.

Sports Illustrated (2002) September.

Stevenson, D. (2002) Women, sport and globalization: competing discourses of sexuality and nation, *Journal of Sport & Social Issues*, 26(2): 209–25.

Stevenson, N. (1995) *Understanding Media Cultures: Social Theory and Mass Communication*. London: Sage.

Stoddart, B. (1979) Cricket's imperial crisis: the 1932–33 MCC tour of Australia, in R. Cashman and M. McKernan (eds) *Sport in History*. St Lucia, QLD: University of Queensland Press.

Stoddart, B. (1986) *Saturday Afternoon Fever: Sport in the Australian Culture*. North Ryde, NSW: Angus & Robertson.

Stoddart, B. (1994a) *Invisible Games: A Report on the Media Coverage of Women's Sport*. Canberra, ACT: Sport and Recreation Ministers' Council.

Stoddart, B. (1994b) Sport, television, interpretation, and practice reconsidered: televised golf and analytical orthodoxies, *Journal of Sport & Social Issues*, 18(1): 76–88.

Stoddart, B. (1994c) Reflections past and present, in W. Vamplew and B. Stoddart (eds) *Sport in Australia: A Social History*. Melbourne, VIC: Cambridge University Press.

Stout, G. (1992) Foreword, in T. McGuane (ed.) *The Best American Sports Writing*. Boston, MA: Houghton Mifflin.

Stratton, J. (1999) Building a better body: male bodybuilding, spectacle and consumption, in R. Martin and T. Miller (eds) *SportCult*. Minneapolis, MN: University of Minnesota Press.

Sugden, J. and Tomlinson, A. (1998) *FIFA and the Contest for World Football: Who Rules the People's Game?* Cambridge: Polity.

Sugden, J. and Tomlinson, A. (1999) *Great Balls of Fire: How Big Money is Hijacking World Football*. Edinburgh: Mainstream.

Sugden, J. and Tomlinson, A. (2002) Theory and method for a critical sociology of sport, in J. Sugden and A. Tomlinson (eds) *Power Games: A Critical Sociology of Sport*. London: Routledge.

Symons, C. (2002) The Gay Games and community, in D. Hemphill and C. Symons (eds) *Gender, Sexuality and Sport: A Dangerous Mix*. Petersham, NSW: Walla Walla Press.

Sydney Morning Herald (1993) Sports computer is write on the ball, 29 May.

Sydney Morning Herald (2000) Man U puts it in the Net, 11 December.

Sydney Morning Herald (2003) AOL Time ponders radical editing to reduce $44bn debt load, 3 February.

Tan, Y.-F. (1990) Space and context, in R. Schechner and W. Appel (eds) *By Means of Performance: Intercultural Studies of Theatre and Ritual*. Cambridge: Cambridge University Press.

The Australian (2002) Murdoch in wings for Lazio, 2 December.

The Sun Newspaper Online (2003) 14 February.

Thompson, E.P. (1967) Time, work-discipline, and industrial capitalism, *Past and Present*, 38: 56–97.

Thompson, J.B. (1997) Scandal and social theory, in J. Lull and S. Hinerman (eds) *Media Scandals: Morality and Desire in the Popular Culture Marketplace*. New York: Columbia University Press.

Throsby, D. (2001) *Economics and Culture*. Cambridge: Cambridge University Press.

Thwaites, T., Davis, L. and Mules, W. (1994) *Tools for Cultural Studies: An Introduction*. Melbourne, VIC: Macmillan Education.

Timms, D. (2002) All eyes are on the ball, *MediaGuardian*, 1 July.

Tomlinson, A. (1996) Olympic spectacle: opening ceremonies and some paradoxes of globalization, *Media, Culture & Society*, 18(4): 583–602.

Tomlinson, A. (1999) *The Game's Up: Essays in the Cultural Analysis of Sport, Leisure and Popular Culture*. Aldershot: Ashgate.

Toohey, K. and Veal, A.J. (2000) *The Olympic Games: A Social Science Perspective*. Wallingford: CABI.

Traub, J. (1991) Please don't mash the sportswriter, *Washington Journalism Review*, July/August, pp. 34–7.

Trotsky, L. (1969) *The Permanent Revolution, and Results and Prospects*. New York: Merit.

Tudor, A. (1992) Them and us: story and stereotype in TV World Cup coverage, *European Journal of Communication*, 7: 391–413.

Tunstall, J. (1996) *Newspaper Power*. Oxford: Oxford University Press,

Turner, B.S. (1990) Australia: the debate about hegemonic culture, in N. Abercrombie, S. Hill and B.S. Turner (eds) *Dominant Ideologies*. London: Unwin Hyman.

Turner, B.S. (1992) *Regulating Bodies: Essays in Medical Sociology*. London: Routledge.

Turner, V. (1990) Are there universals of performance in myth, ritual, and drama?, in R. Schechner and W. Appel (eds) *By Means of Performance: Intercultural Studies of Theatre and Ritual*. Cambridge: Cambridge University Press.

Urry, J. (1990) *The Tourist Gaze: Leisure and Travel in Contemporary Societies*. London: Sage.

Van Zoonen, L. (1991) Feminist perspectives on the media, in J. Curran and M. Gurevitch (eds) *Mass Media and Society*. London: Edward Arnold.

Van Zoonen, L. (1998) A professional, unreliable, heroic marionette (M/F): structure, agency and subjectivity in contemporary journalisms, *European Journal of Cultural Studies*, 1(1): 123–45.

Warren, I. (2002) Hyper-masculinity, Superleague and corporate governance, in D. Hemphill and C. Symons (eds) *Gender, Sexuality and Sport: A Dangerous Mix*. Petersham, NSW: Walla Walla Press.

Weber, M. (1930 [1904/5]) *The Protestant Ethic and the Spirit of Capitalism*. London: Unwin University Books.

Weber, M. (1968 [1922]) *Economy and Society: An Outline of Interpretive Sociology*. New York: Bedminster Press.

Weber, S. (1996) Television: set and screen, in A. Cholodenko (ed.) *Mass Mediauras: Form, Technics, Media*. Sydney, NSW: Power Publications.

Wejbora, P. (2003) 'The global village idiot?': Australian new media policy, 1989–1999. Unpublished doctoral dissertation, University of Newcastle, Newcastle, NSW.

Wenner, L.A. (ed.) (1989) *Media, Sports, and Society*. Newbury Park, CA: Sage.

Wenner, L.A. (ed.) (1998) *MediaSport*. London: Routledge.

Whannel, G. (1992) *Fields in Vision: Television Sport and Cultural Transformation*. London: Routledge.

Whannel, G. (2001a) *Media Sport Stars: Masculinities and Moralities*. London: Routledge.

Whannel, G. (2001b) Punishment, redemption and celebration in the popular press: the case of David Beckham, in D.L. Andrews and S.J. Jackson (eds) *Sport Stars: the Cultural Politics of Sporting Celebrity*. London: Routledge.

Whitson, D. (1998) Circuits of promotion: media marketing and the globalization of sport, in L.A. Wenner (ed.) *MediaSport*. London: Routledge.

Who Weekly (2002) Downfall of a king, 1 April, p. 27.

Wiechula, F. (1997) 'I play in the big league, Gazza Disney!' says Les Ferdinand, *Mirror*, 27 March.

Wild, D. (2002) Networking – goal of the season, *Accountancy Age*, 29 August.

Williams, C.L., Lawrence, G. and Rowe, D. (1986) Patriarchy, media and sport, in G. Lawrence and D. Rowe (eds) *Power Play: Essays in the Sociology of Australian Sport*. Sydney, NSW: Hale & Iremonger.

Williams, L. (1989) *Hard Core: Power, Pleasure and the 'Frenzy of the Visible'*. Berkeley, CA: University of California Press.

Williams, L.D. (1994) Sportswomen in black and white: sports history from an Afro-American perspective, in P.J. Creedon (ed.) *Women, Media and Sport: Challenging Gender Values*. Thousand Oaks, CA: Sage.

Williams, L.D. and Lumpkin, A. (1990) An examination of the sport, gender, race, and sporting role of individuals appearing on the covers of *Sports Illustrated*, 1954–1989. Unpublished paper, New Carolina A & T State University.

Williams, R. (1974) *Television: Technology and Cultural Form*. London: Fontana/Collins.

Williams, R. (1989 [1970]) There's always the sport, in A. O'Connor (ed.) *Raymond Williams on Television: Selected Writings*. London: Routledge.

Wilson, H. (1998) Television's *tour de force*: the nation watches the Olympic Games, in D. Rowe and G. Lawrence (eds) *Tourism, Leisure, Sport: Critical Perspectives*. Melbourne, VIC: Cambridge University Press.

Wilson, N. (1988) *The Sports Business: The Men and the Money*. London: Piatkus.

Windschuttle, K. (1984) *The Media: A New Analysis of the Press, Television, Radio and Advertising in Australia*. Ringwood, VIC: Penguin.

Windschuttle, K. (1998) The poverty of media theory, *Quadrant*, 42(3): 11–18.

Wolf, M.J. (1999) *The Entertainment Economy: The Mega-Media Forces that are Re-Shaping Our Lives*. New York: Random House.

Wolfe, T. and Johnson, E.W. (eds) (1975) *The New Journalism*. London: Pan.

Wolstenholme, K. (1998) *They Think It's All Over . . . Memories of the Greatest Day in English Football*. London: Robson.

Wooldridge, I. (1998) Foreword, in K. Wolstenholme, *They Think It's All Over . . . Memories of the Greatest Day in English Football*. London: Robson.

Wray, R (2003) The great 3G gamble, *MediaGuardian*, 10 February.

Wright, J. and Clarke, G. (1999) Sport, the media and the construction of compulsory heterosexuality: a case of women's Rugby Union, *International Review for the Sociology of Sport*, 34(3): 227–43.

INDEX